Intangible Management

TOOLS FOR SOLVING THE ACCOUNTING AND MANAGEMENT CRISIS

Ken Standfield

*The International Intangible Management
Standards Institute (IIMSI)
San Diego, California*

ACADEMIC PRESS
An imprint of Elsevier Science

Amsterdam   Boston   London   New York   Oxford   Paris
San Diego   San Francisco   Singapore   Sydney   Tokyo

Academic Press
An Elsevier Science Imprint
525 B Street, Suite 1900, San Diego, California 92101–4495, USA
http://www.academicpress.com

Academic Press
84 Theobolds Road, London WC1X 8RR, UK
http://www.academicpress.com

Library of Congress Catalog Card Number: 2002102213

International Standard Book Number: 0–12–663351–7

PRINTED IN THE UNITED STATES OF AMERICA
02 03 04 05 06 07 MM 9 8 7 6 5 4 3 2 1

Intangible Management

TOOLS FOR SOLVING
THE ACCOUNTING AND
MANAGEMENT CRISIS

*To the many wonderful people
who have touched my life and given
me the faith and strength to pursue my dreams.
To the thousands of people I have presented
to over the years that have offered their wisdom.
Especially to Wendy, my soul mate, best friend, and wife*

CONTENTS

6 Intangible Accounting

7 Intangible Bookkeeping

9 Intangible Cost Management

10 Emotion and Time Studies

11 Identifying Nonproductive Time

12 Knowledge Application Costs

13 Intangible Information Management

14 IIS21001 Knowledge Reengineering Standard

15 Examples of IIS21001 Knowledge Reengineering

16 Intangible Cost Structures

Appendix

PREFACE

"The only thing we learn from history is that we learn nothing from history." The notion of wealth and value is a constantly changing one. As new technologies are developed they replace old ones and change our political and social values in the process. Despite overwhelming proof that our lives are filled with disruptive and incomprehensible change, we still insist that the fundamentals of life do not, have not, and cannot change.

We live our professional lives recklessly applying outdated and irrelevant problem-solving techniques to problems that could never have been contemplated by the creators of those techniques. We remain mentally shackled and emotionally imprisoned to obsolete management methods that destroy the very value they seek to enhance. When everything fails, we simply blame "harsh economic conditions" and feel vindicated that we have done our best.

John Naisbitt, the best selling author of *Megatrends*, argued that significant economic growth occurs as one economic system gives way to another. You are uniquely positioned. The Knowledge Age is giving way to the Intangible Age, *right now*. Applying the concepts in this book may make you the next Bill Gates.

All economic eras that follow the Knowledge Economy will rely primarily on a solid understanding of the identification, measurement, and management of *intangibles*. As such, the knowledge in this book will serve you well throughout your professional life.

While conventional theory states that intangibles cannot be measured, the International Intangible Management Standards Institute has developed methods and practices that can give decision makers a clear view of intangibles for the first time. Rather than recommending a solution "here and there" the Standards Institute has developed over 30 international intangible standards that can be applied to *make the invisible visible*, or to *turn soft management into a hard science*, thereby providing a solution to the accounting and management crisis.

Most people have never even looked at the nature of intangibles. We have been researching them for nearly 15 years. This book represents a critical introduction to a new world of possibilities, new skills, new experiences, new products, new services, new revenue streams, and new employment possibilities.

PREVENT YOURSELF FROM BEING
BOILED ALIVE

The Parable of the Boiled Frog describes what is happening to executives, managers, politicians, and other professionals around the world. It even describes what is happening, or about to happen, to you:

> The Parable of the Boiled Frog is a sad story about a frog that was placed in a pot on a stove. The water in the pot was slowly and gradually raised so that the frog did not notice the water getting hotter and hotter. Just before the water boiled, the frog lost consciousness and was literally boiled to death.

The morale of the story is: relentless destructive change is generally only recognized as lethal *after* death has occurred. Think of yourself as the frog. A wise frog can understand when to jump out of the pot when the temperature gets too high, as a frog knows that its purpose is not to be boiled alive.

Many CEOs, executives, managers, politicians, government policy makers, and private individuals are slowly destroying their corporations, economies, and lives because (just like the frog) they don't understand that water is heating up around them. Just as the increasingly hot water sent the frog into unconsciousness; so too does a reliance on obsolete management concepts send decision makers into unconsciousness.

If the frog only had a temperature gauge to understand dangerous temperatures, it could have jumped out and lived. Today, decisions use out-dated and obsolete management methods that were never designed to manage what cannot be seen, cannot be touched, and cannot be owned: *intangibles*.

Today, decision makers have replaced the frogs. The heat of technological, social, and political change has caused the increased heat. Decision makers schooled in the art of reading business temperatures from the industrial era can't understand why they and their organizations are being boiled alive.

The past few years have witnessed a string of "unexplainable" corporate collapses. This book explains how it is possible to look good according to obsolete management methods, while the organization is slowly boiled to death.

Sometimes these organizations are saved before they disappear forever. The rash of downsizing that has infected our planet are witness to the hairbreadth escape of the frog from the boiling pot just before it has been cooked alive by the heat of change. However, such reprieves are typically short lived and ineffective over the long term.

To understand how to read the dials of the new economy we need new tools, new methods, and new systems. Such systems need to be applicable to resources that are fundamentally *intangible*. The fundamental purpose of intangible management (through international intangible standards) is to assist you to accurately read the dials of the new economy.

INCREASE YOUR RADAR'S PRECISION

In today's competitive world, your *success radar* needs to be as accurate as possible. You need to know how factors can hinder or destroy your chances of success. Conventional systems were never designed to detect intangibles or estimate their true impact on your decisions. International Intangible Standards provide you with a powerful new way to increase the precision and range of your decision-making radar. Once you understand the techniques in this book, you will strengthen your ability to understand, respond, and then profit from competitive changes that devastate your competition.

UPGRADE YOUR ENGINE: PUT MORE GAS IN YOUR TANK

The Knowledge Economy and the economic systems that follow it all rely on a strong understanding of how to scientifically manage intangible value. By upgrading your skills, you can build a more powerful success engine and enlarge your capacity to reach your professional and personal goals.

Every time you gain knowledge that your competition does not possess you gain an advantage that can translate into victory. Sun Tzu, in the *Art of War*, stated that any battle requires the use of expected and unexpected tactics and it is the use of unexpected tactics that ultimately determines the outcome of any engagement. International Intangible Standards provide you with powerful new knowledge that can use in unexpected new ways.

INCREASE EMOTIONAL INTELLIGENCE AND QUALITY OF LIFE

If you can scientifically understand *why* you do what you do and scientifically understand why *other* people do what they do, you have the required skills to be an executive. Managers need to manage an increasingly narcissist workforce. The term narcissist comes from the Greek myth of Narcissus, a young man who fell in love with his own *reflection* mirrored in a lake. Captivated by his beauty the young man died of starvation and fell into the water never to be seen again. Narcissists do not love themselves, they love their *reflection*. As reflections more typically reflect fantasy than reality, knowledge managers and knowledge executives need to bring emotional intelligence into their range of executive skills. Today, it is essential to understand that many decisions are more directed at increasing ego than increasing value.

Emotional intelligence is a critical skill to possess when attempting to control a workforce that is increasingly reflective of a group of self-indulgent children than a group of seasoned professionals. International Intangible Standards deals with the scientific study and analysis of emotions and how to better manage those emotions in a workplace environment. This book also covers the detail on how to value intangibles in financial terms and incorporate such decisions into the normal decision-making process.

PAVING THE WAY FORWARD

The concepts you read in this book have been grounded in 15 years of research and development. The total content of intangible management could not be contained within a single book, many books are yet to be written on the subject. For quality control purposes, authors of books on intangible management should at a minimum, be *certified intangible management consultants*. This eLearning qualification ensures that the holder has a deep understanding of international intangible standards and knows how to apply them across a wide variety of different situations.

IN CONCLUSION

This book covers the fundamentals of Intangible Management through an understanding of International Intangible Standards. It provides the foundations needed to gain a solid understanding of how intangibles directly and indirectly influence organizational success. For the avid learner, there are specific qualifications that can be attained through eLearning by visiting *http://www.StandardsInstitute.org*. I welcome your comments and questions by contacting me directly at *ken@StandardsInstitute.org*.

Ken Standfield
San Diego, California
February, 2002

CHAPTER 1

Introduction

Every professional discipline is subject to its own language. Mathematics, accounting, finance, economics, computer science, marketing, chemistry, and physics all have their own language with which practitioners can communicate with each other without the need to explain what they mean and what they are talking about. Like learning to play the piano, each profession requires immersion in a completely new professional language. At first, this language seems alien and daunting. As time progresses, the jargon turns into a shared understanding and the basis of communication with other professionals. Intangibles are no exception. To learn about intangibles requires new skills and a new language with which to describe the problems and solutions that intangibles have created.

A new language is required to explain intangibles because the old rules of conventional management, when applied to intangibles, typically create the opposite outcome of what is expected. Intangibles require a counterintuitive understanding that will allow us to identify, classify, measure, manage, and report intangible value.

This book represents the first consistent attempt to describe the new language of intangibles in a totally structured and logical manner. The study of intangibles has its own language, its own jargon, and its own technical terms. There is no way around this jargon. As you progress through this book, you will learn the new language of intangibles and find that the jargon assists you to better understand divergent areas.

INTANGIBLE STANDARDS

The International Intangible Management Standards Institute (IIMSI) (www.standardsinstitute.org) is the world's leading standards-setting organization in the field of identification and management of intangibles according to the new rules of the Knowledge Economy.

Intangibles cannot be efficiently or effectively identified, managed, measured, or reported using conventional management techniques and methods. To equip executives with the required skills to manage value according to the new rules of the Intangible Age, the IIMSI created numerous intangible standards.

DECODING INTANGIBLE STANDARDS

Intangible standards have a consistent structure:

1. The letters IIS representing International Intangible Standard, followed by
2. A number representing the core standard, followed by
3. A letter to identify a unique reference type, followed by
4. A number to identify a unique reference position.

Core Standards

There are numerous core standards:

IIS1001: Intangible Foundations Standard
IIS2001: Intangible Operating Structures
IIS3001: Intangible Risk Management
IIS4001: Intangible Accounting Standard
IIS4002: Intangible Cost Management Standard
IIS4003: Intangible Cost Quality Standard
IIS4005: Intangible Cost Quantification Standard
IIS5001: Intangible Valuation Standard
IIS6001: Intangible Finance Standard

IIS7001:   Intangible Economics Standard
IIS8001:   Intangible Project Management
IIS9001:   Intangible Marketing Standard
IIS10001: Intangible Knowledge Management
IIS10002: Knowledge Worker Syndrome Standard
IIS10010: Intangible Information Management Standard
IIS11001: Intangible Intellectual Capital Standard
IIS12001: Intangible Return on Investment Standard
IIS13001: Intangible Incentive and Remuneration
IIS14001: Intangible Change Management Standard
IIS15001: Intangible Interaction Management Standard
IIS16001: Intangible Resource Management Standard
IIS17001: Intangible Production Management Standard
IIS18001: Intangible Purchasing Standard
IIS19001: Intangible Mapping Standard
IIS20001: Intangible Consulting Standard
IIS21001: Knowledge Reengineering Standard
IIS22001: Intangible Brand Management Standard
IIS23001: Intangible Product Development Standard
IIS24001: Intangible Law Standard
IIS24002: Intangible Contract Law Standard
IIS25001: Intangible Intelligence Standard

REFERENCE TYPES

Reference types allow people to easily understand the role of the standard they are investigating. Reference types are generally single letters that represent an underpinning structure. Some of these structures are listed next.

Definitions

Reference type: "D"
Example   : IIS1001.D5
Meaning   : The fifth definition in international intangible standards IIS1001
Purpose   : Used to define intangible terminology

Characteristics

Reference type: "C"
Example   : IIS1004.C2

Meaning	: The second characteristic in international intangible standard IIS1004
Purpose	: Used to explain intangible characteristics

Relationships

Reference type:	"R"
Example	: IIS1004.R345
Meaning	: The 345th intangible relationship as detailed in international intangible standard IIS1004
Purpose	: Used to explain relationships between intangibles and other intangibles, or intangibles and other tangibles

Subcategories

Reference type:	"S"
Example	: IIS1001.S5
Meaning	: The fifth subcategory as detailed in international intangible standard IIS1001
Purpose	: Used to explain subcategories that relate to a specific intangible standard

Laws

Reference type:	"L"
Example	: IIS1001.L1
Meaning	: The first intangible law as detailed in international intangible standard IIS1001
Purpose	: Details intangible laws

UNIQUE REFERENCE POSITIONS

Unique reference positions allow professionals skilled in the art of working with intangible standards to refer to the logic that underpins intangible standards without requiring significant amounts of explanation.

For example, IIS1004.D2 may relate to IIS1004.R3 and IIS1005.R4. Being able to make such easy connections between numerous areas assists certified practicing intangible practitioners, certified practicing intangible executives, and certified practicing intangible consultants to ensure that companies are complying with intangible standards.

INTANGIBLE QUALIFICATIONS

The International Intangible Management Standards Institute is also the international certification and accreditation body responsible for ensuring adherence to International Intangible Standards. A range of professional IIS qualifications is available directly from the IIMSI through eLearning: (1) Certified Practicing Intangible Management Practitioner (CPIMP), (2) Certified Practicing Intangible Management Executive (CPIME) and (3) Certified Practicing Intangible Management Consultant (CPIMC). Details are available at www.standardsinstitute.org.

CHAPTER 2

The Failings of Conventional Management

Intention, context, emotional intelligence, escalation, and *sustainability* are words that are typically absent from the operational management techniques of managers around the globe. These words, however, form the foundation of the skills required to manage organizations in today's Knowledge Economy.

CHANGING ECONOMIC SYSTEMS

Economic systems change in response to fundamental changes in the needs of consumers and society. Thousands of years ago, people's most basic instinct was to have food so they could survive. The Agricultural Revolution forced people into communities, away from nomadic life. Land was cultivated and food was grown. This revolution led to the agricultural sector of the economy dominating economic activity (employment and GDP). This revolution continued for thousands of years until the advent of the Industrial Revolution. This shifted the basis of employment from agriculture to manufacturing. When the information technology and communications revolutions occurred in the early 1970s, a quiet Information Revolution occurred as employment fell in manufacturing and was transferred into the service sector. As Table 2.1 illustrates, the bulk of employment and contribution to gross domestic product, is derived from the services sector.

At the dawn of the 21st century, employment is again shifting, this time from service workers to knowledge workers. Knowledge workers create wealth by exchanging knowledge assets and relationship assets using emotions and time. Knowledge managers are responsible for managing knowledge workers. Knowledge managers are therefore responsible for managing the quality of four fundamental factors of production: (1) knowledge assets, (2) relationship assets, (3) emotional assets, and (4) time assets.

International Intangible Standards connect the performance of these intangible assets to the organization's ability to generate financial wealth (for stakeholders), emotional wealth (for employees), and societal wealth (for society at large). Knowledge executives are responsible for managing groups of knowledge managers. Knowledge consultants provide specific methods and practices to assist knowledge workers, knowledge managers, and knowledge executives to better produce, provide, distribute, and share in the tangible and intangible value they create in the specific target market that their organization services.

Intangible management is therefore the management skills and abilities required to sustainably generate financial and emotional wealth from the four

TABLE 2.1   Percentage Employment by Sector

Country	Percent of workforce			Percent of GDP		
	Industry	Agriculture	Services*	Industry	Agriculture	Services*
Australia	22	5	73	26	3	71
United States	24.5	2.6	72.9	18	2	80
Singapore	21.6	1	77.4	28	0	72
Canada	21	3	76	31	3	66
Netherlands	23	2	75	18	4	78
Japan	24	7	69	35	2	63
Germany	41	3	56	34.5	1.1	64.4
United Kingdom	17.5	1.1	81.4	25.3	1.7	73
Luxembourg	14.3	2.5	83.2	23	1	76
Norway	22	4	74	26.3	2.2	71.5
Switzerland	28	5	67	31.1	2.8	66.
Averages	23.5	3.3	73.2	26.9	2.1	71.0

fundamental factors of production listed above that dominate the value creation process in the current economic system.

KNOWLEDGE WORKERS

Doctors, lawyers, teachers, clerks, hospitality staff, tradespeople, programmers, advertising executives, marketers, graphic artists, consultants, and engineers all use knowledge assets, relationship assets, emotional assets, and time assets to create revenue for the organizations they work for and wages for themselves. Knowledge workers use four main intangible assets to create value:

1. *Knowledge assets*: This is the fundamental knowledge that the person requires to deliver value. Knowledge asests have vastly differing qualities ranging from destructive knowledge assets, and diversionary knowledge assets, and obsolete knowledge assets to premium knowledge assets.
2. *Relationship assets*: This is the relationship quality that a person requires to communicate a value proposition to the person seeking the knowledge and the relationship. Relationship asests also have vastly differing qualities ranging from destructive relationship assets, diversionary relationship assets, and obsolete relationship assets to premium relationship assets.
3. *Emotional assets*: Emotional intelligence is essential in the knowledge-based economy. Emotional intelligence is the ability of an individual to manage the emotions of those he or she interacts with in a constructive and sustainable manner. Emotional assets are the key to sustainability, value provision, productivity, and profitability for organizations.
4. *Time assets*: Regarded as the fourth dimension, time is the only universal thing that everyone has access to but no one owns. Every person (regardless of education, profession, religion, industry, country, gender, age, etc.) is given 24 hours each day. Each hour contains 60 minutes and each minute contains 60 seconds. People are free to squander or leverage this invaluable daily resource of 1440 minutes. But once time is spent, it cannot be refunded. Wasted time cannot be reclaimed. Time assets present the only way in which relationship assets, emotional assets, and knowledge assets can be applied and leveraged.

Agricultural workers and manufacturing workers also use knowledge assets, relationship assets, emotional assets, and time assets to create value. Management of intangible assets is therefore critical for all organizations.

Core Value Infrastructures

In the Agricultural Age, value was created from the land. In the Industrial Age, value was created from factories. In the Information Age, value was created from information. The collapse of the global information technology sector heralded the formal end of the Information Age and the start of the Knowledge Age.

> In the knowledge age, value is created from knowledge, emotions, time, and relationships. For the first time in history, organizations cannot own their resource base as they did in all preceding economic ages. Knowledge cannot be owned; only the representation of knowledge can be owned (i.e., intellectual property). Relationships cannot be owned, slavery was abolished hundreds of years ago. People have enough trouble controlling emotions, let alone owning them. No one can own time.

Our current economic system is based on the concept of ownership, referred to as *legal property rights*. Courts allow people to protect these rights and claim damages for their abuse. Legal property rights are often created when a financial transaction (an evidenced exchange of money) occurs. The areas of accounting, finance, and economics have all been built from the foundation that financial transactions capture total value. As you progress through this book, you will see that financial transactions actually carry a very small proportion of total value in the knowledge-based economy. This book outlines the steps required to update the current economic system to reflect the new realities the Intangible Age has brought.

WHY CONVENTIONAL MANAGEMENT IS FAILING

Conventional accounting defines profit as the difference between expenses and revenue. It assumes that assets and equity are used to generate revenue. Measures such as return on assets, return on equity, and return on investment are key metrics. Expenses are used to create prices (cost plus pricing). Margins are the difference between costs and revenues. Conventional businesses, therefore, manage their value creation and sustainability according to the graph shown in Figure 2.1.

The amount of money after expenses (profit) was deemed to be the source of success for Industrial Age and Information Age businesses. Let us assume that there are two organizations, Organization A and Organization B, in the same industry, subject to the same competitive forces. When these two businesses start operations, they have equal cost and revenue structures (Figure 2.2).

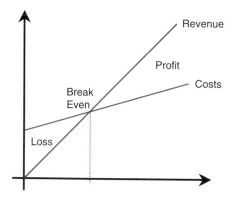

FIGURE 2.1   Conventional value management.

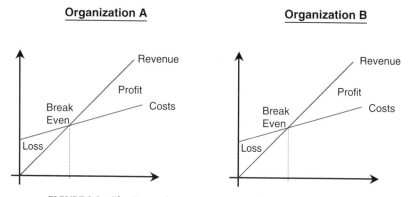

FIGURE 2.2   The Cost and revenue structures of Organizations A and B.

SHORT-TERM IMPACTS: FALSE PROJECTION

As time progresses, Organization A invests in future capabilities while Organization B reduces all possible expenditures. In the short term, Organization A's increase in capabilities comes at a cost. This cost will increase the cost curve in Figure 2.3 from A1 to A2. Organization B's decrease in costs will shift its cost curve down from B1 to B2. Organizaiton A may seem less attractive at this stage and Organization B more attractive. However, it is actually too early to tell. We must understand the intention of the changes in expenditures, not just the fact that they have occurred.

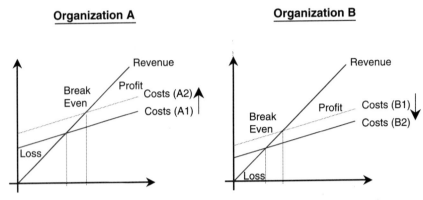

FIGURE 2.3   Short-term changes in the cost structures of Organizations A and B.

Conventional management fails because it confuses short-term impacts with long-term impacts. In short, conventional management uses a method called *false projection* to determine how changes today influence profitability tomorrow.

False Projection

Due to numerous accounting assumptions (we will investigate this later), managers only recognize losses and ignore gains. Law 10 of Intangible Foundations Standard IIS1001 defines *false projection* as:

> False projection occurs when the impact on revenue of short-term cost movements is not determined. This means that changes in short-term cost structures are incorrectly deemed to have zero effect on changes in long-term revenue structures. (IIS1001.L10)

Hence, after the change in costs, Organizations A and B will be perceived to have the *long-term value* structures shown in Figure 2.4. If this were, in fact, the case, then Organization A would be in severe financial difficulty and Organization B would be set to become an economic powerhouse.

Explaining the Foundations of False Projection

False projection occurs because of a set of principles on which accounting, finance, and economics are based: the measurement, recording, and reporting of *financial transactions*. At this early stage, let us revist the 10 fundamental accounting assumptions:

1. *Entity assumption*: Only business transactions (not personal) are recorded in the financial statements. The entity assumption is the foun-

dation of the accounting equation (A = L + C) and is the basis of double-entry conventional accounting.

2. *Continuity assumption*: Organizations are considered to have an indefinite life. This led to the development of the accrual system of accounting.

3. *Accounting period assumption*: Because an organization's life is deemed to be infinite, this assumption is used to divide the life of an entity into arbitrary periods where expenses and revenues can be matched to determine profit. This assumption led to the development of balance day adjustments and depreciation.

4. *Monetary assumption*: All financial information must be presented in monetary format and in aggregated (not individual) terms in accounting reports.

5. *Historical cost assumption*: The information recorded on the receipt of a financial transaction is the amount at which information is entered into financial accounts. If something is purchased for $10,000 but has a current market value of $100,000, the $10,000 is recorded not the $100,000. Inflation and market values are ignored.

6. *Conservatism assumption*: Losses and expenses are written off immediately, but profits are not recorded until actually realized.

7. *Materiality assumption*: Financial transactions are grouped into categories and it is the total of these categories that is reported in financial statements. Only whole dollars are used in reports, because cents are immaterial. The distinction between assets and expenses is material as is the choice to depreciate.

8. *Consistency assumption*: To ensure greater verifiability of data and comparison over different time periods, it is essential to inform the

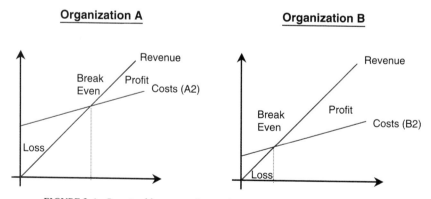

FIGURE 2.4   Perceived long-term financial structures of Organizations A and B.

users of financial statements when there are changes in accounting methods.

9. *Realization assumption*: Revenue is recorded when the transaction is made (i.e., at the point of sale) and not when payment is received.

10. *Objectivity assumption*: Documentary evidence must be produced to validate financial transactions.

Five (50%) of these assumptions are underlined because they cause the problem of false projection.

1. *Conservatism (core assumption 6)*: Expenses must be recognized immediately. This creates a focus on expenses rather than revenue.

2. *Realization (core assumption 9)*: Revenue is only recorded when generated. This creates an understanding in a manager's mind that revenue cannot and should not be predicted because accounting reports will not pay any merit to such projections.

3. *Verifiability (core assumption 10)*: Documentary (historic) evidence must be produced to prove that a financial transaction has occurred. It is only at this stage that a financial transaction is permitted to be recorded in accounting reports.

4. *Historical cost (core assumption 5)*: Only historical, or past, financial events are recognized. This makes managers look toward the past in order to manage the future. Because revenue occurs in the future and is largely outside the control of managers, managers seek to manage expenses over which they have direct control. This core accounting assumption forces managers to manage expenses, not revenue.

5. *Accounting period (core assumption 6)*: All financial transactions that have occurred during a reporting period must be presented for analysis in order to determine taxation liabilities. The accounting period assumption places pressure on managers to determine compliance with taxation laws and government legislation.

What False Projection Looks Like

Most people understand that "it takes money to make money." Few understand that "spending less can cost you more" because reductions in expenditures can actually decrease, or destroy, future revenue-generating capacity. There is always a lag, or time difference, between a change in costs and a change in revenue. Investors, managers, government officials, banks, and others assess *accounting* performance not *business* performance.

Accounting performance is the management of expenses and short-term value.
Business performance is the management of long-term value. Accounting perform-

ance and business performance therefore differ significantly, especially if the organ-ization has significant long term (or intrinsic) value. The *Law of Disassociated Performance (IIS1001.L15)*

While managers seek to manage business performance, taxation laws and archaic recording conventions force managers to focus almost exclusively on managing accounting performance. This creates a focus on short-term performance at the expense of long-term performance. In our knowledge-based economy, the gap between accounting performance and business performance is really a chasm. Accounting performance is measured by financial statements such as the balance sheet and the income statement.

Research by Arthur Andersen of 3500 companies revealed that the balance sheet explained 95% of market value in 1978. In 1998, the balance sheet explained 28% of market value. Currently, the balance sheet explains less than 15% of the market value of the average firm.

THE DECLINING RELEVANCY OF ACCOUNTING PERFORMANCE

The research by Arthur Andersen just mentioned revealed that accounting relevance dropped an average of 3.35% per year during the 20 years of the study. In 2001, the fall to around 15% coincides with a further reduction of 3.35% per year for 3 years.

A natural floor exists to which the relevancy of accounting measures will fall. The International Intangible Management Standards Institute predicts that the relevance of accounting reports will fall to around 5% by 2005. This will mean that if the foundations of tangible accounting are already failing to reflect the realities of the Knowledge Economy, by 2005 it is anticipated that the average accounting report will capture less than 5% of business performance. This also means that accounting reports will fail to capture 95% of the value of a business and its operations. Such a situation will render such reports practically useless.

Professor Baruch Lev, the Philip Bardes Professor of Accounting and Finance at the Stern School of Business, New York University (NYU), and director of the Intangibles Research Project at NYU determined that in 1999, the average market-to-book ratio of the S&P 500 reached 6.26. The market-to-book ratio is defined as the total market value of an organization divided by that organization's book value. The book value of an organization is the balance sheet worth of tangible and financial assets minus liabilities. To interpret this statistic, we need to perform the analysis below:

$$\text{Market value : Book value} = 6.26 : 1 \text{ or } 6.26 \div 1$$

Hence,

$$\text{Book (accounting) value to Market value} = 1 \div 6.26$$
$$\text{Accounting relevance} = 15.97\% \ (1 \div 6.26)$$
$$\text{Relevance of intangibles: } 84.03\% \ [1 - (1 \div 6.26)]$$

This means that accounting performance, as measured by the balance sheet, accounted for less than 16% of the average organization's listed stock market value for the top 500 firms in America in 1999.

The declining relevance of accounting is well known and understood throughout the world. Consider what people within the accounting and finance industries are saying:

> There are going to be a lot of problems in the future as accounting is not tracking investments in knowledge assets. —*Alan Greenspan, Federal Reserve Board Chairman*
>
> As intangible assets grow in size and scope, more and more people are questioning whether the true value—and the drivers of that value—are being reflected in a timely manner in publicly available disclosure. —*Arthur Levitt, Former SEC Chairman*
>
> Good information is vitally important because it reduces the uncertainty associated with making investments, and thus reduces one element of investment risk. Reduced investment risk in turn reduces the cost of capital. If capital costs are low, more capital will be available for companies that need it, capital will be allocated more efficiently, we will have faster and broader-based economic growth, and the welfare of all will be enhanced. —*Peter J. Wallison, Resident Fellow American Enterprise Institute, Congressional Testimony*
>
> The GAAP system has, for all its faults, served business and the public well, like an octogenarian butler. At the same time there's increasing evidence that the faithful servant isn't just misplacing a spoon here or there but has lost track of some valuable jewels, paid no attention to the furnace and the water heater, and put the place at risk. Investors simply don't value what accountants count. —*Thomas Stewart, Fortune*
>
> Accounting is 'lousy.' —*Rajat Gupta, Chairman, McKinsey*
>
> The income statement, balance sheet, and statement of cash flow are about as useful as an 80-year-old road map. —*Robert A. Howell, Professor, Tuck School, Dartmouth University*
>
> Today substantially all of a company's profitability depends on intangible assets, so the accounting problems associated with intangibles become quite serious. —*Peter J. Wallison, Resident Fellow, American Enterprise Institute*

Because nonaccounting value (or intangible value) is now the major value component within organizations around the globe, it is little wonder that the

U.S. Securities and Exchange Commission (SEC) and U.S. Congress are investigating how intangible assets can be accounted for using new reporting formats.

> Since the applicability of the traditional accounting framework is constantly declining, there is no point in trying to include intangible assets on the balance sheet. Instead a whole new framework for measurement will eventually have to be developed. —*Silvia Wompa, American Management Association*

A new value framework is required to protect investors and companies. Companies that do not manage their intangible value creation processes will not be able to sustain returns over the long term and will engage in management practices that inflate short-term financial performance while destroying organizational stability (i.e., Enron). International Intangible Standards detail a completely new framework through which organizations can identify, classify, record, financially report, and manage intangible value.

WHY IS INTANGIBLE VALUE BEING IGNORED?

Every month the International Intangible Management Standards Institute conducts an analysis of the 500 largest firms (by intangible value) listed on U.S. stock exchanges. These firms, referred to as the KNOWCORP 500 are the top 500 knowledge corporations in the United States. Unlike the S&P 500 the KNOWCORP 500 does not exclude non-U.S.-based firms. In March 2002, the KNOWCORP 500 employed 35.94% more employees, generated 38.14% more shareholder value, reported 40.88% more intangible value, and 34.76% more sales than the S&P 500. To qualify for the KNOWCORP 500 a firm must have at least US$2.0 billion of intangible value. Table 2.2 illustrates the results for the top 10 firms in the KNOWCORP 500 for March 2002.

The Accounting Industry

The accounting industry is the custodian of financial reporting for organizations worldwide. According to *Public Accounting Report's* Research Annual Survey of National Accounting Firms and AICPA annual reports, the top eight accounting firms generated $US 67,296 million from global operations in 2000, up 13.4%, or $US 7486 million from the 1999 figure of $US 59,345 million. An analysis of the information is presented in Table 2.3.

The accounting industry generates roughly 25% of its income from taxation services ($US 16,824 million), 30% from management advisory services ($US 20,189 million) with the remaining 45% from accounting and auditing

TABLE 2.2 Examining Intangible Value in Well-Known Firms (KNOWCORP® 500 (March 2002)—Top 20 Listing)

Ticker	Name	Market Value ($U.S. Mil.)	Intangible Value ($U.S. Mil.)	Intangible Value (%)	Employees	Sales Value ($U.S. Mil.)	KNOWCORP 500 Rank	S&P 500 Rank
GE	General Electric Company	$ 376,262	$ 321,414	85.42%	310,000	$ 125,913	1	1
MSFT	Microsoft Corporation	$ 327,242	$ 275,545	84.20%	47,600	$ 26,847	2	2
WMT	Wal-Mart Stores, Inc.	$ 276,562	$ 241,466	87.31%	1,244,000	$ 219,812	3	4
PFE	Pfizer Inc.	$ 254,675	$ 235,782	92.58%	90,000	$ 32,259	4	6
XOM	Exxon Mobil Corporation	$ 297,358	$ 223,572	75.19%	123,000	$ 212,897	5	3
C	Citigroup Inc.	$ 255,576	$ 176,205	68.94%	268,000	$ 66,565	6	5
JNJ	Johnson & Johnson	$ 197,612	$ 173,365	87.73%	101,800	$ 33,004	7	8
INTC	Intel Corporation	$ 205,045	$ 169,135	82.49%	83,400	$ 26,539	8	7
IBM	Int'l Business Machines	$ 181,309	$ 157,793	87.03%	319,876	$ 85,866	9	10
AIG	American Int'l Group, Inc	$ 188,725	$ 137,993	73.12%	61,000	$ 42,426	10	9
GSK	GlaxoSmithKline plc	$ 146,645	$ 134,004	91.38%	107,517	$ 25,735	11	N/A
BP	BP p.l.c.	$ 195,625	$ 118,909	60.78%	88,100	$ 148,062	12	N/A
MRK	Merck & Co., Inc.	$ 132,178	$ 116,137	87.86%	78,100	$ 47,716	13	11
KO	Coca-Cola Company, The	$ 127,342	$ 115,982	91.08%	38,000	$ 20,092	14	12
PG	Procter & Gamble Co., The	$ 116,782	$ 105,378	90.23%	106,000	$ 39,262	15	16
DCM	NTT DoCoMo, Inc. (ADR)	$ 126,906	$ 101,268	79.80%	19,790	$ 38,173	16	N/A
HD	Home Depot, Inc., The	$ 115,667	$ 98,274	84.96%	167,980	$ 40,078	17	17
MO	Philip Morris Companies	$ 114,859	$ 95,292	82.96%	175,000	$ 89,924	18	18
SBC	SBC Communications Inc.	$ 127,109	$ 94,600	74.42%	192,550	$ 45,908	19	13
CSCO	Cisco Systems, Inc.	$ 121,317	$ 93,235	76.85%	38,000	$ 18,290	20	15
		$ 3,884,796	$ 3,185,346	82.00%	3,659,713	$1,385,369		

Source: © International Intangible Management Standards Institute (http://www.StandardsInstitute.org/knowcorp).

TABLE 2.3   Assessing the Value of the Global Accounting Industry

Accounting firm	Global '00	US 2000	Global '99	US 1999
PricewaterhouseCoopers	$19,613	$8,299	$16,879	$7,154
Deloitte & Touche	$11,241	$5,838	$10,605	$5,336
KPMG	$13,500	$4,724	$10,861	$4,111
Ernst & Young	$9,200	$4,271	$8,804	$3,803
Arthur Andersen	$8,400	$3,600	$7,298	$3,300
Grant Thornton	$1,744	$416	$1,616	$375
BDO Seidman	$2,010	$412	$1,763	$298
McGladrey & Pullen	$1,588	$127	$1,520	$127
Totals	$67,296	$27,687	$59,345	$24,505
Growth			$7,951	$3,182
% Growth			13.40%	12.98%

($US 30,283 million). These fees are generated through the application of international accounting standards. These standards are compliant with the 10 fundamental accounting assumptions covered earlier in the Explaining the Foundations of False Projection section. These accounting assumptions are designed to present a true and fair view of an organization's financial health *as dictated by the fundamental accounting assumptions.*

THE PROBLEM WITH ACCOUNTING

The fundamental accounting assumptions only recognize financial receipts that flow from successfully completed contracts for goods or services. Put simply, the cash register must "ring" before accounting "sees" the financial transaction. If the cash register does not ring (a lost sale), or only rings once (a diluted sale) and not again (no repeat business), then accounting will not record these intangible (nonfinancial) transactions. The problem with accounting is that its focus is limited to tracking financial transactions.

How individuals and organizations use knowledge assets, relationship assets, emotional assets, and time assests dictates how many times the cash register bell "rings." Because intangible assets have never been scientifically managed within organizations, intangible costs are not being managed, and any time intangibles are mismanaged, the cash register bell does not ring. Bill Gates always said that when you lose a sale, you lose it twice. If you are going to make a sale for $100, but the competitor gets that sale, you have lost $100 and the competitor gains the $100—according to Gates this creates a $200 difference between where you are and where your competitor is.

WILL THE ACCOUNTING INDUSTRY BECOME OBSOLETE?

The International Intangible Management Standards Institute is uniquely aware that current accounting practices must be fundamental updated to reflect the critical role that intangibles play in winning sales, keeping customers, retaining employees, and building a sustainable business. The greatest risk that the accounting industry faces is in *not* managing the three core value propositions that underpin International Intangible Standards:

1. *Legal intangibles*: This area has been pioneered by the accounting and finance professions. Legal intangibles are legal property rights such as trademarks, patents, and brands. Unfortunately, this pioneering has occurred within the 10 fundamental conventional accounting assumptions. These assumptions (covered previously) explain why intellectual property is so often valued at the financial cost of creating it. The true value of intellectual property is not the costs of creation; it is something fundamentally different: the ability to leverage time capital.

2. *Operational intangibles*: This area is largely unknown to the accounting and finance professions because it involves managing knowledge assets, relationship assets, emotional assets, and time assets on a daily basis. International Intangible Standards deal specifically with the issues relating to operational intangibles.

3. *Market intangibles*: Traditional (accounting commonly) attempts to match intangible value to current market value where market value is evidenced by a financial transaction. Consider goodwill as an example. Goodwill is the difference between the purchase price of a business and the written down asset value of the business's assets. Hence, a business that is sold for $1,000,000 with assets worth $100,000 will have goodwill of $900,000. If the financial transaction does not occur, the goodwill will not occur either. The major problem with market intangibles is that if a sale does not occur, value is not recorded. International Intangible Standards deal specifically with the issues that underpin market intangibles.

As discussed above, accounting listens for the cash register to ring. When it does, accounting swings into full action recording, classifying, reporting, and managing those financial transactions in and out of the business. International Intangible Standards record, classify, report, and manage all the events that (1) prevent the accounting bell from ringing at all, (2) prevent the accounting bell from ringing as often as it should, (3) prevent the accounting bell from ringing in the future, (4) find new ways to ring the bell, and (5) better manage the impact of knowledge assets, relationship assets, emotional assets, and time assets on an organization's cost structure.

ACCOUNTING MEASURES CONTRACTUAL PERFORMANCE

Conceptually, the accounting bell "rings" every time a legal contract is fulfilled. Such contracts do not need to be formally signed by parties. Contracts can be express (represented in writing or orally) or implied (created through conduct). Buying a cup of coffee from a café constitutes an implied contract under common law. For a contract to be legally enforceable, there must be:

1. Two parties who intend to make an agreement
2. An offer
3. An acceptance
4. The capacity to make an agreement
5. Consent of both parties
6. A legal object as the focus of the contract
7. An appropriate format to enforce the agreement
8. Consideration (or payment)

These issues are so important that several paragraphs have been written below to explain their significance.

Offer

For a contract to be legally enforceable, a valid offer must have (1) intent, (2) clear and definite terms, and (3) be communicated. An offer also needs to identify the (1) price of the item to be agreed on, (2) the subject matter, (3) the parties to the contract, and (4) the time of performance.

Acceptance

A legally acceptable offer must be unequivocal and unqualified. It must be in the exact manner prescribed by the offeror. If there is any variance in terms, a counteroffer is deemed to have been made. Silence is not viewed as acceptance.

Consideration

Consideration is payment for entering into a contract. At a fundamental level, each party must give and receive something for a contract to occur. Typically, past consideration, moral obligations, gifts, illusory promises, and legal duties are not regarded as consideration. Critical to the role of consideration is sufficiency: The amount must be sufficient to satisfy the offeror.

Capacity

Factors such as age, mental condition, and the influence of drugs, alcohol, and incapacity will typically destroy contractual capacity and lead to contracts being voided.

Contractual Intent

If material facts are misrepresented through fraudulent or deceptive practices; or physical, economic, or mental distress is caused; or the contract is a result of a mutual mistake contractual intent is deemed not to exist. This therefore invalidates the contract.

The parties to a contract can claim a variety of legally enforceable rights on each other if a breach of contract occurs. A breach of contract (a violation of the agreement) allows the disadvantaged party to enact (1) legal remedies (compensatory damages, punitive damages, consequential damages), (2) equitable remedies (injunctions, specific performance, rescission and restitution, reformation, or (3) remedies for breach of contractual clauses (liquidated damages, limitation of damages, waivers, or arbitration). Accounting therefore measures the financial value of contractual performance. Such contracts occur inside and outside the business.

Contract law is at the heart of conventional accounting, economics, finance, and other business disciplines.

Contract Law and Intangibles

International Intangible Standards cover a specific type of intangible referred to as a level 3 intangible. These intangibles influence the formation of contracts, their dissolution, and future expectations relating to future contracts. In short, the quality of level 3 intangibles determines if the "bell rings" on the cash register in the first place.

Although level 3 intangibles ultimately create financial performance, these intangibles cannot be *initially* evidenced by financial transactions. Typically, numerous intangibles act together to create value and it is this aggregation of intangible value that makes it even harder to understand how intangibles influence financial performance.

The accounting profession has great difficulty reaching consensus on issues involving intangibles. Unlike financial transactions (the bell ringing), intangible transactions (knowledge assets, relationship assets, emotional assets, and time assets) *influence* whether financial transactions *will* occur, *do* occur, or will occur *again*.

It is the lack of consensus and understanding regarding the nature of intangibles that causes the greatest problem for the accounting, finance, economics, and legal industries.

Costs of False Projection

Seemingly financially stable corporations file for bankruptcy every year. As shown by the analysis presented earlier, accounting reports are becoming increasingly irrelevant.

> The problems associated with the discipline of accounting are exceptionally well known. The intellectual capital management industry was founded to address problems with conventional accounting. The increasing irrelevance of tangible accounting is due to changing economic circumstances, not an attempt to mislead investors, managers, or governments by accounting bodies or accounting professionals.

As you progress through this book, you will see how accounting reports have become obsolete and totally unsuited to the measurement of value in a knowledge-based economy. False projection assumes that the past continues into the future. Managers today know that the past is history and even today is uncertain; the past cannot reflect the future.

Long-Term Impacts: Lag +1 Analysis

Because expenses are the seeds of revenue, after a time lag, the true impact of the changes in expenses will become known. Let us assume that after the time lag has passed for organizations A and B (Figure 2.2), the results occur as shown in Figure 2.5. In Organization A, an increase in expenses led to an increase in revenue (due to increased value in the market). In the case of Organization B, the reduction in expenses led to a decrease in revenue (due to decreased value in the market).

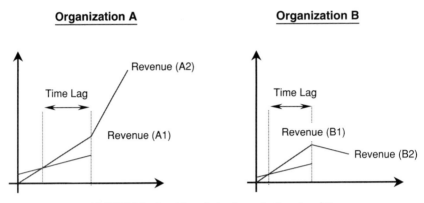

FIGURE 2.5   Lag +1 analysis of organizations A and B.

Expense Types

Expenses, like time, can be either productive or nonproductive (Figure 2.6). Productive expenses are required to grow the value of the organization. Nonproductive expenses destroy organizational value and can be eliminated without loss of revenue potential.

After decades of automation, cost cutting, and headcount reduction, there is simply no "fat to trim" from organizations around the world. The information technology industry was primarily geared toward the reduction of nonproductive expenses.

Expense Conversion

When productive expenses become nonproductive expenses, we state that negative expense conversion has occurred (Figure 2.7). When nonproductive expenses are removed from the organization, we state that positive expense conversion has occurred.

Productive Expenses	Nonproductive Expenses

FIGURE 2.6   Understanding productive and non-productive expenses.

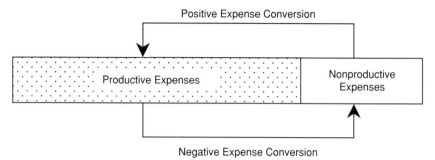

FIGURE 2.7   Understanding expense conversion.

Positive Expense Conversion   Positive expense conversion involves a re-allocation of nonproductive expenses to productive uses. As such, it increases the ability of the organization to create value (IIS4002.D11). Positive conversion expenses create organizational value because they have the ability to increase the amount of productive time in the organizaiton.

Negative Expense Conversion   Negative expense conversion involves a reallocation of productive expenses to nonproductive uses. As such, this type of conversion decreases the ability of the organization to create value (IIS4002.D16). Negative conversion expenses destroy organizational value because they reduce productive expenses, thereby reducing the amount of productive time in the organizaiton.

Linking Expense Conversion with Time

Expenses only have value as they increase the ability of an organization to create value for its customers by increasing productive time (Figure 2.8). Time is the critical link between operational management and financial performance.

Long-Term Impacts: Lag +2 Analysis

Because Organization A has increased productive expenses, its infrastructure now has a greater ability to meet the changing customer demands (Figure 2.9). Increased capacity only becomes valuable if new value propositions can be sold to new and existing customers. Intangible economics is used to assess increased sales potential. As revenue increases, Organization A may

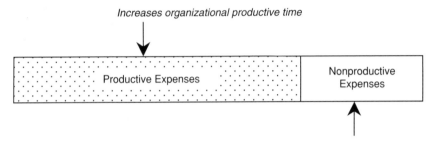

FIGURE 2.8   Linking expenses and time.

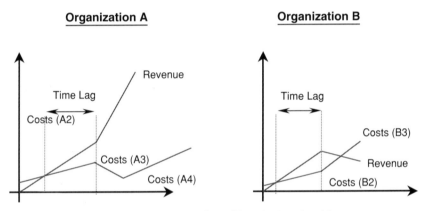

FIGURE 2.9   Lag +2 analysis of Organizations A and B.

decide to harvest profits by reducing expenditures. Such time is generally required to plan the "next big thing." Organization B looked profitable, but now as its relevance in the market has fallen, customers have been seduced by other offerings. As revenue falls, Organization B's costs increase (more advertising, more promotions, etc.) to spark financial interest on the part of customers. This may work for Organization B, but not before revenue continues to fall, putting it in grave danger of financial collapse. In the short-term, Organization B looked superior, but now it is probably headed for bankruptcy.

Societal Concerns with False Projection

The holy grail of management science has always been to predict potential changes in revenue that result from changes in costs. International Intangible Standard IIS5001 deals with the solution to this complex problem.

Organizations exist to increase value for customers, owners, shareholders, the community, and the world. Financial transaction (receipt)-based management frameworks lock managers, employees, investors, government agencies, and other parties into concentrating on the past. The only important thing becomes generating a profit, *at any cost.*

The motion picture *The Bank* was a thriller about a mathematical genius (David Wenham) who is employed by a ruthless bank CEO (Anthony LaPaglia). Using the genius' breakthroughs in mathematics, the CEO predicts the next stock market crash and how the Bank will gain total market dominance in a single day using this new predictive tool. The CEO typifies a man caught in the pressures imposed by traditional accounting measures. Faced with the challenge of publishing greater returns to shareholders or being fired, the CEO did as he was supposed to do: *Make money at any cost.*

> I know of nothing more despicable and pathetic than a man who devotes all the hours of the waking day to the making of money for money's sake. —*John D. Rockefeller*

The concern with managing accounting measures is that actions in the short term can lead to the ultimate destruction of the firm in the long term (as we saw with Organizations A and B earlier).

In the 21st century, we have the unique opportunity of placing humanity back in business. This is not a lofty ideal or a philosophical statement; it is an essential part of creating a stable economic environment where prosperity can be sustained and citizens are fulfilled.

Most people have heard the statement "It's not personal, it's only business." Such statements usually describe malicious and unconscionable attacks on others for the sake of increasing profit *at any cost.* Money, an infinite resource, can never create satisfaction. There is simply no finishing line—people can never have enough money.

In Oliver Stone's famous film *Wall Street*, actor Michael Douglas plays the ruthless, soul-less Wall Street broker Gordon Gekko in the 1980s. Charlie Sheen plays an ambitious young broker who is initially seduced by the power of wealth, but then later understands that "greed is not good"; that there are limits to everything, especially money. In the 21st century, the Gordon Gekkos of the world have left a trail of devastation in their wake. Destroying industries, lives, professions, and organizations for the sake of accumulating money is no longer regarded as an appropriate use of skill and ability.

Today, people have moved through Maslow's hierarchy of needs from survival (the Agricultural Revolution); to shelter, clothing, and possessions (the Industrial Revolution); to connection and communication (the Information Revolution); to self-actualization (the Knowledge Economy). Many business writers have explored the concept of social capital. *Social capital* refers to activities that members of society can conduct in order to increase mutual benefit, trust, security, and cooperation. Sports clubs, neighborhood associations, and cooperatives create channels through which information about the trustworthiness of other individuals and groups can flow and be tested and verified. This increases the potential risks to those who act opportunistically because they risk being omitted from current and future transactions. Such collaboration enhances the value of society and the security and protection of its citizens.

Around the world the profit motive is being replaced by social responsibility, emotional intelligence, cooperation, and other skills that are required if people are to live in prosperity and harmony with each other. As the September 11 terrorist incident at the World Trade Center in New York illustrated, nothing is more valuable than the freedom and security of nations and individuals.

To implement such a global system, requires a fundamental change in the basis of measurement and a change in incentives. This change is brought about through intangibles management.

TWENTY-FIRST-CENTURY VALUE MANAGEMENT

Before the 21st century, managers managed value creation according to the traditional framework shown in Figure 2.10. Expenses were controlled, revenues ignored, and short-term results were all that were required to keep your job. Profit at any cost was the way businesses were run.

In the 21st century, the volatility in the financial markets of the late 20th century (the dot.com bust) created an imperative to manage value on a sustainable level. An investment worth $100 today and $2 within one month's time is only potentially attractive to speculators and day traders. However, the investing community gets financially burned by such speculative ventures. Today, it is more important to achieve moderate growth over a continuous period of time.

In the 21st century, the diagram (Figure 2.11) looks very different. The most well-known example of such curves exists in Hollywood—the movie industry. Films cost millions of dollars to produce, but are relatively inexpensive to replicate and distribute. Movies, as a product, cannot generate money until they are finished. A 95% finished film is still unmarketable because the initial investment has not yet been completed. In knowledge-based businesses, the revenue function does not start from the origin (as it does with conventional management theory). You will notice in Figure 2.11 that losses,

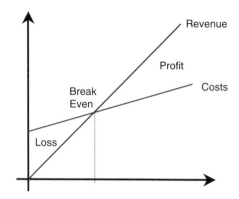

FIGURE 2.10   Pre-21st century profit management.

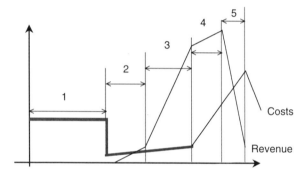

FIGURE 2.11   Knowledge economy value creation process.

break-even points, and profits are not readily determinable from the diagram. After initially high costs, expenses fall to a low maintenance level. Revenue is slow to build initially, but then rapidly increases due to *network effects*. Just before the market is saturated with the value proposition, sales will start to increase at a decreasing rate. At full market saturation, sales will drop off sharply, signaling the end of customer value creation.

VALUE CREATION STAGES IN A KNOWLEDGE-BASED ECONOMY

Value creation in a knowledge-based economy (KBE) takes place according to five stages:

Stage 1: Time-to-market
Stage 2: Market penetration
Stage 3: Market growth
Stage 4: Saturation
Stage 5: Industry obsolescence

Stage 1: Time-to-Market

Time-to-market has always existed, but in the KBE, time-to-market requires a significant amount of time and involves significant unrecoverable expenses and time.

Significant Time

In the KBE the only way to create sustainable competitive advantage is through discontinuous demand. Discontinuous demand involves developing new customers, new markets, new channels to market, new distribution methods, and new alliance partners through the commercialization of new capabilities.

Time-to-market in the Information Economy, Manufacturing Economy, and Agricultural Economy were far shorter than that required in the Knowledge Economy. Today's KBE has a time-to-market in excess of three to four times the length of that in previous economic eras.

Significant Unrecoverable Expenses

To create discontinuous demand in the KBE, significant expenses need to be allocated to knowledge assets and relationship assets. These assets are intangible and therefore cannot be sold like conventional assets. Economists call costs that cannot be reclaimed, even if production ceases, *sunk costs*. Think of a Hollywood movie producer. A movie may cost $200 million to create, but very little of that will be capable of being liquidated in the event the movie is never commercially released.

Unrecoverable expenses have always existed, but in the knowledge-based economy, they dominate the value-creation process. In the Manufacturing Economy, expenses were both fixed and variable in nature. Fixed costs dominated the time-to-market process. If a product line was unsuccessful, the equipment that was purchased could be sold to recover expenses. In the KBE, costs are mainly variable, but they are also nonrecoverable because such expenses are required to build the knowledge assets and relationship assets of employees and supply chains.

Unrecoverable Time

Time is the most important asset in the knowledge-based economy. Today, profit-seeking organizations compete on their efficiency in turning time into revenue and, hence, into profit. Governments compete on the basis of providing high-quality time to industries and encouraging and discouraging the use of time by corporations and individuals through legal means. In an organization, once time is spent it cannot be recovered. If executives make the choice to spend the organization's time on a project with a long time-to-market and unrecoverable costs, significant risks exist if the market changes and consumer demand is satisfied through another source.

Time has always been unrecoverable. Unlike the previous eras, the time required today to bring a product to market is significantly longer. This makes it essential for organizations to focus on current and future markets that can leverage the organization's core competencies. These core competencies then need to be continually increased in order for the organization to remain viable over time.

Stage 2: Market Penetration

People, at a basic level, are fearful of change and act primarily in their own self-interests. As such, if a new technology does not communicate an "imperative" or vital immediate need, it will be difficult for an organization to sell the product that it has developed.

Due to consumer fear, it is important to have organizations with lean cost structures and the ability to financially survive the "long winter" before revenue is reaped from new products. Penetration pricing is a technique used by many businesses to enter a market at a cost that is attractive to potential consumers.

In previous economic eras, market penetration used premium pricing as an entry strategy. In the Information Era, the market penetration method of pricing was to give away value. In the Knowledge Era, organizations must balance premium pricing, free pricing, penetration pricing, and value-based pricing.

Premium Pricing

When an organization engages in premium pricing, it charges the maximum amount for its product or service. Such pricing is sought to maximize the sales value from early adopters (people with a high tolerance to risk).

Free Pricing

When an organization engages in free pricing, it charges nothing for its product or service. Free pricing occurs when an organization gives away its product or service to build potential market sales. The dot.com companies of the late 1990s created price-sensitive consumers and excess choice by using free pricing. The end result was a global market of customers that would not pay for products and expected everything on the internet to be free. In the knowledge-based economy, free pricing is a dangerous process, especially in new markets because it erodes industry value and sustainability. However, it can (and should) be used under a limited set of circumstances.

Penetration Pricing

When an organization engages in penetration pricing, it heavily subsidizes the price of its product or service through discounting. Such discounting is superior to free pricing and should typically generate profitable sales.

In previous eras, penetration pricing was used to cover costs without making a profit margin. In the knowledge-based economy, penetration pricing must create a profitable margin.

Cost Pricing

When an organization engages in cost pricing, it sets the price of its product or service at the cost of production plus a margin. Such pricing is an inferior form of penetration pricing, as most costs today are sunk, not variable.

Liquidation Pricing

When an organization engages in liquidation pricing, it sets the price of its product or service below the cost of production. Such pricing is usually required to clear products or services that no longer have value in the target market.

Value-Based Pricing

When an organization engages in value-based pricing, it sets the price of its product or service through customization. In this sense, the price for each customer is based on the value the customer extracts from the product or service. Value-based pricing will be the dominant form of pricing in the KBE for noncommoditized products and services.

In the Manufacturing Age, fixed and variable costs dominated production. Products were priced in accordance with a "cost plus" basis. Manufacturers charged *margins* to sell their products. For example, cost plus 20% meant that the manufacturer would sell its product at 20% more than the cost of production.

In the KBE, sunk costs are exceptionally high, and variable costs approach zero over time. A cost plus 20% method of pricing makes no sense, because it would yield a zero price. The Information Age was the transition period between the Manufacturing Age and the Knowledge Age. During the Information Age businesses charged nothing for their product because variable costs were practically zero. In the late 1990s, financial analysts understood that such businesses could not sustain performance through such a pricing method.

Stage 3: Market Growth

In the Manufacturing Age, market growth was dominated by supply chains and market relationships. For example, a manufacturer would supply a wholesaler, who would then supply a retailer, who would supply the ultimate consumer. Market growth involved numerous intermediaries ("middlemen"). In the Information Age, computing and telecommunications technologies spelled the death of the middleman and created a process referred to as *disintermediation*. Disintermediation was the process that allowed companies to communicate directly with their customers. Dell computers is a primary example. Dell, with its ability to customize each purchase to the buyer's own exact specifications could supply the end-market with a superior product at a lower price than businesses operating under the manufacturing model of value creation.

The dark side of disintermediation is *commoditization*. Commoditization occurs when a product or service cannot be sold for sustainable profitable margin over time. The information technology (IT) meltdown in 2001 was due primarily to the commoditization of the IT industry. In 2001, computer hardware and software companies found their markets reaching saturation. Practically all consumers who could buy a computer already had several and had no need for more. Upgrades and advances in IT technology were incremental and insufficient to force consumers to repurchase more technology. Faced with falling sales and excess competition, substantial losses, massive layoffs, and mergers followed.

In 2001, the telecommunications industry faced the same problems as the IT industry: *saturation* and *commoditization*. This is not suprising because the IT and communications revolutions worked together to create astronomical value. Facing rising costs, falling customer subscriptions, and price wars, numerous communications companies downsized heavily; many also failed.

Stage 4: Saturation

A market becomes saturated when practically all consumers in a given target market can have have their *needs* satisfied by numerous competitors at a satisfactory level of quality, service, and knowledge.

Price Wars

At the point of saturation, it becomes impossible to sustainably sell the same basic product or service as other competitors at a profitable margin. In saturated markets competitors engage in price wars to force their competitors out of business. Competing organizations should exit industries subject to price wars because saturation is a permament feature and generally cannot be overcome.

In the late 1990s, the airline industry was the subject of fierce price competition by new rivals in established deregulated industries. Price wars can only be survived by organizations with strong cash flows and exceptionally lean cost structures. The lowest-cost supplier is typically the only one to survive in an industry subject to price wars.

Redundancies

An organization that is subject to the effect of saturation will seek to reduce costs dramatically. Such cost reductions typically come from head-count reduction (layoffs and redundancies). Typically, an industry subject to saturation exhibits five primary symptoms:

1. Price wars *that lead to*
2. Cost pricing *that leads to*
3. Fierce cost cutting pressure *that leads to*
4. Significant downsizing *that leads to*
5. Requirement for reinvention or exit

Reinvention

Reinvention is required when an organization's value proposition becomes irrelevant to its target market. Reinvention is the fundamental reshaping of the organization's strategy, where the strategy represents the organization's fundamental value in the market and how it will achieve that vision.

Organizations without the skill to reinvent their operations to changing market needs typically exit the industry through:

1. Mergers or divestitures
2. Liquidation
3. Bankruptcy

Stage 5: Industry Obsolescence

A market becomes obsolete when consumers no longer ascribe value to the products or services that industry provides. When the automobile was first developed, the previous transportation industry (horse and buggies) came under serious threat. Over time, the horse and buggy industry was *marginalized* and transformed into a *cottage industry*. Marginalization occurs when an industry is pushed from its broad focus to a limited focus. For example, horse and buggies still exist today but mainly as tourist attractions run by owner operators.

In the knowledge-based economy, industry obsolescence must always be expected and planned for.

Every organization in the Knowledge Economy progresses through these five stages at varying speeds. Knowledge managers need to understand these phases and profit from each one. The speed at which an organization progresses from Stage 1 of the Knowledge Economy value creation process to the final stage, stage 5, is referred to as the *extinction cycle*.

The Extinction Cycle

All organizations are subject to an extinction cycle. This applies as much to economic systems and countries as it does to organizations, religions, technologies, and professions.

In the management sense, extinction occurs when the customer value proposition of an organization becomes worthless to customers in the target market. Figure 2.12 refers to the Knowledge Economy value creation process just discussed. When organizations enter the final "meltdown" phase (stage 5) of the extinction cycle, they react by downsizing and eliminating employees.Downsizing artificially increases the profitability, stock price, and investment attractiveness of a firm. As costs fall, earnings increase because cost reductions are immediate yet revenue reductions are subject to time lags. The investment community reacts to the news of cost reductions with an increased demand for shares, which increases the stock price.

Many managers still believe—despite overwhelming evidence to the contrary—that the Knowledge Economy is just a variation on the Manufacturing

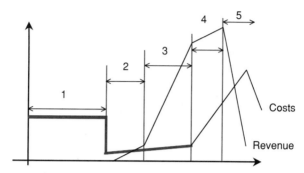

FIGURE 2.12   Knowledge Economy value creation process, with stage 5 shown.

Economy. This would be the same as saying that the Industrial Revolution was a variation on the Agricultural Revolution, which is historically inaccurate. Many believe that the "old rules still apply." This book will prove such assertions are fundamentally incorrect. The greatest risk organizations face is in not understanding the changes that have occurred and the reasons why the world is in a process of "global meltdown."

CHAPTER 3

What Knowledge Managers Need to Know

The knowledge-based economy (KBE) is a fundamentally different economic environment than anything the world has ever experienced. The KBE reverses the fundamental assumptions on which practically all conventional management systems are based. In the KBE, almost none of the conventional assumptions that previously created value are relevant. Specifically, the old assumptions are replaced by new assumptions that are opposite in understanding and application, as shown in Table 3.1.

In the knowledge-based economy, organizations do not own employees or their knowledge or their relationships. Nor do organizations own their customers, suppliers, or partners. As organizations become more knowledge-based (and less production-line based), the means of production (knowledge and relationships) will frequently reside in employees and not in physical systems. In these cases, employee knowledge is not owned by the organization, neither is the means of production. In short, in the KBE, the notion of ownership is an obsolete management concept that is a residual from the manufacturing age. Yet conventional (current) management systems are built on the concepts of ownership and control.

TABLE 3.1   How Conventional Strategy Needs to Change to Remain Relevant

	Conventional view	Intangible Management™
Market change	Slow, predictable	Fast, unpredictable
Global competition	Does not affect local markets	Has a significant effect on local markets
Global economies	Independent	Interdependent and highly connected
Strategic focus	Incremental improvement is sufficient to maintain value	Discontinuous innovation required to maintain value
Employee knowledge and relationships owned by firm	Yes	No
Value of tangible (physical) assets	Primary source of value creation	Unimportant
Value of intangible (nonphysical) assets	Unimportant	Primary source of value creation
Specialization and division of labor	Critical to productivity and performance	Multiskilling, despecialization, and aggregation of labor essential
Role of cost reduction	The only way to manage value	An irresponsible way to manage value
Role of cost quality	Role of organizational champions and visionary leaders who defy common management logic	Only way to manage value
Management structures	Top-down, command and control, ownership based	Bottom-up, complex adaptive systems, innovation based
Management hierarchies	Steep	Flat
Markets	Complicated	Complex
Key economic resources	Land, labor, capital	Knowledge, relationships, emotions, and time
Focus of management processes	Costs	Value
Management focus	Creating value by acquiring then managing physical assets	Creating value in accordance with international intangible standards
Nature of goods and services	Congealed resources	High knowledge quality products and services, low raw material costs
Production cost distribution	Fixed costs and variable costs	Sunk costs, variable costs that approach zero
Most scarce resource	Money	Time

(continues)

TABLE 3.1   (*continues*)

	Conventional view	Intangible Management™
Key management metrics	Return on assets, return on equity, earnings per share	Intangible return on investment, sustainability
Most effective methods to retain staff	More intangibles (pay)	More intangibles (freedom, purpose, flexibility, etc.)
Most effective method to retain customers	Give them discounts and loyalty cards and low prices	Ensure staff know more than the competition and the customers. Treat customers with respect
Pricing systems	Cost plus a margin	Value-based pricing as costs approach zero, so zero + a margin means we give it away
Fundamental basis of management	Demand management (sell more by lowering price)	Intangible management (sell more by ensuring constant relevancy to continually changing needs)
Basis of management decisions	Short-term financial performance	Long-term financial performance, sustainability
Value of staff	Low, or zero	High or mission critical
Importance of "hard" assets	Critical	Irrelevant
Importance of "soft" assets	irrelevant	Critical

In the knowledge-based economy, people are employed primarily due to the quality of two types of employee-owned, but organizationally controlled, intangible assets: knowledge assets and relationship assets. These assets have three fundamental dimensions: (1) creation, (2) expansion, and (3) maintenance. Knowledge processes are used to build and maintain knowledge asset value through these three fundamental dimensions. Relationship processes are used to build and maintain relationship asset value through these three fundamental dimensions.

CONTRARIAN MANAGEMENT

The concept of the "tail wagging the dog" refers to a situation where things are backwards.

In the knowledge-based economy, conventional systems are like the tail wagging the dog. Conventional systems look at financial transactions, the money the business makes and spends, as embodying all that needs to be measured and managed within the organization. Conventional systems assume that if financial figures are managed (expenses minimized) then sustainability and propsperity will naturally follow. In the Industrial Era when assets dominated the production process, this logic made sense. In the knowledge-based economy, however, assets are decreasing in relevance. Armed with superior knowledge and access to cutting-edge technologies, what an organization now *spends money on* is more important than the assets that it purchases.

In the knowledge-based economy, the value of the balance sheet (the organization's assets) has literally nothing to do with that organization's real value. Of even more concern is the fact that in a KBE it is what you spend money on (acquiring knowledge, intangible management of relationships, providing service, creating innovations, etc.) that actually creates value. The very act of reducing expenses today reduces the organization's source of value creation, which leads to a long-term reduction in financial performance and potentially the financial death of the organization.

Due to the now mission-critical nature of intangibles, it can be concluded that conventional systems (1) measure the wrong things, (2) make the wrong conclusions, and (3) force erroneous decisions on organizations. In short, conventional management systems now actually destroy organizational sustainability.

WHAT WENT WRONG?

For the recorded history of management science, the world has managed value creation according to what can be seen, touched, proven, owned, controlled, and *legally protected. Organizations created wealth by owning and controlling assets that it legally owned or could legally protect.* These assets were owned by the business and could be protected from loss (through insurance) or theft (through court action). The balance sheet proved the value of the business by showing the value of its assets. The income statement illustrated how well these assets had been leveraged to create income. Accountants, bankers, and financial analysts assessed financial health by determining ownership ratios such as return on assets (net profit ÷ total assets), return on equity (net profit ÷ shareholders' equity), and others.

With the shift to the KBE, the drivers of value have changed significantly. Robert A. Howell, a professor at the Tuck School at Dartmouth University, stated, "The income statement, balance sheet, and statement of cash flows are about as useful as an 80-year-old road map." Across the globe, the falling relevance of tangibles (assets) is well known. Alan Greenspan, Federal Reserve Board chairman, stated, "There are going to be a lot of problems in the future as accounting is not tracking investments in knowledge assets."

Former Securities Exchange commissioner, Arthur Levitt, stated, "As intangible assets grow in size and scope, more and more people are questioning whether the true value—and the drivers of that value—are being reflected in a timely manner in publicly available disclosure."

THE KNOWLEDGE-BASED ECONOMY

The large capital outlays that signified the Manufacturing Economy are no longer required. In fact, such "tangibles" now explain less than 20% of the value of most publicly listed firms. In Table 2.2 the top 20 firms by intangible value (KNOWCORP 500, March 2002) were listed. Pfizer (PFE) employing 90,000 employees reported 92.58% intangible value ($235.8 billion). Coca-Cola (KO), employing 38,000 employees, reported 91.08% intangible value ($116 billion). Wal-Mart Stores (WMT) employing 1,244,000 employees reported 87.31% intangible value ($241.5 billion). These firms belong to sectors within the economy.

Table 3.2 illustrates the analysis of the KNOWCORP 500 by sector (from transportation to services). The greatest amount of intangible value in March 2002 was generated by the services sector ($1826.1 billion), followed by the financial sector ($1825.8 billion), technology ($1795.6 billion), and health-care ($1723.2 billion). The least amount of intangible value was generated by the transportation sector ($98.2 billion). Full results are available from http://www.StandardsInstitute.org/knowcorp.

As can be seen from this analysis, in today's knowledge-based economy, profitability, productivity, financial performance, and market power are derived from how well companies manage *intangibles* such as knowledge, service, satisfaction, perceptions, expectations, emotions, response time, quality, cycle time, and innovation. Such intangibles generally cannot be owned by the organization, so they do not show up on the balance sheet of the business.

In 1996, the Organization for Economic Co-Operation and Development (OECD) produced a research report entitled the "Knowledge Based Economy." From the OECD's extensive research comes this statement:

> The term *"knowledge-based economy"* results from a fuller recognition of the role of knowledge and technology in economic growth. Knowledge, as embodied in human beings (as *"human capital"*) and in technology, has always been central to economic development. But only over the last few years has its relative importance been recognized, just as that importance is growing. The OECD economies are more strongly dependent on the production, distribution and use of knowledge than ever before.[1]

---

[1]OECD, *The Knowledge Based Economy*, Paris 1996, p. 9.

TABLE 3.2 Examining Intangible Value by Economic Sector (KNOWCORP® 500 (March 2002)—Analysis by Sector)

Economic Sector	Industry Book Value ($M)	Industry Intangible Value ($M)	Industry Market Value ($M)	Industry Sales Value ($M)	Industry Employees	Intangible Value (% of total)	Market Value (% of total)	Employment (% of total)
Transportation	36,149	98,212	134,361	81,885	1,180,736	0.95%	0.93%	4.05%
Capital Goods	61,389	141,518	202,907	191,256	835,076	1.36%	1.40%	2.86%
Utilities	154,823	184,319	339,142	428,037	2,365,445	1.77%	2.34%	8.11%
Consumer Cyclical	201,664	229,095	430,759	869,247	2,601,790	2.21%	2.97%	8.92%
Basic Materials	139,559	255,252	394,812	242,609	2,269,243	2.46%	2.72%	7.78%
Conglomerates	186,687	563,504	750,191	488,436	1,093,240	5.42%	5.18%	3.75%
Energy	420,208	814,102	1,234,310	1,112,597	3,919,890	7.84%	8.52%	13.44%
Consumer/Non-Cyclical	165,294	932,171	1,097,465	618,734	1,630,392	8.97%	7.57%	5.59%
Healthcare	271,119	1,723,225	1,994,344	479,731	8,707,161	16.59%	13.76%	29.85%
Technology	461,335	1,795,603	2,256,938	785,357	3,088,782	17.28%	15.57%	10.59%
Financial	1,161,060	1,825,779	2,986,838	1,499,703	701,011	17.57%	20.61%	2.40%
Services	842,853	1,826,107	2,668,960	1,731,007	775,948	17.58%	18.42%	2.66%
Totals	4,102,139	10,388,887	14,491,026	8,528,599	29,168,714	100.00%	100.00%	100.00%

Source: http://www.StandardsInstitute.org/knowcorp.

CHANGING EMPLOYMENT CONDITIONS

In the knowledge-based economy, the dominant contribution to gross domestic product (GDP) is from service employment. In the Industrial Age, the major GDP contribution was from manufacturing employment. In the Agricultural Age, the major GDP contribution was from agricultural employment.

At present more than 7 out of every 10 employed people work in the service sector of the economy. Service workers, often called knowledge workers, own the means of production (their knowledge, skills, and relationships). Work that is done is complex and complicated and attracts higher wages. The OECD estimated that in 1996, more than 50% of GDP in the major OECD economies was attributable to knowledge and other intangibles.

In the Industrial Age tangible resources such as land, labor, and capital were the primary inputs into the productive process. In the knowledge-based economy, intangible resources such as knowledge, relationships, emotions, and time are the primary inputs into the production process. Intangibles are very different from tangibles. In fact, intangible characteristics often have the opposite characteristics of tangibles.

Employment in the 21st century is unlike what employees experienced in other ages. Today, new technologies are changing the fundamental basis of our economic system:

> Everyone of us lives closer to the brink of obsolescence. Each one of us that is adult and qualified feels menaced in some degree by the push of new developments which establish themselves only by discarding the methods and techniques and theories that he has learnt to master. . . . The rapidity of change in social conventions and moral attitudes, associated with technological transformations in the mode of living, renders a persons experience of the world a generation ago largely irrelevant to the problems of today.[2]

As old skills become obsolete due to the emergence of new technologies, new skills are required. As people heavily resist change the impact of new technologies is often misunderstood or only viewed from a negative perception. Elvin Glaspy once said, "Once technology is out of the jar you cannot put it back in." James Rosenfield, senior vice president of the CBS Broadcasting Group, had this to say about change and new technology:

> Change brought about by a new technology is never seen as important as it may become. For example, when the telephone was invented, the Chief Engineer of the British Post Office said it might be useful in America, but in England, there was no need for telephones, since "we have plenty of messenger boys." A similar view was taken by an officer of Western Union, who expected the phone primarily

[2]Barry Jones, *Sleepers, Wake!: Technology & the Future of work*, Oxford University Press, 1982, p. 181.

would be used to help telegraph operators communicate with each other. He simply could not visualize the elimination of telegraphers by a universal telephone system.[3]

RESOURCE TYPES AND ECONOMIC SYSTEMS

In the 1950s, Sir E. Henry Phelps Brown, a retired professor at the London School of Economics, and his associate, Sheila V. Hopkins, reported their findings to *Economica*, an economics journal, regarding 1000 years of price movements in England. Their research produced an excellent indication of how price *instability* indicates a movement from one economic age to another (see Figure 3.1).

David Warsh, associate editor of *Forbes* in 1977, believed that the sudden price increases (indicative of a change between "Ages") were due to an increase in the complexity of our culture and were required to pay for increased services. The data in Figure 3.1 show that the period of price stability is nearly *halving for each new "Age"*. For example, the Commercial Age had 425 years of price stability, the Market Age had 180 years of price stability, and the Industrial Age had 102 years of price stability. Unfortunately, these data were published in the 1950s, so the start of the Information Age is not presented.

Recent analyses[4] illustrate that it took 46, 38, and 17 years, respectively for electricity, the telephone, and television to reach 30% of U.S. homes (Table 3.3). In contrast, the Internet took only 7 years to reach 30% of households.

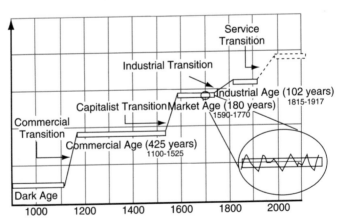

FIGURE 3.1   Economic transitions and price stability in the 1950s.

[3]James Rosenfield, Senior Vice President of the CBS Broadcasting Group.
[4]UCLA Internet Report, "Surveying the Digital Future."

TABLE 3.3   Years to Penetrate 30% of
U.S. Households

Electricity	46 years
Telephone	38 years
Television	17 years
Internet	7 years

As adoption times decrease, we will move through economic transitions more quickly.

INTANGIBLE MANAGEMENT

Intangible management is defined in International Intangible Standard IIS1001 as Follows:

> The concepts, methodologies and tools required for comprehensively identifying, consistently classifying, objectively valuing, scientifically managing, and financially reporting the impact of intangible transactions on long-term and short-term organizational financial performance. (IIS1001. D1)

To understand the application of intangible management, we must first understand intangible characteristics, intangible transactions, and intangible value.

INTANGIBLE CHARACTERISTICS

The knowledge-based economy is forcing a fundamental change in management thought. Intangibles obey very different behavioral laws than do tangibles. In fact, most of the laws governing the behavior of intangibles are the direct opposite of how people have been taught to manage in the past. IIS1001 explores the foundations of the science of intangible management:

1. *Intangibles typically cannot be directly touched.* True intangibles do not have physical form. When an intangible is used (knowledge) it may become part of a tangible, but we cannot touch the knowledge that creates that tangible (IIS1001. C1). Conversely, tangibles can be directly touched.

2. *Intangibles cannot be directly measured.* Tangibles have always been directly measured through financial transactions generated via market exchanges (trading). Your satisfaction (a soft intangible) cannot be measured directly and typically cannot be sold through the market

system (IIS1001.C2). Conversely, the traditional way to measure a tangible is directly.

3. *Intangibles are not evidenced by financial transactions.* It is incorrect to perceive that the value of a financial transaction can embody the total value of an intangible. Consider an expenditure of $1000 to gain new skills. The value of this knowledge is not $1000; it is what you do with it after you have gained it. As accounting looks backwards (into historical transactions), it ignores the fact that intangibles create their value in the future (IIS1001.C3). Conversely, tangibles are always evidenced by historical financial transactions.

4. *Intangibles create future value.* Examples of intangibles such as knowledge, relationships, expectations, service, quality, and speed create future value as they influence expectations about the future. Because all intangible transactions are future orientated, conventional accounting and management systems ignore their potential impact due to the *conservatism concept* (do not recognize it until it happens) and the *materiality concept* (exchanges of money must occur because the result must be auditable) (IIS1001.C4). Assets are deemed as a source of future value. Conventional management practices deem that assets are turned into revenue at a cost (expenses). Profitability defines the rate at which realized asset value (revenue) exceeds asset costs (expenses).

5. *Intangibles cannot be owned.* Legal (hard) intangibles, also known as intellectual assets, are a trick of the law to create ownership where none actually exists (IIS1001.C5). As tangibles are evidenced by financial transactions (exchanges of money), they fall within the definition of a legal property right under legal practice.

6. *Intangibles cannot be voluntarily extinguished.* Under accounting rules an asset must have a useful life at which it no longer has value. This allows assets to be *depreciated* or *amortized* over a period of time. Intangibles cannot be extinguished like tangibles. Intangibles are viewed under intangible standards as having an infinite life. As such, depreciation and amortization do not apply to intangibles (IIS1001.C6). A $20,000 computer may be deemed to have a useful life of 5 years under taxation laws. Using various depreciation methods, the $20,000 expenditure will be turned into an expense at a specified rate until the claims over the asset are extinguished.

7. *Intangibles do not diminish with use; instead, they increase.* A fundamental foundation of economic theory is that when you add more and more of a resource to a productive process the incremental gain out of adding each successive unit of the resource decreases (the law of diminishing marginal utility). Intangibles behave in the opposite way. The more knowledge you have, the more knowledge you can gain as you talk

with others and share your knowledge. Intangibles are subject to increasing returns (IIS1001.C7). Unlike an intangible, if you use a tangible, it literally "wears out" with that use.

8. *Intangibles are typically felt when they are removed, not when they are present.* If you love someone and they leave you, you might say, "I didn't realize what I had until it was gone." Intangible standards primarily measure and manage the absence of intangible value, not the presence of that value. Such a management concept is counterintuitive to most (IIS1001.C8). Conversely, tangibles are defined by their presence, not their absence.

9. *The true impact of intangibles is typically not understood or recognized due to the impact of derived demand.* Derived demand has always been one of the most powerful competitive forces in existence. *Derived demand* is demand that is literally "derived" or "created" from a *new* technology, product, or service. Derived demand does *not* exist *before* the product is produced, only *after* the technology has been released and used in the market. Television, the telephone, computers, automobiles, and airplanes were innovations initially rejected by the market ("if man was meant to fly he would have been given wings"), but grew to become billion dollar industries due to the impacts of derived demand. Intangibles that create significantly changed perceptions, that threaten existing knowledge infrastructures, are the intangibles that underpin new industries and new career paths (IIS1001.C12).

10. *Intangibles can be simultaneously deployed without loss of value.* Tangible assets can only exist in one point in space and at one time. In this sense, you cannot drive a car that someone else is driving in another country. Intangibles are very different. Information on the Internet can be read by 100,000 people at once without loss of value. If correct mechanisms are in place, intangible value can actually increase with multiple usage (IIS1001.C16).

Considering these points, it is little wonder that current management and value systems do not, and cannot, measure the value of intangibles or manage them correctly.

THE SOLUTION

As you progress through this book you will frequently refer to the IIS5001 system. The IIS5001 system is at the heart of intangible standards and provides a practical perspective and framework with which to implement and enforce intangible standards within an organization. All the chapters in this book will assist you in understanding how to apply the IIS5001 system to an organization.

The system requires a new language to describe the problems faced by knowledge-based organizations so this text will frequently refer you to numerous intangible standards that you can use, to build that language.

INTANGIBLE VALUE

There are two types of intangibles: (1) hard intangibles—those that the law states can be owned (trademarks, patents, copyrights, etc.) and (2) soft intangibles—those that cannot be owned, only managed and leveraged (service, satisfaction, knowledge, quality, etc.). What is typically not known is that intangibles that can be owned [legal (or hard) intangibles] are actually created from intangibles that cannot be owned [competitive (or soft) intangibles]. Because conventional systems only measure changes in ownership as evidenced by financial transactions, *competitive intangibles typically are not recorded in financial reports*. Because we only manage what we measure, a failure to measure becomes a failure to manage.

In Table 3.2, the value of competitive intangibles can be approximated by the difference between market value and book value. In the next chapter we will investigate the nature of intangibles in far greater detail.

UNDERSTANDING INTANGIBLES

Conventional management systems are specifically designed to manage "the bottom line," or financial performance, of an organization by identifying, reporting, and managing financial transactions. The income statement (or profit and loss statement) shows the revenue and expense financial transactions over a period of time. The balance sheet shows the financial transactions relating to assets, liabilities, and capital. The cash flow statement shows the financial transactions relating to cash inflows and cash outflows.

THE BOTTOM LINE

The bottom line occurs when financial transactions (exchanges of money) are aggregated into financial performance and represented in financial reports (see Figure 3.2).

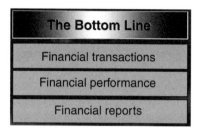

FIGURE 3.2   Explaining the bottom line.

FINANCIAL TRANSACTIONS AND INTANGIBLE TRANSACTIONS

Intangible Standard IIS1001 defines an *intangible* as follows:

> An intangible is defined as any event that creates or modifies perceptions or expectations of the future behavior, value or relevance, of an individual, group, or otherwise constituted organization. (IIS1001.D2)

An intangible can be a *source intangible or a destination intangible*:

> A source intangible is defined as the source from which soft (competitive) intangibles are generated. (IIS1001.D3)
> A destination intangible is the embodiment of a source intangible. Such embodiments typically give rise to the creation of hard (legal) intangibles. (IIS1001.D4)

Source Intangibles

Source intangibles include knowledge, service, quality, employee morale, systems, turnover, strategy, quality, and other sources of intangible value. Source intangibles are literally the *source* of competitive intangibles and legal intangibles.

Customer service is a source intangible. Customer service exists in a neutral state until an *interaction* changes perceptions or expectations. According to IIS1001.C9, all source intangibles exist in a neutral state until influenced by an interaction. An interaction is defined by IIS1001.D5 as any human or nonhuman intervention, *or lack thereof*, which alters perceptions or expectations. Whenever there is a change in a perception or an expectation, an intangible transaction occurs. Intangible Standard IIS1001.D6 defines intangible transactions:

> An intangible transaction is defined as the change in perceptions or expectations that occur when interactions alter the quality or quantity of source, or destination, intangibles. (IIS1001.D6)

For example, *poor customer service* is problematic for an organization, because customers perceive that future customer service will *also* be of low value. As perceptions and expectations have changed, an intangible transaction is deemed to have occurred. Intangible transactions directly influence the allocation of time capital between productive and nonproductive time. Time capital is defined in IIS1001.D7 as:

> Time Capital is the total amount of productive and non-productive time available to an entity, measured in hours. (IIS1001.D7)

Productive time capital is defined by reference to nonproductive time capital (compare IIS1001.C2 and IIS1001.C8). To explain the concept of *by reference* let us consider an employee, Bob. Bob may be employed to work 2000 hours by an organization, but may only be productive for 900 hours due to various overheads present within the business (see Figure 3.3).

In Bob's example, we have actually determined productive time by reference to nonproductive time. It is the 1100 hours of nonproductive time that allows us to understand how much productive time Bob actually leveraged, given a total time of 2000 hours. In this sense, the flow is actually that shown in Figure 3.4.

The term *entity* in IIS1001.D7 is also significant. Time capital can apply to many entities such as (1) an individual, (2) a group of people, (3) an organization, (4) an industry, (5) an economy, (6) the global economy, or some other entity.

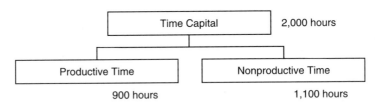

FIGURE 3.3   Productive time and nonproductive time.

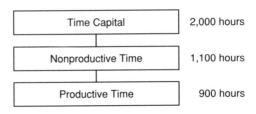

FIGURE 3.4   Determining productive time by reference to nonproductive time.

Intangible Source Analysis

There are numerous types of intangible sources. Each source has a varying degree of value in reference to different comparative dimensions, as shown in Table 3.4.

Superior Sources (IIS1001.D40)

A *superior source* is a source intangible that has high quality across internal dimensions (IIS1001.C45 to IIS1001.C48) and medium quality across external dimensions (IIS1001.C49 to IIS1001.D52). Superior source intangibles create *cash cows* within an organization and also create *competitive blinding* because new knowledge is ignored if it does not fit within the established confines of superior source knowledge.

In the KBE, organizations must ensure that superior source knowledge is constantly expanded by inversion sources.

Inversion Sources (IIS1001.D44)

Inversion sources literally redefine conventional wisdom through new advances in knowledge. *Inversion sources* are typically disregarded by organizations when they first impact the organization because inversion sources typically undermine superior sources. Intangible Standard IIS14001 (Intangible

TABLE 3.4   Better Understanding of Intangible Sources and Intangible Source Quality

Intangible standard:	Intangible standard: IIS1001	Superior source .D40	Average source .D41	Deficient source .D42	Obsolete source .D43	Inversion source .D44
Internal dimensions	.D38					
Quality	.C45	High	Medium	Low	Negative	Highest
Relevance	.C46	High	Medium	Low	Negative	None
Cost efficiency	.C47	High	Medium	Negative	Negative	Negative
Profitability	.C48	High	None	Negative	Negative	Low
External Dimensions	.D39					
Sustainability	.C49	Medium	None	Negative	Negative	Highest
Customer value	.C50	Medium	None	None	None	Highest
Societal value	.C51	Medium	None	None	None	Highest
Investor value	.C52	Medium	None	None	None	Highest

Change Management) deals with the reasons why inversion sources are typically disregarded by organizations. To understand the typical reaction to inversion sources, consider the following quotations:

> Who in the hell wants actors to talk? —*Harry Warner, founder of Warner Bros.
> Studio, 1927*
> There is no reason for any individual to have a computer in their home. —*Ken
> Olsen, President of Digital Equipment, 1977*
> Get that toy of my desk!! —*Said by an irate banker to Alexander Graham Bell, the
> inventor of the telephone*
> For God's sake, go down to reception and get rid of a lunatic who's down there.
> He says he's got a machine for seeing wireless! Watch him—he may have a razor on
> him."—*Said by the editor of* the London Daily Express *when refusing to see John
> Baird, inventor of television in 1925*
> I think there is a world market for about five computers. —*Thomas J. Watson,
> Chairman of IBM, 1943*
> Innovative technologies also have another very important effect. They fre-
> quently create their own demand. The modern jet airliner is a case in point. The
> rapid spread of national and international air travel could barely have been im-
> agined 20 or 30 years ago. Consumer durables such as television receivers are
> also examples of significant new industries which have developed as a result of
> technical innovation.—*Hansard, House of Representatives, 18 September 1980,
> p. 1518*

Inversion sources give rise to disruptive technologies that destroy the value of
superior sources. The Intangible Change Management Standard (IIS14001)
details methods and procedures to harness the economic power of inversion
sources.

Destination Intangibles

Knowledge is not valuable in its source form, only in its applied form. Conventional management assumes that the applied form of knowledge (information) is totally representative of the knowledge that created it. This is
incorrect. Destination intangibles, like the information contained on a page,
represents a small fraction of a person's knowledge in that specific area. There
are many reasons for this.

> When source intangibles are exchanged (i.e., knowledge is shared) each
> exchangee has their source intangible potentially increased or decreased.
> (IIS1001.R1)

Whether or not a source intangible increases or decreases is due primarily to
what intangibles are transferred (see IIS10001, Intangible Knowledge Management Standard).

Knowledge Assets

Organizations have two fundamental resources in the knowledge economy: *knowledge assets* and *relationship assets*. The definition of knowledge assets is as follows:

> Knowledge assets occur when source intangibles interact with destination intangibles to modify, or otherwise change, source intangibles or destination intangibles. (IIS1001.D9)

To explain this critical concept, refer to Figure 3.5. Let us assume that Bob (owner 1) uses his knowledge (source intangible 1) to find information (destination intangible, Dest 2) on the Internet that belongs to Fred (owner 2). Bob then *integrates* this knowledge into his own source knowledge to formulate new source knowledge (source 1m). Bob then uses this knowledge to create information (destination intangible, Dest 3).

The critical factor of a knowledge asset is that it involves dealing directly with a destination intangible, not another source intangible.

Relationship assets are defined as follows:

> Relationship assets occur when source intangibles interact with other source intangibles to modify, or otherwise change, source intangibles or destination intangibles. (IIS1001.D10)

Let us return to our earlier example of Bob and Fred. If Bob (owner 1) *interacts* directly with Fred (owner 2) then the asset is a *relationship asset* as shown in Figure 3.6. The benefit of a relationship asset is that both source intangibles are modified for participants involved in the interaction. The benefits of this exchange can be exponential as one source intangible (Bob's knowledge) interacts with another source intangible (Fred's knowledge), leading to a modification of both source intangibles (both Bob and Fred can potentially benefit).

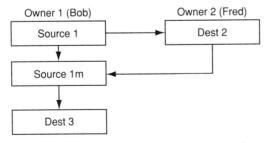

FIGURE 3.5   Understanding how knowledge assets are formed.

FIGURE 3.6   Understanding the nature of relationship assets.

Knowledge assets occur through *information infrastructures* and relationship assets occur through *interaction infrastructures*.

Information Infrastructures

Knowledge assets are created through information infrastructures:

> Information infrastructures allow the creation, Intangible Management and dissemination of knowledge assets within a specified event space. Information infrastructures can be structured (formal) or unstructured (informal). (IIS1001.D15)

The importance of information infrastructures cannot be underestimated. Consider why:

> The sum total of human knowledge changed very slowly prior to the relatively recent beginnings of scientific thought. It has been estimated that by 1800 it was doubling every 50 years; by 1950, doubling every 10 years; and that presently [1972] it is doubling every 5 years. Computer technology may make a frighteningly high rate of increase possible for centuries. —*J. Martinand and A. Norman, The Computer Society, Penguin, 1973*
>
> The volume of information is estimated to be doubling every 20 months. — *New Scientist, 9 January 1993*

In 2001 Internet information was estimated to be doubling every 90 days. It is estimated that for the typical enterprise, the amount of unstructured information doubles every 3 months. Organizations must be constantly aware of the burden placed on existing information infrastructures.

Interaction Infrastructures

Relationship assets are created through interaction infrastructures:

> Interaction infrastructures allow the creation, Intangible Management and dissemination of relationship assets within a specified event space. Relationship infrastructures can be structured (formal) or unstructured (informal). (IIS1001.D16)

Interaction infrastructures facilitate the interaction of source intangibles. Communications, computing, and human infrastructures are essential to the creation and sustenance of relationship assets.

MAKING IT PRACTICAL

Let us assume that you have just taken over a café called "Your Café." This café is deep in the heart of the café district of your city. You have at least 10 direct competitors (other cafés) on your street and 10 indirect competitors (hotels, restaurants, etc.). Irrespective of this competition, business is brisk and you are set to make good returns. Your Café is staffed by a chef, two waiters, and you (the cashier and boss). You are interested in understanding how intangible standards could be applied to Your Café to assist you to better manage and improve financial performance.

It is the first day of the operation of Your Café and a regular customer (Joe) of the old owner enters to buy a cup of coffee. The coffee costs $2.50. Joe didn't have to pick Your Café, especially with 20 other direct and indirect competitors close by. You greet Joe and show him to a table. After looking at a menu, Joe makes a decision and calls the waiter for service. After the order is placed, Joe waits until the coffee arrives. If the coffee is not what he ordered, he'll send it back. Satisfied with his order, Joe drinks the coffee, gets the bill, approaches the cashier and then *pays the bill* (the financial transaction occurs). It is only when *money changes hands* that conventional management recognizes that value has been created. If Joe were to walk out of Your Café without making a purchase, the financial accounts would not reflect this fact.

After Joe pays the bill, he leaves Your Café. He assesses the experience and creates and stores the knowledge of that experience. If Joe likes you, or your staff, and the quality of the coffee, he may choose to share that knowledge with his network of contacts. Conversely, if Joe dislikes you, or your staff, or Your Café, or your coffee, he is likely to share that knowledge with his network of contacts.

As an owner, you know that a substantial cost is involved with poor service. You know that poor service can reduce current business, repeat business, and referred business.

Intangible Mapping™ Analysis

The International Intangible Management Standards Institute developed *Intangible Mapping™* to assist organizations to better understand how financial transactions are created, lost, and prevented from reoccurring. As can be seen in Figure 3.7, the financial transaction of $2.50 was the 17th transaction (what conventional systems record). The remaining 22 transactions are unmanaged by conventional systems, *but are the core of the value creation process for the organization.*

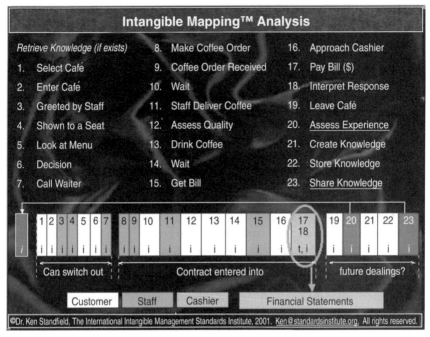

FIGURE 3.7 Intangible Mapping® Analysis.

The process of identifying and mapping intangible transactions using transaction management is referred to as *intangible mapping*. Transactions 3, 4, 7, 8, 9, 11, 15, and 16 indicate transactions that involve customers interacting with Café staff. The 17th transaction identifies the financial transaction ($2.50). All remaining transactions are shown in white, indicating that they are customer-specific transactions.

As can be seen from this analysis, *immediate* financial results (the $2.50) are the accumulation of numerous intangible transactions. *Repeat business* and *referred business* are the result of intangible transactions that occur after the financial (17th) transaction.

DOUBLE-ENTRY INTANGIBLE ACCOUNTING

Double-entry intangible accounting was developed[5] to provide organizations with a way to account for intangible transactions in an era where the source

[5]Dr. Ken Standfield, Chairman of the International Intangible Standards Institute, 1992.

of value creation (source intangibles) could not be owned. Double-entry intangible accounting will be covered in later chapters.

LINKING INTANGIBLE TRANSACTIONS TO FINANCIAL PERFORMANCE

A direct, casual relationship exists between intangible transactions and short-term and long-term financial performance. According to Intangible Standard IIS1001.C11:

> Financial transactions and financial performance are the end result (or accumulation and translation) of numerous intangible transactions. (IIS1001.C11)

As we witnessed in the Your Café example, it is the quality of the expectations and perceptions that an entity creates that dictates if that entity receives financial value in the form of financial transactions.

The link between intangible transactions and financial transactions is easy to understand if you view financial transactions as the outcome of the *contract process*.

CONTRACTS AND THE KBE

In the knowledge-based economy, organizations enter into *promises* with entities (customers, suppliers, employees, partners, etc.). Because promises establish perceptions and expectations, promises are the purest form of intangible transactions (compare IIS1001.D6).

Precontractual Assessments

When a customer visits Your Café, it is because that customer believes that the demand for time capital they demand will be matched by the supply of time capital the organization supplies.

It is the demand and supply of time capital that dictates if promises are kept, contracts are fulfilled, and financial transactions occur. Intangible economics[6] was developed to assist organizations to better manage time capital as a strategic resource.

---

[6]Dr. Ken Standfield, Chairman of the International Intangible Standards Institute, 1992.

Practically Applying Intangible Economics

When a customer approaches an organization they will determine if their price for time capital is *consistent* with the organization supplying the time capital. In such a situation several things can happen:

- *The customer walks out without buying.* The price of time capital is greater than the customer could afford. In the knowledge-based economy, people are so busy that if their needs cannot be met, they simply go somewhere where they can be. There is no need to stay with an underperforming organization if substitute competitors can be found.
- *The customer believes that the promise will be kept.* The price of time capital is affordable by the customer. In this case the business has enough time to deliver the promises at the level the customer requires to satisfy that customer's perceptions and expectations.

We will look at intangible economics in later chapters. IIS7001 is the international intangible standard that deals with intangible economics. In the Your Café example (Figure 3.7), intangible transactions 1 to 7 were the precontractual intangible transactions.

Contractual Assessments

In the Your Café example (Figure 3.7), intangible transactions 8 to 18 were the contractual intangible transactions. If the customer has become locked into the transaction with the assumption that his demand for time capital will be satisfied by the organization's supply of time capital, then the interactions that occur up to the point of the financial transaction (the conclusion of the contract) will fundamentally dictate repeat business and referred business.

Repeat Business

Repeat business is a major determinant of an organization's profitability and sustainability in the KBE. When customers give an entity repeat business, the organization effectively eliminates the advertising costs required to gain a new customer. Repeat business customers usually buy more from a business and do so more frequently than other types of customers. Intangible standards define repeat business as follows:

> Repeat business is defined as the willingness to re-supply time capital demand to a specific entity. IIS1001.D15

Referred Business

If a business is successful at gaining repeat business, it may also be successful in encouraging repeat clientele to recommend the organization to their network of contacts. Personal referrals are the most powerful form of marketing in all economic eras, especially in the KBE. Referred business is therefore the most effective form of marketing, because it is not conducted by the business, but by the clients of the business. Intangible standards define it as follows:

> Referred business is defined as the willingness to recommend an entity's intangible supply to contacts within personal relationship networks. (IIS1001.D16)

Both repeat and referred business are essential to the financial health of organizations in the knowledge-based economy.

Postcontractual Assessments

After the financial transaction has been completed, the quality of all of the intangible transactions will be assessed. It is at this stage that the decision on repeat business and referred business is made. Transactions 19 to 23 in the Your Café example (Figure 3.7) represent the period in which postcontractual assessments occur.

Competitive barriers exist around all organizations, regardless of industry sector. Competitive barriers come into existence due to the effects of *positive and negative interpretation distortion*. Intangible standards define competitive barriers as follows:

> Competitive barriers occur when violations in expectations, promises and perceptions translate into a psychological aversion of supplying a particular entity with time capital. (IIS1001.D17)

For example, if Joe purchases the cup of coffee for $2.50 and perceives the event subject to positive interpretation distortion then the competitive barrier on Your Café will fall relative to the competitive barriers of all other direct, and indirect, competitors. If Joe purchases the cup of coffee for $2.50 and perceives the event subject to negative interpretation distortion, then the competitive barrier on Your Café will increase relative to the competitive barrier of all other direct, and indirect, competitors.

Transactions 20 and 22 in the Intangible Mapping™ diagram (Figure 3.7) explore how the assessment of intangibles can lead to the creation of a competitive barrier. Negative customer experiences give rise to *competitive barriers*. Competitive barriers are the dark side of the knowledge-based economy, because they are not seen by the affected organization. To understand psychological aversion, it is important to understand interpretation distortion.

Interpretation Distortion

Customers are no longer prepared to give the benefit of the doubt to any person or organization for poor service, deficient knowledge, low quality, negative interactions, or other *perceived* transgressions. Intangible Standard IIS1001.D21 defines *experience* as either a positive or negative interpretation distortion. IIS1001.D20 defines these subterms as:

> *Negative interpretation distortion* is the personal assessment that negative short-term events will be encountered in all future organizational interactions (IIS1001.D20a). *Positive interpretation distortion* is the personal assessment that positive short-term events will be encountered in all future organizational interactions. (IIS1001.D20b)

Interpretation distortion is a double-edged sword for organizations in the knowledge-based economy. Negative interpretation distortion explains the "one strike and you're out" mentality of customers in this day and age.

For example, if Joe receives poor treatment by Your Café, or the coffee quality is not as he expects, then it is likely that Joe will subject Your Café to negative interpretation distortion. It is also likely that Joe will advise his network of contacts not to visit Your Café also. It is also unlikely that Joe will visit Your Café again.

If Joe receives excellent treatment from Your Café, Joe will undergo positive interpretation distortion. It is likely that Joe will again visit Your Café and tell his network of contacts to do likewise.

Comprehensive Value

Comprehensive value is defined in Intangible Standard IIS1001.D25:

> Comprehensive value is the total effect of all intangible transactions on a specific value creation process. Comprehensive value is assessed by how well an organization creates perceptions and expectations of consistent behavior. (IIS1001.D25)

Intangibles such as knowledge, service, quality, and employee morale specifically affect long-term customer and employee value *perceptions* and *expectations* about the future. Comprehensive value therefore refers to the effectiveness and efficiency of all intangible transactions used to generate a current financial transaction and facilitate repeat and referred business.

To track comprehensive value, we need a solid scientific framework with which to analyze intangible interactions. This framework is made possible by grouping intangible transactions by intangible categories.

Intangible Categories

Just as conventional systems group expenses, assets, liabilities, revenue, and capital into categories when they are similar in nature, so too does intangible management group different intangible transactions into similar categories, referred to as *intangible categories*. Intangible Standard IIS1001 identifies numerous intangible categories including the following.

- **Customer Intangibles (IIS1001.S10).** Customer intangibles relate to *customer-only* interactions with the organization. In the Your Café example (Figure 3.7), customer intangibles are referenced by the following transactions: 1, 2, 5, 6, 10, 12, 13, 14, 16, 19, 21, and 22.
- **Employee Intangibles (IIS1001.S11).** Employee intangibles relate to *employee* interactions with the organization.
- **Supplier Intangibles (IIS1001.S12).** Supplier intangibles relate to *supplier* interactions with the organization.
- **Organizational Intangibles (IIS1001.S13).** Organizational intangibles relate to *organizational* interactions with employees, customers, or other groups and the organization. In the Your Café example all transactions relate to organizational intangibles.
- **External Intangibles (IIS1001.S14).** External intangibles relate to *nonorganizational* interactions with employees, customers, or other groups of other organizations. In the Your Café example, external intangibles are the intangibles that are designed to move business away from Your Café to that of the competition.
- **Relational Intangibles (IIS1001.S15).** Relational intangibles occur when one group interacts with another. For the categories listed above each can have a relational category. For example, transaction 3 (greeted by staff) is an employee–customer relational transaction. Whoever initiates the interaction is the first to be presented, hence, employee–customer means the employee initiates the relationship with the customer, whereas customer–employee means the customer initiates the relationship with the employee.
- **Repeat Intangibles (IIS1001.S16).** Not all intangibles can, or will, be sufficient to attract a customer back to the business after a value transaction has been completed. This return business, also known as repeat business, is actually the only real source of sustainability for knowledge-based businesses.

- **Referred Intangibles** (IIS1001.S17). Not all intangibles can, or will, be sufficient to motivate customers to recommend an organization to that customer's network of contacts. Referred business is the most powerful form of marketing in the knowledge-based economy.

Having high-quality repeat and referred intangibles is essential for organizations wishing to succeed in the knowledge-based economy. To understand why these intangible categories are critical to an organization's continued existence, we need to investigate competitive barriers.

INTANGIBLES CREATE TANGIBLES

This chapter has proven that financial results are the accumulation of numerous intangible transactions. Intangible transactions (or expectations of current and future organizational behavior and value) create intangible performance (service, satisfaction, knowledge, quality, etc.) that gives an organization the ability to *make and receive* financial transactions. The impact of this concept is substantial.

> To manage financial transactions, we must first manage intangible transactions.

THE IIS5001 MODEL

After 15 years of research and development, the International Intangible Management Standards Institute (http://www.StandardsInstitute.org) is the world's first organization to be able to identify, classify, measure, value, manage, report, and manage intangible transactions in familiar financial terms using the new financial reporting and management systems based on international intangible standards. The IIS5001 model manages, values, and reports intangible value to create reliable and objective financial measures that can be used to comprehensively compare intangible value in different industries so that investor confidence is safeguarded and there is reduced opportunity of fraud, misrepresentation, or creative accounting by organizations (i.e., Enron). Referred to as the IIS5001 model, this system connects an organization's top line (strategy) to the bottom line (financial performance) through the middle line (intangible performance) (see Figure 3.8).

INTEGRATING IIS5001 INTO CURRENT SYSTEMS

The integration of IIS5001 into current management systems requires knowledge of intangible standards. Once this knowledge is gained, IIS5001 becomes an addition to existing systems, *not* a replacement.

INPUTS INTO THE IIS5001 SYSTEM

To operate the IIS5001 system, the organization must collect four types of data: (1) operational data, (2) financial data, (3) human resource data, and (4) intangible mapping and benchmarking data (see Figure 3.9). While the first three data sources exist within traditional organizations, the fourth data source (intangible benchmarking data) can only be collected through IIS5001 approved software programs.

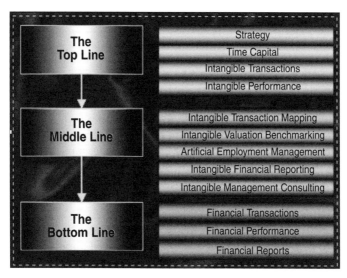

FIGURE 3.8   The IIS5001 model.

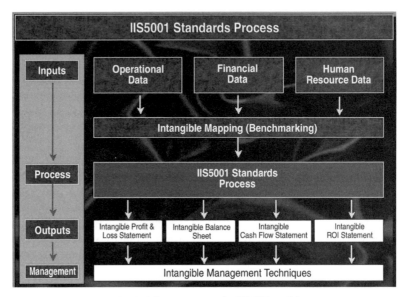

FIGURE 3.9   Inputs into the IIS5001 model.

The IIS5001 system initially uses the IIS5001 Intangible Valuation Standard to *benchmark* the translation of time capital into financial performance. By financially measuring the ability of the organization to translate time capital into financial performance (based on objective financial and operational data), we create benchmarks through which we can assess future uses of time capital.

To assess the financial quality of time capital, IIS5001 tracks value changes in knowledge assets and relationship assets. Operational management and changes in strategy alter allocations in time capital and alter intangible transactions, thereby changing financial performance. The IIS5001 system financially estimates how changes in time capital will impact financial performance given current operational data. This acts as an *early-warning system* and *opportunity identification system* for organizations. This information can be used for:

1. Determining intangible return on investment (intangibleROI)
2. Creating artificial employment
3. Identifying, financially measuring, reducing, and managing intangible costs
4. Performing intangible scenario analysis on how different strategies could alter financial performance
5. Financially valuing the knowledge within the organization

6. Financially valuing the information within the organization
7. Financially valuing the relationships within the organization
8. Preparing intangible financial statements that financially measure all of the above factors and report value changes to management on a periodic basis
9. Better managing competitive actions by assessing how those actions could impact the value of the intangible transactions the organization currently makes
10. Much more

All of these uses give executives, managers, and employees new tools to increase profitability, reduce costs, and increase sustainability.

CHAPTER 4

Intangible Operating Structures

In the last chapter we learned that financial transactions were the end result of numerous intangible transactions. The quality of those intangible transactions determines current business, repeat business, and referred business. Intangible transactions are responsible for creating financial transactions and future profitability.

Because conventional management systems only measure financial transactions and specifically exclude the systematic capture of intangible transactions, conventional systems do not measure the source of value creation, only its manifestation.

This chapter will illustrate that of the three categories and 18 core resource types that organizations can manage in the knowledge-based economy (KBE), conventional management systems only manage one category and 6 core resources. Assuming consistent resource value across all 18 core resource types, conventional management techniques fail to even acknowledge more than 60% of an organization's resources.

APPLICATION OF INTANGIBLE STANDARDS

Intangible management applies to all organizations. Intangible management concerns itself with the scientific management of *all* tangible and intangible resources at an organization's disposal. Organizations have access to two basic types of resources: *tangible* and *intangible*.

THREE-LEVEL MANAGEMENT

Figure 4.1 illustrates that organizations manage three levels of resources in order to create effectiveness, efficiency, and sustainability. These three levels are defined by IIS2001, the Intangible Operating Structures Standard, as follows:

- *Level 1 Resources (IIS2001.S1)*. Level 1 (L1) resources are legal property rights. IIS2001.D1 defines *legal property rights* as the right of an entity to own, otherwise control, and protect an item of identified value (as evidenced by a financial transaction). The current legal system assists organizations and individuals to enforce their legal property rights. Examples of level 1 resources include conventional management's

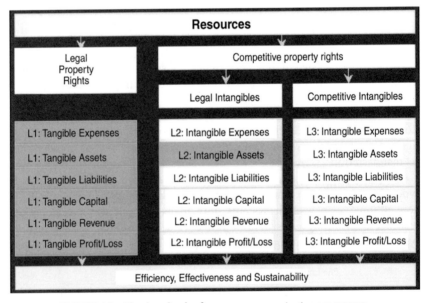

FIGURE 4.1   The three levels of resources an organization can manage.

understanding of (tangible) assets, (tangible) liabilities, (tangible) expenses, (tangible) revenue, and (tangible) capital.

- *Level 2 Resources (IIS2001.S2).* Level 2 (L2) resources represent legal intangibles. *Legal intangibles* are defined as ownership rights that are conferred by an act of Parliament, or by national or international agreement, and that create legal ownership in the *represented form* of an applied *intangible competitive right* (IIS2001.D2). Conventional management acknowledges legal intangibles as "intangible assets." The concept of legal intangibles has been systematically expanded[1] to extend legal intangibles to the categories of intangible expenses, intangible liabilities, intangible revenue, and intangible capital. Legal ownership allows the represented form (trademark, copyright, patent, etc.) of the intangible to be sold, licensed, or otherwise controlled as though the intangible were tangible in nature.

- *Level 3 Resources (IIS2001.S3).* Level 3 (L3) resources represent competitive intangibles. *Competitive intangibles* are defined as the source from which legal intangibles are *created, maintained,* and *enhanced* over time (IIS2001.D3).

How the Three Levels Relate

In the knowledge-based economy, Intangible Standard IIS2001.R1 defines the fundamental interaction between the three levels of resources present within all organizations (see Figure 4.2). L3 resources (competitive intangibles) are the source of all value creation. L3 resources, when applied through decisions, create L2 resources (legal intangibles). Level 1 resources are then required for production.

Exploring Causal Relationships

Sometimes, a decision (L3) will lead directly to the purchase of a L1 resource (for example, an asset) without any L2 resource being created. In fact, L2 resources are always created, but many are not formally acknowledged, or

FIGURE 4.2   The fundamental causal associations between resource levels (IIS2001.R1).

[1]Developed by Dr. Ken StandField, Chairman of the International Intangible Standards Institute, 1995.

protection is not sought. In such cases, the relationship in IIS2001.R1 holds true.

OPERATING STRUCTURES

The IIS5001 system manages two operating structures, tangible operating structures (IIS2001.S10) and intangible operating structures (IIS2001.S20), as discussed next.

TANGIBLE OPERATING STRUCTURES

Within every firm, level 1 assets, liabilities, expenses, revenue, (etc.) interact to form that company's *tangible operating structure*. This structure is captured in the balance sheet and the profit and loss statement. IIS2001.D10 defines a tangible operating structure as follows:

> The term tangible operating structure refers to the identification, classification, measurement, reporting and management of Level 1 resources. (IIS2001.D10)

Tangible Resources

Level 1 resources are tangible by nature. In one form or another, tangible resources involve ownership and legal property rights. For example, a notebook computer is a tangible resource because it can be touched and it has a value evidenced by a financial transaction (i.e., it costs $3500).

> *Tangible resources* are defined by IIS2001.D11 as components of the value creation process that have a physical form and substance and are evidenced by financial transactions and ownership that permit the business to generate value, efficiency, and effectiveness. Tangible resources include tangible assets, tangible liabilities, tangible capital, tangible expenses, and tangible revenue.
> IIS1001.D12 defines *financial transactions* as exchanges of money that result in changes in legal property rights (ownership).

INTANGIBLE OPERATING STRUCTURES

The *intangible operating structure* represents the interaction of L2 and L3 intangible resources with each other, leading to the development or use of L1 tangible resources. IIS2001.D20 defines an intangible operating structure as follows:

The term intangible operating structure refers to the identification, classification, measurement, reporting and management of L2 and L3 resources. (IIS2001.D20)

Tangible resources (L1) are therefore the *visible resource base* of an organization. Just like an iceberg, this visible portion is only a fraction of the total resource base of the organization.

INTANGIBLE RESOURCES

Organizations seek to manage two types of intangible resources: legal intangibles and competitive intangibles.

LEGAL INTANGIBLES

Intangible Standard IIS2001.D2 defines legal intangibles. Legal intangibles confer ownership in the *represented value* of the specific application of a *competitive intangible* to a specific issue. This definition may seem confusing at first, but once it is broken into its components, as discussed next, the concept is made more understandable.

Ownership

Typically, intangibles cannot be owned by organizations. To make intangibles fit into the current legal system of legal property rights, governments passed laws and acts of Parliament to create ownership in intangibles. Intangible standards refer to legal intangibles as conferring *artificial ownership* to an organization. Artificial ownership can be contested in a court of law.

The legal profession typically refers to artificially owned intangibles as *intangible assets*. Intangible assets are the end product of applying knowledge, relationships, time, and other intangibles to create *represented value*.

Represented Value

Represented value is a unique term that explains that the value of intangible assets is in what they represent, not how they are embodied. For example, if the intangible asset is a trademark, the value of that trademark is stopping other organizations from using certain words, or symbols, to communicate with a particular market. If the intangible asset is a patent, the physical embodiment of a patent on paper is not the value of the intangible asset: The value of the patent is the degree to which the competition can be prevented in a new and valuable market.

Legal intangibles are typically conferred by common law or by an act of Parliament. When a legal right is attached to an intangible, we refer to that intangible as an intangible asset. In the text *Valuing Intangible Assets*,[2] six specific characteristics are required in order to qualify something as an intangible asset:

1. It should be subject to specific identification and a recognizable description
2. It should be subject to legal existence and protection
3. It should be subject to the right of private ownership, and the private ownership should be legally transferable.
4. There should be some tangible evidence or manifestation of the existence of the intangible asset (e.g., a contract, a license, a registration document, a computer diskette, a listing of customers, a set of financial statements, etc.)
5. It should have been created or have come into existence at an identifiable time or as the result of an identifiable event
6. It should be subject to being destroyed or to a termination of existence at an identifiable time or as the result of an identifiable event

The essential issue is that for something to qualify as an intangible asset it must be capable of being owned, transferred, and extinguished. Trademarks, patents, copyright, and other forms of intellectual property are all intangible assets. Goodwill is created when a financial transaction occurs regarding the sale of a business. When the government passes legal acts to protect intangibles we refer to those assets as intangible assets and we refer to the rights conferred by an act of Parliament as legal property rights.

Intangible Standard IIS2001 defines intangible assets as they are known in current accounting, legal, and finance industries as a level 2 intangible asset. This is to differentiate them from level 3 intangible assets, which will be discussed in the next section.

Classifying Legal Intangibles

When an intangible falls inside the accounting definition of an intangible asset, it falls within the definition of a *legal intangible*. According to international intangible standards, level 2 intangibles can be classified under six categories:

[2]Robert F. Reily and Robert Schweihs, *Valuing Intangible Assets*, McGraw-Hill, 1999, p. 5.

1. Level 2 intangible assets
2. Level 2 intangible liabilities
3. Level 2 intangible revenues
4. Level 2 intangible expenses
5. Level 2 intangible capital
6. Level 2 intangible profits or intangible losses

Intangible Standard IIS2001 defines these categories. We will investigate these categories in Chapter 6.

COMPETITIVE INTANGIBLES

Ownership of intangibles can be even more confusing. When a customer is given customer service, or an employee attains employee satisfaction, these intangibles are not owned by the organization. They are also not owned in the real sense by the customer or the employee. These intangibles relate more to *perceptual changes* than increases or decreases in intellectual property (intangible assets) or changes in legal property rights.

Customer retention and staff retention are intangibles that are neither identifiable nor owned by an organization. Customer retention is a function of many different issues that lead a customer to repeat purchases and referred purchases from the same company.

An organization may pay for an employee to increase their *personal knowledge* through training, but the employee and not the organization ultimately owns that knowledge. Employment contracts may seek to own any *intellectual property* the employee creates during work hours by transforming that knowledge into products and services for the organization. However, with continued downsizing, restructuring, and job losses, employment security is missing from most organizations. Many organizations increase employment when times are good and let employees go when times are bad, so employees naturally seek to establish a safety net when things go bad for the company. In a KBE, the only real safety net is knowledge. Hence, an employee with a multibillion dollar invention may seek to develop that invention without the knowledge of the organization they work for.

Another contentious KBE issue is who owns *employee relationships*: the employee or the organization? If an employee leaves a business do the relationships stay with the organization or do they leave with the employee? Various nondisclosure and restraint-of-trade clauses in employment contracts seek to retain employee relationships as an organization's intellectual property, and may result in lawsuits. In some court cases employees have won; in others, the organization has won—the jury is still out on a definitive answer.

Quality is an intangible that is a by-product of the application of many tangible and intangible factors. As such, it eludes definition as a level 2 intangible asset.

Time is the most intangible of all intangibles. Time is an abstract notion made concrete through various time-keeping devices (clocks, watches, etc.). Issues such as cycletime, time-to-market, and downtime are all the end product of many tangible and intangible events. For example, cycletime is the amount of time required to produce a measure of value. That measure of value could be a car from a production line, a cup of coffee from a café, or anything else that creates value. Time-to-market is the cycletime required to move an idea from concept to implementation. Downtime is the amount of time productive activities cease as the result of tangible inefficiencies (a machine blowing up) or intangible inefficiencies (a network going down). Employees, suppliers, or customers do not own time. Time is not an intangible asset or subject to legal property rights.

Recognizing Competitive Intangibles

Competitive intangibles (L3 resources) are the true source of value creation in all organizations. These intangibles have characteristics that do not permit organizations to own them. Typically, competitive intangibles:

1. Cannot be specifically identified or accurately described
2. Are not subject to legal existence and protection in the traditional sense
3. Are not subject to the right of private ownership and cannot be reasonably transferred to another party
4. Are evidenced by intangible, or nonfinancial, transactions, not by tangible financial transactions.
5. Can have associated financial value, but this value is a minor part of the represented value of the intangible.
6. Are created at unidentifiable times or by an unidentifiable event
7. Cannot be physically destroyed and are not subject to termination of existence at an identifiable time or by an identifiable event

The Link between Competitive and Legal Intangibles

Competitive intangibles are the source from which legal intangibles are created, maintained, and enhanced. Legal intangibles are therefore a subset of competitive intangibles (see Figure 4.3). It is competitive intangibles that

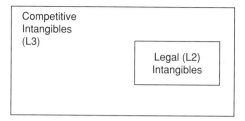

FIGURE 4.3   The relationship between competitive and legal intangibles.

continually renew the value of legal intangibles. For example, a trademark has little value if it is not used or continually kept relevant. It is the implementation of competitive intangibles that creates value.

Identifying the Impact of Competitive Intangibles

Competitive intangibles directly influence:

1. Current revenue
2. Repeat business
3. Referred business
4. Cost efficiency
5. Customer retention
6. Employee retention
7. Responsiveness to change
8. Innovation ability
9. Employee satisfaction
10. Customer satisfaction
11. Employee knowledge
12. Quality
13. Brand image
14. Share price

Although a specific organization may not create, leverage, or license legal intangibles, all organizations are subject to the bottom line effects of the management or mismanagement of competitive intangibles.

Classifying Competitive Intangibles

When an intangible falls outside the accounting definition of an intangible asset, it falls within the definition of a competitive intangible under international intangible standards. Intangible competitive rights classify intangibles under six categories:

1. Level 3 intangible assets
2. Level 3 intangible liabilities
3. Level 3 intangible revenues
4. Level 3 intangible expenses
5. Level 3 intangible capital
6. Level 3 intangible profits or intangible losses

Intangible Standard IIS2001 defines these categories. We will investigate these categories in Chapter 6.

INTANGIBLE LAWS

IIS2001 also deals with a number of intangible laws. These laws have been designed to enhance people's perception regarding the behavior of level 3 intangibles.

THE FIRST LAW OF INTANGIBLES

Intangible Standard IIS2001.L1 defines the first law of intangibles as follows: (see Figure 4.4):

> Intangible performance causes financial performance.

Think of an intangible as a *decision*. A decision is a *selection*, or choice, of one option over less viable options. Once a decision is made, it must then be implemented. In this sense, the core value creation process is intangible by its very nature. To implement a decision, a series of financial and nonfinancial transactions must often be made. In this sense, people may spend a great deal of time talking to others, seeking advice from various online and offline networks and other sources before a financial transaction ever occurs. Depending on the complexity of the decision, numerous financial transactions at numerous points of time may need to be made to support the decision.

Using intangible standards, we now have ways to track intangible transactions, intangible performance, and changes in intangible performance. Using intangible accounting, it is possible to develop intangible financial statements to represent intangible performance. Conventional management systems do not record the *loss of financial value* caused by low-quality intangible transactions.

Returning to the previous chapter, if Your Café has poor service, then the $2.50 sale may not even occur. Conventional systems *do not record* the

FIGURE 4.4   The first law of intangibles.

financial cost of poor service; they merely record the receipt of the $2.50 (if it occurs). If the staff of Your Café have poor knowledge, they will produce inferior quality coffee and give poor service. These factors could also lead to a lost sale or loss of repeat or referred business. If Your Café is dirty, disorganized, unclean, or poorly presented, customers may not even step in the door. Even if a customer were to enter Your Café under such conditions, if employee satisfaction were low, staff could be unattentive (perhaps even rude), which could prevent the sale or any repeat or referred business.

THE SECOND LAW OF INTANGIBLES

Intangible Standard IIS2001.L2 defines the second law of intangibles as follows:

> Conventional management records do not reflect negative intangible transactions or negative intangible performance.

In the Your Café example, if poor customer service resulted in a lost sale, the value of that lost sale would not be recorded in the café's financial records. However, poor customer service is a *real cost*. For many organizations it is the major cost incurred on a daily basis. Such costs directly influence the profitability of Your Café. Poor customer service is a level 3 *intangible expense* to the Café. Conversely, superior customer service is a level 3 *intangible asset* to Your Café because it provides a source of current value and future value (repeat and referred business).

There is a critical requirement for organizations to identify, measure, and understand how intangible transactions influence financial performance. Intangible accounting assists organizations value the financial impact of intangible transactions on financial performance.

THE THIRD LAW OF INTANGIBLES

Intangible Standard IIS2001.L3 defines the third law of intangibles as follows:

> Immediate and future financial transactions occur in accordance with the aggregated quality of perceptions and expectations from all intangible transactions relevant to those transactions.

Financial performance is therefore the end product of a series of intangible transactions. Due to the nature of financial transactions, monetary-based receipts cannot and do not attempt to capture the complexities of intangible transactions.

This law has significant ramifications for executives in the knowledge-based economy. If the quality of intangible transactions is not consistent across multiple interactions with customers negative interpretation distortion (IIS1001.D20a) will occur, generating level 3 intangible liabilities and level 3 intangible expenses for the organization.

THE FOURTH LAW OF INTANGIBLES

Intangible Standard IIS2001.L4 defines the fourth law of intangibles as follows:

> Immediate financial transactions only occur if the perceived return on intangible investment is greater than the perceived cost of intangible investment.

In the Your Café example from Chapter 3 (Figure 3.7), the financial transaction occurred on the 17th transaction. This transaction only occurred because Joe, the customer, perceived that the return on his time was greater than the cost of his time for that *event sequence* (the total number of intangible plus tangible transactions per IIS1001.D30).

THE FIFTH LAW OF INTANGIBLES

Intangible Standard IIS2001.L5 defines the fifth law of intangibles as follows:

> As individual intangible transactions are not directly evidenced by financial transactions, financial transactions are not tied to the decisions that create them.

Because conventional systems do not link intangible transactions to financial transactions, such systems are prevented by their fundamental nature from measuring value changes in the organization's core value creation process (which is intrinsically intangible). Managers therefore, cannot readily understand how financial performance is derived from intangibles. It is this fundamental disconnection that prevents organizations from determining the rate of return on knowledge-based projects.

THE SIXTH LAW OF INTANGIBLES

Intangible Standard IIS2001.L6 defines the sixth law of intangibles as follows:

> The financial value of level 3 intangibles cannot be measured directly. Level 3 intangibles can only be financially valued by assessing changes in the quality of Time Capital™.

To understand this sequence, think of Mozart composing a symphony. He first uses his skills and talents to represent the music as he directs (these ideas are level 3 intangibles). The music, once written down, becomes a level 2 intangible. An orchestra, singers, set painters, an auditorium, (etc.) is hired to play that music (these tangibles are level 1 transactions). The financial value of the symphony is not just the receipts from the sale of tickets, it is much more. We will investigate these issues when we investigate the intangible accounting standard, IIS5001, and the intangible finance standard, IIS6001.

THE SEVENTH LAW OF INTANGIBLES

Intangible Standard IIS2001.L7 defines the seventh law of intangibles as follows:

> It is the use of intangibles over productive time that creates organizational value. Any usage of intangibles in a non-productive manner leads to a loss of organizational efficiency, effectiveness, and value. When such losses create the potential for lost business an intangible liability is incurred. When such losses create actual lost business, an intangible expense is incurred.

Time is the scarcest productive resource for all organizations in today's economy. Productive time is the component of time capital and is responsible for an organization's productivity and revenue generating ability. Nonproductive time is the component of time capital responsible for a *competitor's* productivity and revenue-generating ability.

THE EIGHTH LAW OF INTANGIBLES

Intangible Standard IIS2001.L8 defines the eighth law of intangibles as follows:

> The accumulation of Expenses, Liabilities, Revenue and Assets are the result of Intangible Management L3 and L2 intangibles during productive time.

CHAPTER 5

The Asset versus Expense Debate

The significant problems we face cannot be solved at the same level of thinking we were at when we created them. —*Albert Einstein*

It is common to use conventional frameworks to solve new problems. The solution to the intangible problem is not to try to adapt existing management frameworks to solve the problem. Existing systems are hindered by the very rules that create them.

Whenever a system becomes completely defined, someone discovers something which either abolishes the system, or expands it beyond recognition. —*Brooke's Law*

ANOMALIES AND EXCEPTION CLASSES

When conventional systems encounter unexplainable events (anomalies) the conventional system creates an *exception class* to capture that anomaly and its potential solution. Anomalies generally do not fit in the exception classes. For this reason, existing specialists tend to label anomalies as "fads" or "buzz words" at best, or falsehoods or impossibilities at worst.

By incorporating information in the category of intangibles and goodwill the problem of valuing information has been neatly avoided. However, the increasing importance of information as a factor of production in today's economic scene means that this position cannot be sustained for very much longer. —*Bill Mayon-White, London School of Economics*

THE PROBLEMS WITH ACCOUNTING

The problems with accounting for intangibles are well known. In fact, a whole discipline has been created, which is referred to as *intellectual capital management*, to attempt to repair the problems accounting faces when attempting to measure intangibles. In the groundbreaking work of Kaplan and Norton, developers of the Balanced Scorecard, it is acknowledged that accounting systems are unlikely to evolve the way they need to in order to cope with the demands of the 21st century:

> If intangible assets and company capabilities could be valued within the financial accounting model, organizations that enhanced these assets and capabilities could communicate this improvement to employees, shareholders, creditors and communities. Conversely, when companies depleted their stock of intangible assets and capabilities, the negative effects could be reflected immediately in the income statement. Realistically, however, difficulties in placing a reliable financial value on such assets as the new product pipeline; process capabilities; employee skills, motivation, and flexibility; customer loyalty; databases; and systems will likely preclude them from ever being recognized in organizational balance sheets. Yet these are the very assets and capabilities that are critical for success in today's and tomorrow's competitive environment.[1]

FORM VS. SUBSTANCE

In 1997, Thomas Stewart explored the concept of intangibles and accounting:

> We manage the forms rather than the substance, which is like a viticulturist [someone who grows grapes to make wine] paying more attention to the bottle than the wine. It's easier, after all, to count the bottles than to describe the wine, and in the old economy of "congealed resources," it was also a reasonable thing to do: Accounting for forms—the costs and materials of labor—captured most of the value of the product. But in the economy of "congealed knowledge," it doesn't come close... Moreover, the digitization of everything often removes the wrapper entirely. It no longer makes sense to manage the production of intangible goods and services solely by measuring and managing the process of putting wrapping paper and a ribbon on them.[2]

[1] Robert S. Kaplan and David P. Norton, *The Balanced Scorecard: Translating Strategy into Action*, Harvard Business School Press, 1996.

[2] Thomas Stewart, *The Intellectual Capital, The New Wealth of Nations*, Doubleday, 1997.

In an era where there is literally no bottle and only the perception of wine, the complications surrounding the management of intangibles have become even more problematic. Most people regard money as one of the most tangible of tangibles. However, Walter Wriston the former CEO and chairman of Citibank looks at things differently:

> Information about money has become almost as important as money itself. Money today flows in waves of bits and bytes that wash over the globe in 24-hour cycles. As markets in Osaka and Singapore pass the book to London and on from there to New York and Chicago, great pools of speculative capital churn on rumors, political events, and feedback mechanisms endemic to the markets themselves. The rules for understanding this flow of money seem to come more from the study of turbulence and fluid dynamics than from dry economic theory. Short of laws for predicting the motion of money, what we have to work with are approximations—and for that, you need good information.[3]

THE ACCOUNTING VIEWPOINT

Perhaps one of the best indications of a professional accounting practitioner commenting on the accounting framework comes from David Wilson, a CPA and partner at Ernst and Young, an international accounting and consulting firm:

> It has been 500 years since Pacioli published his seminal work on accounting and we have seen virtually no innovation in the practice of accounting—just more rules—none of them which has changed the framework of measurement.[3]

In accounting terminology financial transactions can be *capitalized* (presented as an asset) or *expensed* (written off immediately). Assets make their way into the balance sheet to show the financial health of the organization. Expenses make their way into the income statement as a reduction against any income generated from the sale of assets by the business. If the business holds onto assets for more than 12 months, these assets are depreciated. Depreciation represents the lowering of the value of the assets in accordance with an estimated loss of value through usage and obsolescence. Depreciation makes its way into the income statement as an expense.

The choice between how a business classifies a financial transaction (an exchange of money) is largely dependent on what the business does. For example, store that sells office supplies would classify the purchase of office supplies as an asset because it will turn this purchase into a sale within a period of time. For another business, say, an information technology (IT)

---

[3]*Wired Magazine*, Issue 4.10, Oct. 1996. http://hotwired.lycos.com/wired_online/4.10/wriston/.

firm, the purchase of office supplies constitutes an expense, because office supplies will not be sold by the IT firm to generate revenue.

To understand the asset vs. expense debate, we nee to understand why we must go beyond conventional strategy to manage the value creation process.

BEYOND CONVENTIONAL STRATEGY

In the past companies made money by following, at a fundamental level, the basic process shown in Figure 5.1. The company would need to obtain the vast amounts of capital (money) required to build factories and production lines and buy the equipment required to transform tangible inputs (raw materials) into finished (tangible) products. Products were created through production processes that heavily relied on tangible assets.

Capital could be acquired from borrowing (debt) or from investors/shareholders (equity), which led to the formation of the concept of the *cost of capital* and the weighted average cost of capital (WACC). The metrics of return on assets, return on capital, and return on investment were created to assist managers to understand how to allocate resources to their most profitable uses.

The first factory appeared in 1760 in England. At that time the vast majority of the population could not read or write, few went to school, and most worked 14-hour days in mines. Even so, money was scarce and people lived without luxuries. Most people had a standard of living far below today's poverty line. The gap between the "haves" and the "have nots" was significant.

Faced with an uneducated and unskilled workforce, managers could *not* rely on their employees. People who were educated became managers and all others became workers (also known as employees). Managers invented ways to ensure that employees would minimize errors when they worked. Because employees were unskilled, managers needed to manage them very closely.

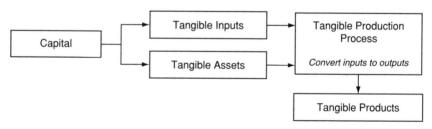

FIGURE 5.1   The conventional strategy process

Production was made *linear* and *sequential*. If there were 20 steps in the production process, workers would specialize in just 1 or 2 of these steps so that they would gain mastery over that stage of production. This is what Adam Smith referred to as *specialization* and *division of labor*. The work of one worker depended almost exclusively on the output of the worker before them. As such, bottlenecks often occurred in the industrial organizational structure when one worker was either too fast or too slow for the other workers in the process.

As workers became proficient in their tasks, each detail of those tasks became known and routine. Routine tasks required no real problem-solving ability on the part of workers. Managers soon found ways to develop machines to replicate these routine tasks through mechanical means. Soon automation had spread through factories around the world, replacing workers with machines. What followed were layoffs of unskilled and low-skilled workers. Automation became so common that economists termed the job losses due to technological advancement as *structural unemployment*.

As routine tasks were automated, the need to control individual workers fell dramatically. This led to a *flattening* of managerial hierarchies as the *span of control* (the number of workers that a manager was responsible for) was reduced. Soon lower and middle managers found themselves out of work also, because they no longer had workers to supervise.

In the 1970s, the information and communications revolutions occurred. These revolutions led to the creation of numerous new industries. Many of these industries that came into existence removed unskilled and semiskilled workers, directly or indirectly, from organizations.

Check Point

When implementing a new technology, the first issue senior managers raise is that of *cost justification* and *return on investment*. For example, if a business is to spend $250,000 on a project the cost justification for this is typically cost savings brought about by a reduction in the headcount (the total number of employees in the firm). If headcount cannot be reduced, then the next significant place for executives to look is the reduction of expenses (closing factories, buying cheaper materials, etc.). If the $250,000 project is estimated to decrease costs by $1,000,000, then the return on investment is 400%. This means that for each $1 the business outlays on the project, they expect to receive a reduction in expenses of $4. There are many different ways to calculate return on investment.

ASSETS AND EXPENSES

For industrial companies the distinction between assets and capital is critical for income tax and investment purposes.

Assets

Assets are converted into expenses over time using *depreciation*. Depreciation involves writing down the value of an asset to reflect its loss of value on a periodic basis. Accumulated depreciation is subtracted from the value of the asset in the company's *balance sheet*. For example, if you buy a machine for $14 million, wear and tear will decrease the value of that asset. Accountants use depreciation to reflect this loss of value in accordance with prevailing taxation laws. If depreciation of 20% per year over 5 years were suitable, then the asset's value would fall to zero (be fully expensed) after 5 years (see Table 5.1).

However, it would be highly likely that the machine could be sold at the end of its useful life for scrap (spare parts, etc.). The amount of money a business expects to obtain by selling a fully depreciated asset is referred to as *scrap value*.

Depreciation does not measure changes in market value; it merely recognizes reductions in asset value brought about by wear and tear, obsolescence, erosion, etc. Depreciation is often referred to as a noncash expense. Consider the $14 million machine. In year 1, $2 million of depreciation has been written off, taking the written-down value, or book value, of the machine to $12 million. The $2 million of depreciation is regarded as a noncash expense because the $2 million will be deducted from income. No funds were spent each year to acquire this deduction. Because this $2 million deduction reduces the tax burden, it is common for finance and accounting practitioners to calculate the tax saving from depreciation and use this in free cash flow analysis to better determine how organizations are using their resources.

TABLE 5.1 Value Analysis

Year	Depreciation ($ million)	Accumulated depreciation	Book value	Total value
0	$ 0	$ 0	$ 14	$ 14
1	$ 2	$ 2	$ 12	$ 14
2	$ 2	$ 4	$ 10	$ 14
3	$ 2	$ 6	$ 8	$ 14
4	$ 2	$ 8	$ 6	$ 14
5	$ 2	$ 10	$ 4	$ 14

Expenses

From an intangible management perspective, it is useful to think of expenses as assets that have no scrap value and 100% depreciation. Hence, if you spend $1 million on electricity to power the $14 million machine, the $1 million will be written off immediately with a book value of zero, and the $14 million will be depreciated and have a scrap value.

Why Make This Distinction?

The current accounting and finance debate is that intangibles should not be expensed, they should instead be treated as assets.

The argument is made that a software firm that spends $14 million creating new software should be able to treat this expense as an asset and place the $14 million in the balance sheet to more accurately reflect the value of the business (especially because software companies have so few tangible assets). It is argued that *capitalization of expenses*, or turning expenses into assets, is the only way for a firm to more accurately reflect its value in a knowledge-based economy.

Assets, Expenses: Why the Big Deal?

To explain the real issues underpinning the debate concerning assets and expenses, let's consider the case of Christine.

Christine, the teenager, is given $15 pocket money each week. Skilled in the art of living beyond her means, Christine manages to spend $20 each week. Each week she spends $10 on assets (depreciated at 10% per week) and $10 on expenses. Each week she needs to borrow $5 to support her spending addiction.

In the first week, Christine will receive $15, but $20 will go out and she will need to borrow $5 to cover the spending shortfall. In the second week, Christine makes $15 and spends $20. She needs to borrow another $5 to cover this week's shortfall. As the weeks progress, she makes $15, spends $20, and borrows an additional $5.

As time progresses, her debt will increase by $5 a week. Soon a time will come when she cannot borrow anymore and she will either try to repay the debt or go bankrupt. After 3 weeks, Christine's debts will have accumulated to $15 (equal to her weekly income). Christine's way of managing her finances is not sensible. Excessive spending leads to excessive debt and finally foreclosure and bankruptcy.

Enter Accounting and Finance

Accounting records financial transactions (exchanges of money documented by receipts) and generates accounting reports to monitor the financial health of an organization. For our purposes, Christine's organization is herself and she calls it *Christine Enterprises*.

The profit and loss statement shows the aggregation of financial transactions relating to revenue and expenses. The balance sheet shows the aggregation of financial transactions relating to assets, liabilities, and capital.

The Assets–Expenses Distinction

Assets are depreciated and expenses are written off immediately. Asset values are measured in the balance sheet to show what an organization owns. Expenses make their way into the profit and loss statement to be deducted from revenue to show how much money capital holders have made from the organization's operations. Depreciation reduces the value of the asset in the balance sheet and reduces profit in the profit and loss statement.

Conventional Accounting Treatment. Let's assume Christine uses conventional accounting treatment to show the financial health of Christine Enterprises, as evidenced by Table 5.2.

Each week Christine receives $15 in revenue. She has $10 in expenses and $1 in depreciation for each $10 she spends on assets. Total expenses are therefore $11 in the first week, leaving a profit of $4. If we continue the analysis for 4 weeks, we see that it is only the increased depreciation that is driving weekly profit down. Irrespective, a profit is made each week.

Over the same 4 weeks, Christine's balance sheet looks like the one shown in Table 5.3. We can see that even though Christine's spending is resulting in $5 of increasing debt each week, she still looks financially good on paper.

TABLE 5.2   The Financial Health of Christine Enterprises (Income Statement)

Income Statement	1	2	3	4
Revenue (1)	15	15	15	15
Expenses (1)	10	10	10	10
Depreciation (1)	1	2	3	4
Total Expenses (1)	11	12	13	14
Profit (1)	4	3	2	1
		−25.0%	−33.3%	−50.0%

TABLE 5.3   The Financial Health of Christine Enterprises (Balance Sheet)

Balance Sheet	1	2	3	4
Assets (1)	10	20	30	40
less Depreciation (1)	1	2	3	4
Book Value (1)	9	18	27	36
		100.0%	50.0%	33.3%

What about Her Growing Debt?   Christine is borrowing from friends, relatives, or anyone else who will give her money in order to spend the $20 each week. At the end of the first week she has spent the $5 given to her that week. Just before the end of the first week she borrows enough money to repay her debt and enough to cover her spending habit. Christine's debt is shown in Table 5.4. By paying the debt before the end of each week and borrowing enough to pay past debts and cover future purchasing requirements, Christine avoids debt showing up in her financial statements.

Christine's Bottom Line (1).   No matter how good Christine looks financially on paper, she is actually experiencing a loss of $5 per week; not a profit as shown in the income statement of Table 5.2. As each week progresses, the debt burden will grow increasingly painful for her. Eventually, Christine will not be able to borrow to repay those who loan her the money.

Proposed Intangible Treatment.   It is argued that money spent on increasing a firm's intangible assets should be regarded as an asset (and not an expense). Currently the accounting industry has resisted such attempts. To see why, suppose that Christine can now convert all her expenses into assets. Balance sheet (2) is shown in Table 5.5, which shows that Christine has managed to increase the value of her assets 100% from traditional accounting conventions. The percentage weekly change in assets is the same for the conventional treatment and the intangible treatment.

Income Statement (2).   Because the $10 in expenses has been relabeled as an asset, the $10 expense will be missing from each income statement. As assets are depreciated, increased depreciation will show up in the income

TABLE 5.4   Christine Enterprises—The Growth of Debt

	1	2	3	4
Debt	$ 5.00	$ 10.00	$ 15.00	$ 20.00

TABLE 5.5   Christine Enterprises—Current Proposed Intangible Treatment

Balance Sheet (2)	1	2	3	4
Assets (2)	20	40	60	80
less Depreciation (2)	2	4	6	8
Book Value (2)	18	36	54	72
% Weekly Change		100.0%	50.0%	33.3%
Book Value (1)	9	18	27	36
% Change (1) to (2)	100.0%	100.0%	100.0%	100.0%

statement. Irrespective, the profit will be much greater under this arrangement as income statement (2) in Table 5.6 shows.

The differences between the two methods are not easily seen through this analysis. Table 5.7 illustrates this.

We can make several conclusions from this information, as discussed next.

TABLE 5.6   Christine Enterprises—Current Proposed Intangible Treatment
(Income Statement)

Income Statement (2)	1	2	3	4
Revenue (2)	15	15	15	15
Expenses (2)	0	0	0	0
Depreciation (2)	2	4	6	8
Total Expenses (2)	2	4	6	8
Profit (2)	13	11	9	7
% Weekly Change (2)		−15.4%	−18.2%	−22.2%

TABLE 5.7   Christine Enterprises—Assessing the Differences

Intangible Analysis	1	2	3	4
% Weekly Change (2)		−15.4%	−18.2%	−22.2%
% Weekly Change (1)		−25.0%	−33.3%	−50.0%
Change in Growth Rates (2,1)		62.5%	83.3%	125.0%
Change in Growth Rates (1,1)			33.3%	50.0%
Profit (1)	4	3	2	1
Profit (2)	13	11	9	7
% Chg (1) to (2)	225.0%	266.7%	350.0%	600.0%

Artificial Profit. Under conventional accounting practices, Christine would have a total "paper" profit of $40 over the 4 weeks. If expenses were transformed into assets, Christine would amass a staggering $40 in profit (revenue after expenses). In practice, in week 5 Christine will have to borrow $25 to repay $20 in debt and borrow $5 for that week.

Artificial Effectiveness. If expenses are turned to assets then profit will be significantly higher in absolute terms and the reduction in profitability will be significantly suppressed. This makes it appear that Christine is more effective at preventing losses because the reduction in losses under method 2 is about half that of method 1. As Table 5.8 shows, instead of a reduction in profit of 25% in week 2, the reduction is just 15.4%. During the 4 weeks, the average reduction in profitability is more accurate under conventional accounting practices.

Christine's Bottom Line (2). From a personal perspective, Christine is actually experiencing a loss of $5 each week because she is spending $5 more than she earns. How the expenditure is treated in an accounting sense will not change the fundamental fact that as each week progresses Christine's financial health is deteriorating.

If we consider Christine's real position to be a $5 loss each week (profit 0) we can then compare it to the current accounting treatment (profit 1) and the proposed intangible treatment (profit 2), as done in Table 5.9.

Over the 4 weeks, Christine is actually worse off to the tune of $20. Neither the paper profit of $10 under method 1, or the $40 profit under method 2, accurately details Christine's true position: a loss of $20.

UNCOVERING FINANCIAL HEALTH

We now have three primary scenarios through which we can assess Christine's financial performance:

TABLE 5.8   Assessing Artificial Effectiveness

	Week 1	Week 2	Week 3	Week 4	Tot/Avg
Profit (1)	4	3	2	1	10
		−25.0%	−33.3%	−50.0%	−36.1%
Profit (2)	13	11	9	7	40
		−15.4%	−18.2%	−22.2%	−18.6%

TABLE 5.9   Assessing Potential Reporting Differences

	Week 1	Week 2	Week 3	Week 4	Tot/Avg
Profit (0)	−5	−5	−5	−5	−20
		0.0%	0.0%	0.0%	0.0%
Profit (1)	4	3	2	1	10
		−25.0%	−33.3%	−50.0%	−36.1%
Profit (2)	13	11	9	7	40
		−15.4%	−18.2%	−22.2%	−18.6%

1. *Assets are expenses.*This accurately reflects that Christine is losing $5 each week because she is spending $5 more than she earns.
2. *Normal accounting treatment.*This assumes that Christine will continue as a *going concern* (viable business) for many years to come. As such, the *matching concept* is used to apportion expense and asset payments to income. As assets are depreciated, profit does not reflect that Christine is making a loss of $5 per week.
3. *Expenses are assets.* Like fitting a large round peg into a small round hole, many accounting practitioners have tried to make intangibles "fit" into existing frameworks. The concept of pretending an expense is an asset makes logical sense, but financially the long-term consequences could be economically destabilizing.

POTENTIAL ECONOMIC DESTABILIZATION

You have seen that representing an expense as an asset significantly increases profit. Because many investors look to profitability as a measure of financial health, it is highly likely that this *asset conversion* process would result in many organizations gaining access to investment funds that they would find increasingly difficult to repay.

Imagine having millions of businesses run by Christine. The longer such businesses operate, the greater the potential for a significant economic downturn due to defaulting on loans. Assuming the global economy moved to such a standard, the end result would be significant destabilization in financial markets, increased volatility in capital markets, increased bankruptcies, and less investor security.

CONCLUSION

The debate on how conventional accounting will treat intangibles has not been decided. Each of the methods has advantages and disadvantages as mentioned in this chapter depending on who benefits from the changes.

INTANGIBLES AS ASSETS

Businesses seeking finance would prefer to treat intangibles as assets because it increases reporting earnings and artificially increases profitability. Governments would like the idea also because more tax revenue is generated. Investors and shareholders would not like the idea because it creates distortion in actual financial performance. Regulators would be against this due to the potential of economic destabilization.

INTANGIBLES AS EXPENSES

Investors stand to gain the most from this method, because businesses are less able to engage in creative accounting practices that artificially increase the financial attractiveness of the firm. Business would be against this because such a move reduces reported earnings and therefore decreases the potential investment attractiveness of the firm. Governments would initially be apprehensive of the reduction in traditional tax revenues because reported earnings are the source of income tax. The natural response to this would be to create an updated taxation system that reflects the realities of operating in an economic environment in which intangibles dominate the value process.

NO CHANGE

The current system has significant problems. It is unlikely that the traditional accounting framework will continue to be used in its current form, but classifying financial transactions according to expenses and assets is making less and less sense as time progresses. International intangible standards offer the long-awaited update to conventional management, reporting, and valuation systems.

CHAPTER 6

Intangible Accounting

In 1494, Italian mathematician, scholar, and philosopher Fra Luca Pacioli published the first account of a new method of bookkeeping in his book *Summma de Arithmetica, Geometria: Proportioni et Proportionalita*. Pacioli, a colleague of Leonardo da Vinci, never claimed to have invented double-entry bookkeeping; he simply detailed its use and structure. The system of bookkeeping underpins the system of accounting, finance, and economics that is used by practically all organizations around the world today.

Nearly 510 years later another mathematician, scholar, and philosopher, Dr. Ken Standfield, published a completely new form of measurement and reporting system that can account for intangibles and link those accounts to financial changes in monetary value. Regarded as the holy grail of management science, the consistent valuation of intangibles has eluded the world for hundreds of years.

BOOKKEEPERS AND ACCOUNTANTS

Conventional bookkeepers record business transactions and conventional accountants know these recording techniques, but specialize in creating and interpreting financial statements. Accountants use their skills to forecast, report, analyze, and interpret, where as bookkeepers use their skills to record financial information. Accountants use accounting systems to produce information that is:

- Relevant to making informed and high-quality business decisions
- Timely and current so that its value is maximized
- Verifiable and therefore free of bias
- Comparable over different time periods

All conventional accounting systems are based on accounting standards and accounting conventions. The 10 fundamental conventional accounting assumptions are as follows:

1. *Entity assumption.* Only business transactions (not personal) are recorded in the financial statements. The entity assumption is the foundation of the accounting equation $(A = L + C)$ and is the basis of double-entry conventional accounting.
2. *Continuity (or going concern) assumption.* Organizations are considered to have an indefinite life. This led to the development of the accrual system of accounting.
3. *Accounting period assumption.* As an organization's life is deemed to be infinite. This assumption is used to divide the life of an entity into arbitrary periods where expenses and revenues can be matched to determine profit. This assumption led to the development of balance day adjustments and depreciation.
4. *Monetary assumption.* All financial information must be presented in monetary format and in aggregated (not individual) terms in accounting reports.
5. *Historical cost assumption.* The information recorded on the receipt of a financial transaction is the amount at which information is entered into financial accounts. If something is purchased for $10,000 but has a current market value of $100,000, the $10,000 is recorded not the $100,000. Inflation and market values are ignored.
6. *Conservatism (or prudence) assumption.* Losses and expenses are written off immediately, but profits are not recorded until actually realized.
7. *Materiality assumption.* Financial transactions are grouped into categories and it is the total of these categories that is reported in financial statements. Only whole dollars are used in reports, because cents are immaterial. The distinction between assets and expenses is material as is the choice to depreciate.
8. *Consistency assumption.* To ensure greater verifiability of data and comparison over different time periods, it is essential to inform the

users of financial statements when there are changes in accounting methods.

9. *Realization assumption.* Revenue is recorded when the transaction is made (i.e., at the point of sale) and not when payment is received.

10. *Verifiability (or objectivity) assumption.* Documentary evidence must be produced to validate financial transactions.

NEW BASIS OF MEASUREMENT

Intangible bookkeeping and intangible accounting have their origins in the understanding that all organizations experience two types of transactions: financial (money) transactions and intangible (time) transactions.

A government organization experiences money and time transactions. A nonprofit organization experiences money and time transactions. A publicly listed corporation experiences money and time transactions. A bank experiences money and time transactions. A small corner store experiences money and time transactions. A person selling secondhand goods experiences money and time transactions. All entities experience money and time transactions.

Financial (money) transactions and intangible (time) transactions involve either an expenditure or receipt of money or time (IIS4001.L10). Intangible bookkeeping identifies, classifies, and records an organization's time-based expenditures and receipts (IIS4001.D5). Intangible accounting values reports and analyzes how time-based expenditures and receipts increase or decrease the financial performance, cost effectiveness, value creation ability, and sustainability of organizations (IIS4001.D10).

TIME TRANSACTIONS

Organizations make two types of time transactions: a productive time transaction and a nonproductive time transaction (IIS4001.L20).

When an organization *acquires* time (through employment, automation benefits, alliances, etc.), time is received by the organization. When the firm is subject to increased nonproductive time (due to lack of knowledge in staff, increased information requirements, substandard process speed, etc.), the organization makes an expenditure of time. Time receipts can increase productivity and revenue generation and time expenditures can decrease productivity and revenue generation.

INTANGIBLE ACCOUNTING

Just as conventional bookkeeping records financial transactions and conventional accounting presents financial records for reporting and analysis, intangible bookkeeping and intangible accounting do the same.

To apply intangible accounting, time-specific allocations must be categorized. This method of viewing time assumes that every organizational event has a productive and a nonproductive time component. If a task takes 60 minutes to perform, then these 60 minutes will represent some mixture of productive and nonproductive time. Intangible accounting determines what those time allocations are and assigns them values. Intangible accounting records time-based transactions and estimates the financial impact on the organization.

Highly accurate time-specific allocations of time (second by second) are required because nonproductive time forces productivity to zero when experienced. Due to the impact of compounding, even a 1-minute overhead per hour in an organization of 250,000 staff, translates to a loss of productive capacity (across the whole organization) of 4167 hours for each organizational hour. At a marginal wage cost of $18 per hour, the wage cost alone is $75,006 per hour of organizational time. In a single 8-hour day, the organization will experience a nonproductive wage allocation cost of $600,048— simply from 1 minute per hour of nonproductive time.

In any tasks staff perform, they will continually accumulate both productive time and nonproductive time. As such, they will continually be contributing and not contributing value to the organization.

Intangible Accounting Standards

Intangible accounting standards provide a firm foundation and infrastructure to assist organizations in correctly specifying the allocation of time for individual and aggregate employees, in a format compliant with intangible accounting practices.

Organizations and Staffing Levels

According to Intangible Economics (IIS7001) an organization has an optimal time level at which intangible demand (demand for organizational time) and intangible supply (supply of organizational time) are in equilibrium. In practice, the real optimal employment level (ROEL) indicates the ideal balance between intangible demand and intangible supply. Employment below the ROEL indicates an understaffed organization. Employment above the ROEL indicates an overstaffed organization. At points above the ROEL, extra time cannot be readily translated into increased organizational value. The ROEL is also referred to as the optimal productive time level.

As an organization grows, the demand for productive time increases, thereby increasing the optimal productive time level. The supply of productive time is acquired from a number of different sources: employees, partnerships, alliances, strategic relationships, etc. The supply of productive time is relatively inelastic due to high resource costs and knowledge switching costs. The demand for productive time also drops to zero shortly after the optimal productive time level because any increases in time above the optimal level cannot be translated into benefits.

Understanding Revenue

Revenue can be *employee contributed* or *derived* from investments. For example, a firm generating $100 million in gross revenue with a $10 million contribution from investment income generates $90 million in employee-contributed revenue.

Linking Revenue and Time

Intangible accounting analyzes changes in financial transactions according to their impact on productive and nonproductive time. If 100 staff employed for 2000 hours only work 1200 hours on average, then the *money value of time* is $90 million $\div$ (1200 $\times$ 100 staff) = $90 million $\div$ 120,000 = $750 revenue contribution per productive hour. The figure of $750 per productive hour is referred to as the *money value of time*. The actual calculation of the money value of time is more complicated, but this illustrates the concept.

Linking Expenses and Time

If an expense reduces productive time, it is referred to as *negative conversion expense*. For example, reducing staff in an understaffed organization gives rise to negative conversion expenses. If increasing an expense results in more productive time becoming available to the organization, it is referred to as a *positive conversion expense*.

Linking Changes in Expenses to Changes in Revenue

By attaching a time dimension to expenses, intangible accounting assesses expenditure quality and demonstrates how revenue and expenses are interdependent (reliant on each other).

For example, consider a company making $100 million in revenue, with $60 million in expenses that seeks to reduce expenses by 20% ($12 million). Intangible accounting systems can be used to determine the potential reduction in productive time (negative conversion) using the procedures discussed below.

Assuming that the $12 million cost reduction causes a $16 million decrease in revenue, the ultimate change in revenue is $100 million − $60 million + $12 million − $16 million = $36 million. Hence, where traditional accounting analysis estimates new profit to be $52 million (as revenue and expenses are treated as independent), the new valuation system estimates new profit to be $36 million (because revenue and expenses are interdependent). To determine potential changes in profit, intangible accounting operates in the following manner:

$$\text{Profit}_{\text{New}} = (R_o - E_o) + (\Delta R_{\text{Est}} - \Delta E_{\text{Est}})$$
$$= ([\textstyle\sum PT_o \times MVT] - E_o) + ([\Delta PT_{\text{Est}} \times MVT] - [E_o - E_n]),$$

where

$R_o = \text{Revenue}_{\text{Original}} = \sum PT_o \times MVT_o$ $\Delta R_{\text{Est}} = \text{Change\_in\_Revenue} = [\Delta PT_{\text{Est}} \times MVT_o]$

$E_o = \text{Expenses}_{\text{Original}} = E_o$ $\Delta E_{\text{Est}} = \text{Change\_in\_Expenses} = [E_o - E_n]$

$PT_o = \text{Productive\_Time}_{\text{Original}}$ $MVT_o = \text{Money\_Value\_of\_Time}_{\text{Original}}$

$PT_{\text{Est}} = \text{Productive\_Time}_{\text{Estimated}}$ $\Delta PT_{\text{Est}} = \text{Change\_in\_Productive\_Time}_{\text{Estimated}}$

$E_n = \text{Expenses}_{\text{New}}$

This approximates the financial impact on revenue if expenses are increased or decreased. Organizations have traditionally associated changes in profitability with changes in expenses. That is:

$$\text{Profit}_{\text{New}} = \text{Profit}_{\text{Original}} - [E_o - E_n] = \text{Profit}_{\text{Original}} - \Delta E_{\text{Est}},$$

where

$$E_o = \text{Expenses}_{\text{Original}} = E_o$$
$$E_n = \text{Expenses}_{\text{New}} = E_n$$
$$\Delta E_{\text{Est}} = \text{Change\_in\_Expenses} = [E_o - E_n]$$

This traditional view asserts that profit will increase as expenses are decreased. For example, a firm generating $100 million in revenue with expenses of $60 million would have a profit of $40 million. If expenses were estimated to decrease by 20% ($12 million), it would be estimated that profit would increase by $12 million, from $40 million to $52 million.

Expense Quality

However, the preceding analysis neglects the quality of the expense(s) being reduced. If reducing an expense increases nonproductive time, then the cost reduction will have a revenue contribution cost equivalent to the money value of time (MVT) multiplied by the productive hours that have been converted into nonproductive hours. The adjustment executed by an intangible accounting system allows organizations to better estimate the impact of changes in the qualities of expenditures on profitability. Returning to the previous example, the $100 million firm with $40 million in expenses, seeking a 20% reduction in costs, would be analyzed as follows:

$$
\begin{aligned}
\text{Profit}_{\text{New}} &= (R_o - E_o) + (\Delta R_{\text{Est}} - \Delta E_{\text{Est}}) \\
&= ([\textstyle\sum PT_o \times MVT_o] - E_o) + ([\Delta PT_{\text{Est}} \times MVT_o] - [E_o - E_n]) \\
&= (\$100\,\text{million} - \$60\,\text{million}) + (-\$16\,\text{million} - (-\$12\,\text{million})) \\
&= (\$40\,\text{million}) + (-\$16\,\text{million} + \$12\,\text{million}) \\
&= (\$40\,\text{million}) + (-\$4\,\text{million}) \\
&= \$36\,\text{million},
\end{aligned}
$$

where

$$
\begin{aligned}
R_o &= \text{Revenue}_{\text{Original}} = [\textstyle\sum PT_o \times MVT_o] = \$100\,\text{million} \\
E_o &= \text{Expenses}_{\text{Original}} = E_o = \$40\,\text{million} \\
\Delta R_{\text{Est}} &= \text{Change\_in\_Revenue} = [\Delta PT_{\text{Est}} \times MVT_o] = -\$16\,\text{million} \\
\Delta E_{\text{Est}} &= \text{Change\_in\_Expenses} = [E_o - E_n] = -\$12\,\text{million} \\
m &= \text{million}
\end{aligned}
$$

Profit Is Not a Function of Expenses

The preceding equation demonstrates that profit is not simply a function of a change in expenses, but is determined in relation to the quality of cost reduction and the impact on organizational productive time. This functional form also allows increased expenditures to increase profitability due to their impact on productive time.

Mutual Codependence

Organizations have always relied on recording and analyzing financial transactions. As such, it has been considered that "only sales staff made revenue." Such a proposition is as flawed as the traditional approach of treating expenses and revenues as independent. In the networked economy, *all employees* participate in the value production process and their total contribution creates the money value of time.

Whereas a secretary picking up a phone and answering a call may not seem to generate immediate value, it captures customer time. It is customer time that the organization converts into revenue. Attention is required to gain customer time. As such, any time a customer interacts with the business (either verbally, digitally, or otherwise), customer time may be acquired or lost. Once acquired, customer time can be translated into revenue or lost to the competition through competitive switching. It is the translation of acquired and translated customer time into revenue that determines an organization's market share. Hence every employee at every level of business has the potential to add to or subtract from customer time. As such, an increase in customer time leads to an increase in productivity, while a decrease in customer time leads to a decrease in productivity. Intangible accounting uses the term "mutual codependence" to refer to the fact that all people are responsible for value creation within organizations.

By making a mathematical connection between time, productivity, and revenue, intangible accounting estimates how changes in expenses influence changes in time, which influence changes in productivity and revenue.

Using Intangible Accounting Systems

Because share price is the market value of a firm divided by the shares outstanding, the valuation system can predict how changes in market value affect share price. For example, the chief financial officer (CFO) of a business may wish to evaluate the effect of a particular business decision on the value of the business. The CFO can connect to the International Intangible Management Standards Institute intangible accounting server via the Internet. After submitting a username and password, the CFO enters the intangible accounting valuation system The intangible accounting system executes tangible and intangible accounting processes to value the business based on time transactions. The time transactions have a financial value and may be used to estimate the impact of changes in intangibles (knowledge, relationships, service, expectations, quality, etc.) on the organization's performance (productivity, revenue, market value, and share price). The intangible (time-based) transactions are separated into two principal categories: (1) information assets and (2) relationship assets. It is assumed that all activities that occur within a business organization can be categorized in one of these core areas. For example, consider the various transactions discussed next.

Staff Conflict. Conventional accounting only records a cost associated with staff conflict when a financial transaction occurs. For example, the cost of staff conflict to a conventional accounting system would be composed of all the financial transactions associated with staff conflict (mediation costs, training, etc.). Such costs are not representative of the true costs of staff conflict. The translation of productive time into nonproductive time is the major cost of staff conflict. This translation represents a decrease in productive capacity and translates into decreased productivity and revenue.

Addition and Removal of Staff. Conventional accounting represents employees as an expense. Assuming that expenses directly reduce profit, many organizations fail to acknowledge that employees are actually the source of revenue as employees create and convert productive time into revenue. By reducing headcount below optimal employment levels, organizations also reduce their earning capacity and devalue their companies in the market.

Absenteeism. Companies often provide for a certain amount of leave (sick leave, compassionate leave, etc.) from the firm each year. When absenteeism strikes, conventional accounting may record a tangible cost (a wage cost), but this is unlikely because full-time wages are already accounted for. Intangible accounting records the loss of productive time and estimates what this loss of time will translate to in terms of time, productivity, and revenue.

Poor Customer Service. Organizational market share continually erodes due to competitive pressure. Poor customer service accelerates loss of market share. Conventional accounting generally ignores all forms of human interaction until it results in a financial transaction. If human interactions result in an expenditure not being made, conventional accounting ignores the transaction. Intangible accounting records the transaction as a *never sale* (a sale that was never made), a *diluted sale* (a sale that was made where the customer remains unsatisfied in whole or in part), a *destructive sale* (one where the customer will leave the business forever and inform others not to shop there also), or a *constructive sale* (one where the customer favors the business and recommends others to buy there also). Because sales are a key issue for the majority of organizations, never sales, diluted sales, and destructive sales, must be measured. Management should record the potential impact on productivity, revenue, market value, and share price assessed of such sales.

Upgrade of a Computer. Expenditures to increase the speed of a computer are looked on as luxury expenditures by most accountants. However, such expenditures decrease the amount of nonproductive time within the business and have the potential to increase productivity, revenue, market value, and share price. By assessing the potential time changes it is possible to determine expense quality and the influence on profit and profitability.

Free Vendor-Held Training. Training is never free, even when there is no monetary cost to an organization. The cost associated with training must always be justified against the potential for improved productivity (through increased knowledge, increased network relationships, etc.). If a "free" training seminar occurs during working hours, the conversion of productive time into nonproductive time must be assessed. Estimates should also be made regarding the security of investing organizational time in the knowledge activity. If the incremental productivity gain over time is higher than the productivity loss, then the organization will increase revenue, market value, and share price.

Decision Profitability. Conventional accounting does not draw logical connections between expenses and other expenses, expenses and revenues, revenues and revenues, and so on. For example, if an executive decision is made to perform training, the (tangible) cost of the training is recorded as an expense and the revenues that flow from that training (if any) are not typically identified, categorized, or associated as being derived from that particular activity. In this sense, there is no connection between financial cause-and-effect relationships. Intangible accounting seeks to create significant awareness that time changes, brought about by intangibles, create flow-through (or "run on") effects that are felt over days, months, or years. By linking tangible flows with intangible flows, executives can understand how their business operates more effectively.

Process Improvement. Typically, process improvement undertaken by management consultants results in decreased tangible costs. Because consultants do not understand the nature, role, or importance of intangibles, it is easy to remove tangible cost centers that are actually mission-critical value creation sources. It is not uncommon for companies to downsize profitable sales forces to reduce wage costs. These actions occur due to society's preoccupation with tangibles (costs) and misunderstanding and ignorance of the fact that intangibles are responsible for financial performance.

CHAPTER 7

Intangible Bookkeeping

Intangible accounting performs six core tasks:

1. Identification of intangibles
2. Classification of intangibles
3. Recording of intangibles
4. Measurement of intangibles
5. Financial reporting of changes in cost quality
6. Analysis of intangible transactions

Adherence to international intangible standards relating to intangible accounting and intangible bookkeeping is made easy by using software that has been certified and accredited by the International Intangible Management Standards Institute. For a list of such software, please refer to http://www.StandardsInstitute.org/software. Such software performs the collection, categorization, measurement, valuation and reporting of intangible transactions.

INTANGIBLE ACCOUNTING REPORTS

This classification scheme allows organizations to formulate four primary intangible accounting statements:

1. Intangible balance sheet
2. Intangible income statement
3. Intangible time flow statement
4. Intangible Management statement

By 2004 it is expected that traditional accounting reports will be capturing less than 5% of the true value of the organizations for which they are created. Because 95% of the value creation process will be unaccounted for, it is essential that traditional accounting reports be supplemented with intangible accounting reports.

INTANGIBLE T-ACCOUNTS

Conventional (tangible) accounting reports are built on a bookkeeping foundation that measures and records financial transactions. Intangible accounting is built on a bookkeeping foundation that measures and records intangible transactions.

The fundamental building block of bookkeeping is the T-account. The T-account allows a bookkeeper to place data into a structured format so that it can be used by then transferred to journals, ledgers, and finally financial reports.

Intangible T-accounts record the daily flows of productive and nonproductive time in hours. As such, time, not value, is measured. Intangible T-accounts have the form shown in Figure 7.1. The only difference between an intangible T-account and a conventional (tangible) T-account is seen in what data are recorded. In a tangible T-account financial transaction data are recorded, as shown in Figure 7.2.

	Intangible Accounting Account	
Debit		Credit
Year	Hours	Year	Hours
Date Cross Reference Time	Date Cross Reference Time
Account	Account

FIGURE 7.1   The structure of an intangible T-account.

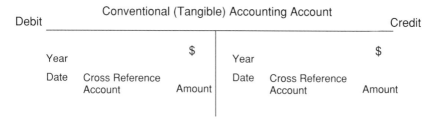

FIGURE 7.2   The structure of a conventional (tangible) T-account.

Hence, tangible bookkeeping records financial transactions and intangible bookkeeping records time transactions.

TANGIBLE T-ACCOUNT TYPES

In tangible accounting, financial transactions are recorded and classified according to what the result of the financial transaction means to the organization. For instance, if the financial transaction evidences an expenditure of $2500 cash on a new computer system, then two accounts are involved:

- The source of the $2500 cash, i.e., the Bank Account
- The destination of the $2500 cash, i.e., the Computer Account.

If the financial transaction results in the organization acquiring something of value, then an asset account has been used. T-accounts can represent a wide variety of components, such as those discussed next.

CONVENTIONAL ASSETS

Conventional assets consist of any item of economic value owned by an organization, especially those that can be converted to cash. For example, cash, securities, office equipment, and computers are all examples of assets. On the Balance Sheet assets are equal to the sum of liabilities, common stock, preferred stock, and retained earnings. Conventional assets have many classifications, such as:

- *Current assets* are a balance sheet item that is equal to (1) cash and cash equivalents plus (2) accounts receivable plus (3) inventory plus (4) marketable securities plus (5) prepaid expenses plus (6) all other assets that could be converted into cash in less than 12 months.
- *Fixed assets* (also referred to as capital assets, plant, or noncurrent assets) are not expected to be converted into cash within 12 months.

Hence, real estate, furniture, fixtures and fittings, and leasehold improvements are all examples of fixed assets.

- *Active assets* are those assets used in the daily operation of the organization.
- *Operating assets* are those assets that regularly generate revenue for the organization.
- *Earning assets* provide income.
- *Wasting assets* have a limited life and decrease in value over time.
- *Tangible assets* have physical form and can be touched. Under conventional tangible accounting standards, *intangible assets* cannot be physically touched and include trademarks, brands, patents, and franchises.

CONVENTIONAL LIABILITIES

A conventional liability is a debt, claim, potential loss, or other obligation that will consume financial resources within a specified period of time. Conventional liabilities have numerous categories, such as:

- *Current liabilities* are the total of financial transactions relating to the total value of all money owed by the organization to other parties that is due for payment within one financial year.
- *Noncurrent liabilities* are the total of financial transactions relating to the total value of all money owed by the organization less the value of money owed to other parties that is due for payment within one financial year.
- *Contingent liabilities* are liabilities that may occur but are extremely difficult to quantify (such as an outstanding lawsuit).

CAPITAL

Capital relates to the financial transactions used to generate income. Under conventional management, capital is defined as assets minus liabilities. This is also referred to as the accounting equation and is the basis of tangible bookkeeping and tangible double-entry accounting. The net worth of a business is the amount by which asset value exceeds liability value.

- *Invested capital* is the sum of an organization's (1) long-term debt, (2) stock, and (3) retained earnings.
- *Market capitalization* is the market price of an organization based on the product of the number of shares outstanding times the share price.
- *Book value* is the organization's common stock equity, which is equal to (1) total assets less (2) liabilities, (3) preferred stock, and (4) intangible

assets. Book value is derived from an organization's balance sheet. *Modified book value* (or *adjusted book value*) is the adjusted value of book value after factoring in current market prices for the organization's assets and liabilities. *Intrinsic value* is the perceived value of an organization and is different from the organization's market value. *Market value* is the value of the number of shares outstanding times the share price. The *price to book ratio* is the market capitalization of a firm divided by its book value. The *price to cash flow* ratio is the market capitalization of a firm divided by its cash flow for the latest fiscal year. The *price to sales ratio* is the market capitalization of a firm divided by its sales for the latest fiscal year.

REVENUE

Revenue is the total value of financial transactions collected regarding the exchange of money for the goods and services provided by the organization.

- *Gross revenue* is the total financial value of all sales made. *Marginal revenue* is the additional income generated from one additional unit of production. *Deferred revenue* is revenue that is considered a liability until payment for work done has actually been completed.
- *Earnings* represent revenue less the (1) the cost of sales, (2) operating expenses, and (3) taxes. *Normalized earnings* are earnings adjusted for the effects of economic cycles. *Cash earnings* are cash revenues less (1) cash expenses, not including noncash expenses such as depreciation. *Retained earnings* (or *earned surplus, accumulated earnings, unappropriated profit*) are earnings reinvested in the core business to fund future growth and repay debt.
- *Operating income* (or *operating profit* or *EBIT, earnings before interest and tax*) represents earnings less (1) interest payments and (2) income taxes. *Gross income* (or *gross profit*) is (1) pretax net sales less (2) the cost of sales.
- *Operating margin* measures an organization's earnings power by dividing (1) operating income by (2) revenues to arrive at a percentage measure of value creation.

EXPENSES

An expense is any cost incurred in running an organization, such as wages, light and power, and rent. Capital expenditures are expenses that are assigned to assets.

- *Accrual accounting* recognizes costs when incurred and revenue when earned.

- *Cash accounting* recognizes expenses when paid and revenue when received.
- *Accrued expenses* are expenditures incurred but not yet paid.
- *Operating expenses* (or *operating costs*) are expenses incurred in running the business on a day-to-day basis.
- *Marginal cost* (or *incremental cost*) is the cost associated with an additional unit of production.

PROFIT OR LOSS

If the difference between revenue and expenses is positive, a profit occurs. If the difference is negative, a loss occurs.

- *Net profit* (or *net income* or *the bottom line* or *net earnings*) is equal to (1) gross sales less (2) taxes, (3) interest, (4) depreciation, and (5) other expenses.
- *Net profit margin* (or *net margin*) is (1) net profit divided by (2) net revenues expressed as a percentage.

TANGIBLE DOUBLE-ENTRY BOOKKEEPING

Double-entry bookkeeping on financial transactions is the backbone of the accounting profession. Double-entry bookkeeping means that for every financial transaction incurred, there is a corresponding balancing financial transaction in an associated account. Consider the fundamental double entries shown in Table 7.1.

VALUE DOUBLE ENTRY

Bookkeeping is therefore the recording and presentation of the interaction between the sources and uses of financial transactions. For each debit value there is a corresponding credit value. The value of the financial transactions on both the debit and the credit side must match (see Table 7.2).

DOUBLE-ENTRY BOOKKEEPING RULES

Bookkeeping deals with five fundamental account types: assets, liabilities, capital, revenue and expenses. For convenience, the bookkeeping rules for these five account types are given in Table 7.3.

TABLE 7.1   How Debit and Credit Entries Balance

Action	Debit transaction	Credit transaction
Buy		
Asset on credit	Asset increases (debit)	Liability increases (credit)
Asset for cash	Asset increases (debit)	Asset decreases (credit)
Sell		
Asset on credit	Asset increases (debit)	Asset decreases (credit)
Asset for cash	Asset increases (debit)	Asset decreases (credit)
Repay liability	Liability decreases (debit)	Asset decreases (credit)

TABLE 7.2   How Debit Values and Credit Values Balance

Action	Debit transaction	Credit transaction	Credit transaction
Buy			
Asset for $1000 partly with cash ($250) and partly on credit ($750)	Asset increases (debit: $1000: purchased asset)	Liability increases (credit: $750 creditor)	Asset decreases (credit: $250 Bank account)

TABLE 7.3   Double-Entry Bookkeeping Rules

Account type	If increases	If decreases	Usual balance	Report
Asset	Debit	Credit	Debit	BS
Liability	Credit	Debit	Credit	BS
Capital	Credit	Debit	Credit	BS
Expenses	Debit	Credit	Debit	P & L
Revenue	Credit	Debit	Credit	P&L

VALUE MANAGEMENT STAGES

There are many variations of the five fundamental account types. These different types are captured by the chart of accounts.

Chart of Accounts

To make auditing easier, a *chart of accounts* assigns a unique identification number to each account for which an organization records data. For example, current assets may be numbered between 1 and 50, with cash on hand assigned the chart of accounts number "1." Debtors could be assigned a value of "10," etc. Fixed assets may have the range of values from 51 to 100 with motor vehicles assigned a unique identifier of "60," furniture a unique identifier of "70," and land and buildings a unique identifier of "80." The unique identifier system represented by the chart of accounts allows organizations to cross-reference various account types in journals and ledgers. At the end of the reporting period, accounts are balanced and a trial balance is created.

Trial Balance

The *trial balance* lists the total value of each individual account and its corresponding debit or credit balance. As we know, the total value of the debit balance must equal the total value of the credit balance in the trial balance. These amounts are then closed off and posted to financial statements.

Financial Statements

Organizations use numerous *financial statements* to understand how they have allocated financial transactions over a certain period of time. The two most critical financial statements are as follows:

- *Tangible balance sheet.* The tangible balance sheet measures the financial transactions relating to assets (A), liabilities (L), and capital (C) for the accounting period under analysis. The balance sheet is based on the equation $A = L + C$.
- *Tangible income statement.* The tangible income statement (or the tangible profit and loss statement) is based on the equation revenue (R) less expenses (E) equals profit or loss (P/L), or $R - E = P/L$.

ENTER ACCOUNTING

Accountants then take the results of bookkeepers and analyze the aggregated amounts. The primary job of an accountant is to ensure that the government obtains the correct amount of taxation from an organization. For many organizations, accounting has more to do with taxation assessment than business performance. Accountants have a legal responsibility to present a true and fair view of the flows of an organization's financial transactions.

For managers, accounting information is often used as the basis of *return on investment* (ROI) analyses. Accountants seek to cost-justify investments based on potential returns to the organizations making investments. Because accounting information looks primarily at financial transactions and not time transactions, a large part of the understanding of the business is missing. This

TABLE 7.4   Conventional Bookkeeping and Intangible Bookkeeping

Conventional bookkeeping	Intangible bookkeeping
Tangible assets	Intangible assets
Tangible liabilities	Intangible liabilities
Tangible capital	Intangible capital
Tangible revenue	Intangible revenue
Tangible expenses	Intangible expenses

fundamental weakness in conventional accounting is addressed by supplementing conventional reports with intangible bookkeeping and intangible accounting[1] reports.

INTANGIBLE BOOKKEEPING

As seen earlier, and as presented in Table 7.4, the fundamental intangible accounts have the same basic composition as the five fundamental tangible accounts. When people refer to tangibles, they are actually speaking about financial transactions. Financial transactions involve allocations of money and transfers of legal property rights. As such, financial transactions are the foundation of contract law. A contract is an agreement to do, or not to do, something given specific and adequate monetary consideration.

We also know that intangibles are not tangibles; they are activities that involve allocations of time. Such allocations of time involve the appreciation or depreciation of competitive (or market) rights. Contract law does not typically cover such rights as market rights prevent financial transactions from occurring either immediately or at future points of time. It is the very nature of competitive rights to directly affect the chance of a financial transaction, which makes them so essential to control. Because competitive rights are not observable by exchanges of money, we have to use a nonfinancial indicator: time.

INTANGIBLE CLASSIFICATION SYSTEM

Intangible accounting redefines many traditional terms by basing them on time transactions rather than on financial transactions. These new terms are discussed next.

[1] The intangible bookkeeping and intangible accounting reports were developed by Dr. Ken Standfield.

Intangible Assets

In previous chapters, you were introduced to the concept of a level 3 intangible. Level 3 intangibles are intentions to allocate time in a specific way for a specific objective. These objectives are financial and nonfinancial and are realized only after a significant amount of time.

> Any amount of time that has the potential to increase, leverage or create long-term or short-term financial transactions is referred to as an intangible asset.

Because intangible assets are level 3 intangibles they are *not owned* by the business. Such intangibles can only be controlled and managed through intangible management methods and standards.

Intangible Liabilities

Some expenditures of time have the ability to reduce, disrupt, or destroy financial transactions in the short term or long term. As a result such time expenditures need to be made visible so that an organization can take corrective action.

> Any amount of time that has the potential to reduce, disrupt or destroy long-term or short-term financial transactions is referred to as an intangible liability.

Intangible Capital

Just as tangible capital is the defined by the accounting equation $A = L + C$, the intangible accounting equation[2] defines how intangible capital is determined. The intangible accounting equation is

$$iAssets = iLiabilities + iCapital$$

Hence, iCapital is equal to iAssets less iLiabilities. According to international intangible standards:

> Intangible capital is defined as the total of (1) any amount of time that has the potential to increase, leverage or create long-term or short-term financial transactions is referred to as an intangible asset, less (2) any amount of time that has the potential to reduce, disrupt, or destroy long-term or short-term financial transactions. (IISD4001.D50)

Intangible Revenue

Tangible revenue is the aggregation of financial transactions relating to revenue accounts. This revenue is generated from the financial transactions of level

[2]Developed by Dr. Ken Standfield.

1 (tangible) assets. Intangible revenue is the translation of intangible assets into financial transactions. According to international intangible standards:

> Intangible revenue occurs when Intangible Assets are translated into actual financial transactions.

Intangible assets therefore create intangible revenues.

Intangible Expenses

Tangible (level 1) expenses can be broken into two fundamental categories: (1) productive expense financial transactions and (2) nonproductive expense financial transactions. Intangible (level 3) expenses have exactly the same characteristic. Intangible expenses have two fundamental categories: (1) productive time financial transactions and (2) nonproductive time financial transactions.

> Intangible expenses occur when Intangible Liabilities are translated into opportunity costs. Intangible expenses are therefore the cost of non-productive time.

Intangible liabilities therefore create intangible expenses.

Intangible Profit and Loss

Just as tangible profit (or loss) is defined by the profit equation $R - E = P$, the intangible accounting profit equation[3] defines how intangible profit (or loss) is determined. The intangible accounting profit equation is

$$iProfit = iReveue - iExpenses$$

Hence, iProfit is the difference between iRevenues and iExpenses. According to international intangible standards:

> Intangible Profit is defined as the positive difference between intangible revenue and intangible expenses. Intangible Loss is defined as the negative difference between intangible revenue and intangible expenses.

INTANGIBLE BOOKKEEPING IN PRACTICE

Whereas tangible bookkeeping records financial transactions, intangible bookkeeping records time transactions.

Suppose that a company spent 10,000 hours on Project X. The intangible bookkeeping entry is shown in Figure 7.3.

[3]Developed by Dr. Ken Standfield.

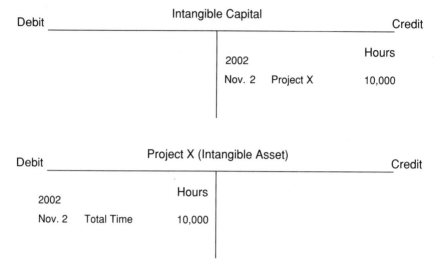

FIGURE 7.3   Double-entry intangible bookkeeping.

To determine the productive and nonproductive time impacts, the following analysis is performed. Assuming that 2000 hours of this 10,000 hours were nonproductive (due to knowledge overheads); then the next transaction is recorded in Figure 7.4.

Project X (Intangible Asset)

Debit _____ Credit

2002		Hours	2002		Hours
Nov. 2	Total Time	10,000	Nov.2	Knowledge Overheads	2,000

Knowledge Overheads (Intangible Expense)

Debit _____ Credit

2002		Hours
Nov. 2	Project X	2,000

FIGURE 7.4   Double-entry intangible bookkeeping.

If Project X attracted other overheads such as information overheads of 1750 hours, communications overheads of 1500 hours, and process overheads of 500 hours, then the Project X intangible T-account appears as: would look like that shown in Figure 7.5. The 10,000 hours allocated to Project X have been diluted by 5750 hours of overhead (nonproductive) time. This leaves a balance of 4250 hours of productive time in Project X's account. As time progresses the receipts of Project X must be matched to the investments of time, from all sources, in the project. It is only at this point that we can understand how organizations can manage and value intangible costs.

Debit			Project X (Intangible Asset)		Credit
2001		Hours	2001		Hours
Nov. 2	Total Time	10,000	Nov. 2	Knowledge Overheads	2,000
				Information Overheads	1,750
				Communications Overheads	1,500
				Process Overheads	500

FIGURE 7.5   Double-entry intangible bookkeeping.

CHAPTER 8

Foundations of Intangible Management

Today, intangibles dominate the inputs and outputs of the production process. Service workers dominate employment and service industries dominate in their contribution to gross domestic product. In the manufacturing age, financial (tangible) cost management was a major determinant of an organization's profitability. Now, however, intangible cost management is the major determinant of organizational profitability and sustainability.

Intangible cost analysis when applied to everyday activities arms executives with powerful tools to manage and control according to the new principles of the Intangible Economy.

Around the world, concern is growing that employees are not using time productively. Management guru Peter Drucker has found that staff can be nonproductive, or be engaging in tasks that create little, if any, value, for up to 70% of each workday.

> ... the people who actually do most of the knowledge and service work in organizations ... carry a steadily growing load of busy work, additional activities that contribute little or no value and that have little or nothing to do with what these people are qualified and paid for. —*Peter Drucker*, Managing for the Future

James Field, a noted management consultant, also supports this stance:

> The average worker is productive only 55 per cent of the time. —*Los Angeles Times*

WHAT THIS REALLY MEANS

Consider an organization where 1000 employees are capable of generating $250,000,000 of revenue each year. Let us assume that staff are only operating at 55% productivity. Hence, actual revenue generation of $137.5 million is therefore significantly below total potential revenue of $250 million, as shown in Figure 8.1.

We can therefore state that the 45% non-productivity is costing the business $112.5 million in revenue. Hence,

$$1\% \text{ of Nonproductivity} = \$2,500,000 \text{ of Revenue.}$$

Intangible Management Potential

For each 1% of nonproductivity the business converts into an *additional* 1% of productivity, the firm should generate an *additional* $2.5 million of annual revenue. Hence, if the firm could convert all 45 points of nonproductivity into productivity, the firm should expand revenue by 45 × $2.5 million, or $112.5 million.

The Employee Dilemma

Employees will always have *some* nonproductive time (talking to other staff, coffee/tea breaks, toilet breaks, etc.). This means that a firm can never fully

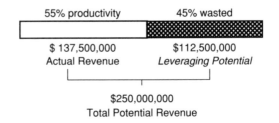

FIGURE 8.1   Determining intangible Management potential.

convert nonproductive time to productive time. However, by applying intangible management to existing processes to relieve employees of nonproductive and non-value-added tasks, your firm should be able to increase productivity to between 75 and 90%. Some firms may be capable of going even further.

It is theoretically possible to push productivity to 99%, but the cost of attaining this level of productivity would almost certainly lead to the generation of significant intangible costs (turnover, human interaction costs, quality costs, etc.) and the strong possibility of the firm reverting to more comfortable levels (75 to 90%).

Minimizing Ongoing Intangible Costs

The costs involved with internal and external human interactions can be substantial. Any attempt to reach *unsustainable* productivity levels will cause employees to revert to earlier, less satisfactory, productivity levels. Managers responsible for intangible management must ensure that they circumvent this "reversion process" by *adding* to employee security, *not* eliminating it. The role of intangible management is to make employees feel safe with the changes intangible management practices generate.

Most importantly, intangible management can be applied on an ongoing basis through the application of the software certified as conforming to international intangible standards. Management's role then becomes one of facilitating the intangible management process by assisting employees to manage intangibles so they can perform their work more productively and efficiently.

HOW TO IMPLEMENT
INTANGIBLE MANAGEMENT

Intangible management is an exceptionally powerful management consulting technique because it creates increased productivity and organizational value by removing nonproductive work from the employee's workload. To gain the benefits that intangible management can create, it is essential to understand nine fundamental propositions as discussed in the following subsections.

PROPOSITION 1: MONEY IS TIME

Time is the currency of today's economic system. When the currency of time is matched to the currency of money we can link financial performance to operational performance. Just as we say that "time is money" we can also state "money is time." The monetary value of time is estimated through IIS5001, the Intangible Reporting Standard. IIS5001.D1 defines the money value of time as follows:

> The money value of time is determined when financial performance is matched to organization's time performance. (IIS5001.D1)

PROPOSITION 2: EMPLOYEES CREATE TIME

The average staff member has approximately 1800 hours in which to be productive or nonproductive. Because time is money, every hour of capacity available to the firm represents revenue potential. If an organization hires one employee, then *the organization* will have a total of 1800 hours in which to generate revenue. If the organization employs 50 staff, then the organization will have 50 × 1800 hours or 90,000 hours in which to generate revenue each year. If the organization employs 1000 staff, the organization will have 1,800,000 (1000 × 1800) hours each year to generate organizational wealth. The greater the number of employees, the more time capital will be at the organization's disposal.

Another Example

Let us assume that a services firm charges clients an average of $125 per hour. If the firm can charge for every hour of employee work, then an employee working 1800 hours will generate $225,000 for the firm. However, if we assume that employee productivity runs at 55%, then the firm will only generate $123,750 from each employee. The difference of $101,250 is *intangible management potential*. Table 8.1 illustrates the relationship between time and value at different firm sizes. By releasing intangible management potential (by converting nonproductive time into productive time), firms can dramatically increase their market power.

PROPOSITION 3: EMPLOYEE VALUE IS MISUNDERSTOOD

Every organization has two main revenue (or income) streams: employee-generated income (sales, consulting, etc.) and non-employee-generated income (investment interest, etc.).

- *Employee-generated revenue streams.* Often 95–100% of revenue generated by an organization will come from the effort of existing employees.

TABLE 8.1   Relationship between Time and Value at Different Firm Sizes

Firm size (staff)	Firm size (at 1800 hours per employee)	Firm value (estimated) (at $ 125/hr @100%)	Firm value (actual) (at 55% productivity)	Intangible management potential (at 45% productivity)
1	1,800	$ 225,000	$ 123,750	$ 101,250
5	9,000	$ 1,125,000	$ 618,750	$ 506,250
10	18,000	$ 2,250,000	$ 1,237,500	$ 1,012,500
50	90,000	$ 11,250,000	$ 6,187,500	$ 5,062,500

- *Non-employee-generated revenue streams.* For a revenue stream to qualify as a non-employee-generated revenue stream staff must not contribute *any time* to the derivation of that income. For example, if a business invests in the stock market and makes a $500,000 return, that return was principally generated by fund managers and stockbrokers and not by the efforts of internal staff. Such a return is non-employee generated. In the majority of organizations non-employee-generated revenue accounts for less than 5% of organizational income.

Valuing Employee Contributions

To *benchmark* employee value requires an understanding of mutual codependence and relative performance.

Mutual Codependence

Organizations are collective entities—they work as a whole to produce value. Typically, the Research and Development Division supplies information and knowledge to the Engineering Division, which then acts on this knowledge, combined with its own, to create specifications for the Manufacturing Department to make. The Marketing Department and Sales Department then package and sell produced goods and services. The Quality Assurance Department determines if the quality of the product is sufficient to pass customer tests.

Underpinning all of this, the Human Resources Department ensures that the right employees with the right skill sets are distributed to the right departments. In short, every department is *mutually codependent*, or reliant, on every other department. This also means that individual staff members are codependent on each other.

Relative Performance

In 1996, General Motors (GM) generated revenue of $168,369M from 647,000 employees. In 2002, GM generated revenue of $177,270M from 365,000 employees. Relative performance (the ratio of gross revenue to employees) for GM was $260,230.29 in 1996 and $485,671.23 in 2002.

Benchmarking Employee Performance

The *hourly productivity formula* allows corporations to benchmark hourly employee productivity.

Applying the Hourly Productivity Formula

Let us assume that a firm generates $137.50 million in annual revenue, with $7.50 million generated from non-employee-related activities (investment returns, etc.). The firm employs 1000 employees who work an average of 38 hours a week over 5 days. Each employee averages 14 days of annual leave: 3 days sick leave, 1 day of absenteeism, 8 days of holidays, and 1 day of other leave. Management determined that the results of redundancies, layoffs, and retrenchments from the previous year decreased the productive time of the remaining staff by 2 days per staff member. The hourly productivity formula would deduce that each staff member contributes $73.73 each hour toward revenue.

Capturing Net Employee Benefit

The *employee benefit ratio* measures the ratio of productivity to wages. If the above firm paid wages and associated employee benefits of $50 million to generate $130 million in employee revenue contributions, then the firm has an employee benefit ratio of 2.6 to 1 ($130 million/$50 million). The employee benefit ratio is calculated by dividing the employee-generated contribution to revenue by the total wage cost.

We have therefore determined that the relationship between wages and productivity is 2.6 to 1. This means that for every $1 of wages paid to an employee the organization can expect $2.60 of employee revenue contribution in return.

Applying the hourly productivity formula and the employee benefit ratio to your business should be the first thing you do. These measures allow you to manage your business with greater strategic insight. You will know how much staff contribute to revenue each hour and the efficiency of that contribution.

PROPOSITION 4: REDUCING WAGE COSTS CAN UNDERMINE LONG-TERM CORPORATE VIABILITY

Consider two identical firms in the same market. Both firms operate at 55% productivity with 1000 employees and generate $137.50 million per year in revenue. Each firm spends $50 million each year on employee remuneration. To determine the total potential revenue-generating capability of each firm (if nonproductivity were eliminated) at the current employment level, the *potential gross revenue (PGR) formula* is used:

$$PGR = \left(\frac{\sum R}{\text{Productivity rate}} \right)$$

Using the figures above, we determine that each firm could generate, with 1000 employees, $250 million each year:

$$PGR = \left(\frac{\sum R}{\text{Productivity rate}} \right)$$
$$= (\$137.50 \text{ million}) \, (1/0.55)$$
$$= \$250 \text{ million}$$

Hence, at 100% productivity 1000 staff should generate $250 million in annual revenue (or $250,000 per staff member).

Dual Scenario Analysis

The presidents of both of the identical firms mentioned above have decided to apply intangible management to create their preferred competitive position. President A, in addition to intangible management, decides to downsize to 550 staff to reduce costs. President B applies intangible management, but chooses not to use downsizing. The questions now become which organization will be better off, by how much, and why?

President A—Intangible Management + Downsizing

If 1000 staff are paid $50 million in wages, then making 450 staff redundant should create an annual wage saving (WS) of approximately $22.50 million.

$$WS = 450 \times (\$50,000,000/1000)$$
$$= 450 \times (\$50,000)$$
$$= \$22,500,000$$
$$= \$22.50 \text{ million}$$

However, redundancies also generate other payments, such as "golden parachutes," long service payments, sick pay, annual leave payments and other loadings. These could potentially drain the company's cash position significantly. If we assume that the downsizing firm is required to pay a total of $9.50 million in *additional* redundancy costs, then it would cost the business $9.50 million to reduce wages by $22.50 million. Hence, a net savings of $13 million ($22.50 million–$9.50 million) would be expected.

Downsizing also tends to create significant *human interaction costs* because remaining employees may feel psychologically threatened that they will made redundant. As such, many employees will work more slowly, have higher error rates, and lose their commitment to the organization. This tends to generate poor customer service, higher internal stress, greater turnover, and numerous other factors that can further decrease productivity.

Although intangible management can increase productivity to higher levels, the intangible costs generated by downsizing would lead to an increase in nonproductive time and intangible expenses. This may result in productivity falling to 85%. A fall of 15% would cost the business $20.63 million ($137.50 × 0.15) in intangible costs. As we saw with GM earlier, it is possible to maintain revenue levels at lower employment levels, but only through artificial employment, better workplace practices, and other intangible management strategies

President B—Intangible Management Only

The second firm does *not* downsize after intangible management, so this firm allows 1000 staff to generate $250 million in revenue contributions. President A has contracted the firm to $137.50 million, whereas President B has expanded the firm to $250 million (a difference of $112.50 million).

On a percentage basis, Firm B will now be 45% more attractive to investors because it is 45% more powerful than Firm A.

Flow-Through Intangible Benefits. Because employees are not being retrenched, their commitment to the organization grows stronger, which is reflected in increased customer service, lower internal stress, and less turnover. President B will therefore increase productivity without experiencing the intangible costs that generally follow downsizing.

Moreover, market investors will be more inclined to invest in President B's organization because it is growing. This may lead to other intangible benefits (greater sales, previously unattainable contracts becoming attainable, etc.). Additional intangible benefits of 5 to 10% may push the company into its next growth phase. Hence, by focusing on nonwage factors, the intangible management – only company has dramatically outperformed its competitor.

PROPOSITION 5: CHANGE AND INNOVATION MUST BE HARNESSED

Today's economy is ever changing. New technologies and new methods continually impact market power and market profitability. In this sense, organizations operate in an environment where the rug is continually being pulled from underneath their feet.

> Once technology is out of the jar, you can't put it back in. —*Ervin L. Glaspy*

Organizations are now faced with a choice—do they react to changes or do they create change for a living?

> Most economists concur that 50 to 60 per cent of our economic growth can be attributed to technological innovations. —*Ian M. Ross, President, AT&T Bell Laboratories*

By using intangible management to harness change and innovation, organizations can enhance long-term viability and investor security.

> Economic power changes as markets and technology change. Big companies cannot prevent change. Even they will be bypassed unless they keep on top of changing markets and technology. —*Alfred D. Chandler, The Wall Street Journal, February 15, 1981*

The most important issue organizations face today is how to integrate change and innovation into their corporate structure while maintaining corporate stability and long-term viability.

> Our commercial history is filled with companies that failed to change with a changing world, and became tombstones in the corporate graveyard. —*Walter B. Wriston, Chairman, Citicorp, 1981*

Intangible management proposes two methods: (1) innovation adoption policy and (2) change integration policy, both of which are discussed in the following subsections.

Innovation Adoption Policy

We are living in an age of exponential change, where the future cannot be determined by projecting *past* trends. It is useful to keep a few quotes in mind when forming your understanding of innovation adoption policy:

> To succeed, jump as quickly at opportunities as you do at conclusions. —*Benjamin Franklin*
> We live in the present with our feet firmly planted in the past. —*Ken Standfield*
> The significant problems we face cannot be solved at the same level of thinking we were at when we created them. —*Albert Einstein*

Intangible management is a management consulting discipline with a solid grounding in reality. Innovations are not adopted for many reasons. The *law of derived demand* captures the main reason:

> *New* technologies (innovations, methods, etc.) create demand, uses, applications and benefits that previously *did not exist*. As new uses must be *experienced* to be understood, new products are often misunderstood and seriously undervalued.

Change Integration Policy

To leverage innovation correctly, it is essential to understand change and how it affects individuals, organizations, and the economy.

> When you're through changing, you're through. —*Bruce Barton*

In many ways, nearly everything we use and take for granted has been created within the past 100 years—computers, VCRs, televisions, microwave ovens, etc. This led Alvin Toffler, author of the best selling book *Future Shock* to write the following:

> It has been observed, for example, that if the last 50,000 years of man's existence were divided into lifetimes of approximately 62 years each, there have been about 800 such lifetimes. Of these 800, fully 650 were spent in caves.
> Only during the last 70 lifetimes has it been possible to communicate effectively from one lifetime to another—as writing made it possible to do. Only during the last 6 lifetimes did masses of men ever see a printed word. Only during the last 4 has it been possible to measure time with any precision. Only in the last 2 has anyone anywhere used an electric motor. And the overwhelming majority of all the material goods we use in daily life today have been developed within the present, 800th, lifetime. —*Alvin Toffler*, Future Shock, 1974, p. 22

The pace of change is *not going to decrease*; it will increase. Change integration policy assists organizations to profit from change.

> The art of progress is to preserve order amid change and to preserve change amid order. —*Alfred North Whitehead*

Proposition 6: Organizational Value Only Occurs in Productive Time

Employee revenue generation (organizational value) *only* occurs in productive time. To apply intangible management correctly, it is essential to understand the *law of time productivity*:

> Every organizational task has a productive and a nonproductive time component. (IIS8001.L1)

A major focus of intangible management is to minimize, or eliminate, the nonproductive time associated with employee tasks.

Consider a normal operational task—writing a memo. Gone are the days when an employee could simply write a memo by hand on a piece of paper, photocopy it, and wait for the mailroom to collect and distribute it. To write a simple memo today an employee must understand:

1. Computer *hardware* (to turn on the computer and operate the printer— if the memo is to be printed)
2. The computer's *operating system* (to start the software)
3. The *software package(s)* used (word processor, graphics, e-mail program, intranet publishing software, etc.)
4. As well as an understanding of *what* needs to be written
5. *How* the memo should be formed (company guidelines, etc.)

The task (writing a memo) will be generating productive and nonproductive time at each stage of fulfillment. To illustrate the law of time productivity, we will investigate two employees working for two different organizations. One organization uses old methods and old technologies (i.e., is change resistant); the other organization uses new methods and new technologies. The task of both employees is to write and distribute a memo; *how the organization allows each to accomplish that task* will be significantly different.

Employee A—Old Methods, Old Technology

This employee starts the 286 computer with 4 MB of RAM and goes into Windows 3.0 to start a word processor. After a minute the program loads and the employee starts to type. The employee, when finished, prints the memo to a dot-matrix printer (remember those?). This report is then printed and taken to the manager's office for approval. Along the way, the employee catches up on the local gossip. After 20 minutes the manager finds the time to look at the memo. Spelling mistakes are corrected and the employee is given the memo to redraft. The employee retypes the memo with the changes, prints the memo, and places it in the internal mail to be distributed to other the employees on the distribution list. The Mail Department picks up the mail, photocopies the required number of copies, and distributes the mail to the required personnel (who are on different floors of the building). In total, the process takes approximately half a day.

Employee B—New Methods, New Technology

This employee starts the latest computer, launches into the latest version of a word processor with integrated grammar correction and spell-checking capabilities. This employee will distribute the memo by e-mail. Managerial input is not required because employees use templates to write memos. A template is much like a preconstructed memo where employees simply need to fill in the required fields. Within a few minutes, the memo has been written according to organizational policy. Spell checking ensures that the employee does not make any typing mistakes. The completed memo is then distributed by e-mail to required recipients at the click of a button. *In total, the task takes under 10 minutes.*

Applying the Law of Time Productivity

Employee B was more productive because "performance lags"—waiting for the manager to correct the work, retyping the memo and waiting for the printed materials to be distributed—were practically eliminated.

Employee B's use of latest technology also allowed "technological lags" to be minimized (e.g., Employee B's computer was significantly faster than that of Employee A's).

Intangible management aims at eliminating performance, technological, and other lags.

Lags or Time Delays

The Intangible Project Management Standard (IIS8001) defines a number of organizational lags:

1. Performance lags (IIS8001.D20)
2. Technological lags (IIS8001.D21)

3. Knowledge lags (IIS8001.D22)
4. Cultural lags (IIS8001.D23)
5. Organizational lags (IIS8001.D24)
6. Operational lags (IIS8001.D25)
7. Relational lags (IIS8001.D26)

By attempting to subclassify time delays (or lags) into functional groups, we can assess where bottlenecks occur. For example, *knowledge lags* occur when people do not have the required knowledge to perform the task efficiently. *Cultural lags* occur when the country of business suspends productivity in accordance with the religious, political, cultural, or business practices of the country in question. *Organizational lags* occur when outdated policies and operating procedures slow down the flow of work (e.g., work has to be signed off by two supervisors). Operational lags are the organizational and performance lags when applied to a specific task or process.

> Intangible management minimizes time lags so that organizations can maximize productive time and profitability.

PROPOSITION 7: HUMAN INTERACTION COSTS MUST BE MANAGED

Employee stress, in-fighting, and internal politics all create financial costs and competitive costs. These intangible costs, while not viewable on a conventional profit and loss statement, can now be identified and valued through intangible cost analysis. Because human interaction costs are major generators of nonproductive time, it is vital that organizations identify, manage, and reduce human interaction costs. Several chapters in this book are devoted to the issue of valuing and reducing human interaction costs.

PROPOSITION 8: 55% PRODUCTIVITY

As a benchmark most organizations—despite how *busy* staff appear—are only operating at approximately 55% productivity. The transition from the Manufacturing Age to the Intangible Age (not managers, executives, employees, or organizations) is fully responsible for this 55% worldwide productivity benchmark.

> Within your organization your employees may exhibit more, or less, than 55% productivity. Later chapters will show that productivity is measured by the amount of time employees spend performing value-added tasks for which they are qualified.

Value Addition, Not Activity

Peter Drucker in his book *Managing for the Future* (pp. 86–87) says that managers, nurses, academics, salespeople, engineers, and other employees are spending a large proportion of their time in activities that generate little if any organizational value. He argues that if knowledge and service productivity are not increased, then "Developed countries will face economic stagnation" (p. 92). He goes on to state that:

> Raising the productivity of knowledge and service work must therefore be an economic priority for developed countries. Whichever country first succeeds in satisfying it will economically dominate the twenty-first century. And the key is raising the productivity of knowledge work, on all levels. (p. 92)

Intangible management is the way to increase the productivity of knowledge and service work on all levels. Intangible management focuses on value addition, not activity. Being busy is no guarantee of being productive; in fact, usually it is an indication of lack of organization, planning, and time management. Intangible management starts by eliminating activities that cause staff to be busy, but not productive.

Busy Activities

Consider information as an example. Regardless of your occupation, you could spend every working hour just "keeping current" and never do any real work. This is because the Intangible Age has resulted in an explosion of information and complexity. Significant amounts of information are now required to make decisions. As decisions become increasingly more complex, even more information is required to make an informed decision.

Technology is also at fault. To perform simple tasks, employees must now understand numerous complex computer packages and be familiar with computer hardware. Because most staff only understand 10% of the features of the average computer program, it is little wonder that staff are busy but lack productivity.

As the two simple examples above illustrate, employees, managers, executives, and organizations are not to blame for the productivity problem. Executives and managers can only *become* responsible for the productivity problem if they do nothing to solve it.

PROPOSITION 9: EQUAL APPLICATION

Intangible Management creates enterprise-wide benefits. Applying intangible management to employees involved in revenue-generating activities ignores mutual codependence. Intangible management is equally applicable to all staff. In truth, client contact is simply the outcome of organizational processes. This outcome cannot be logically isolated and dissected from the other sections of the organization.

To understand the true place of revenue-generating staff (sales), let us assume that a corporation is like a person. The heart is sales, the brains are management, and the body parts (arms, legs, etc.) are employees. Movement is generated by the brain (management) and the speed of movement (progress) by the body (employees)—everything is interconnected, interrelated, and not capable of standing alone.

- If the brain (management) were removed, the heart (sales) and body (employees) would die (insolvency).
- If the heart (sales) were removed, the brain (management) and body (employees) would also die (insolvency).
- If the body (employees) were removed, the brain (management) and the heart (sales) would cease to have use (insolvency).

Intangible management can potentially create benefits throughout every part of an organization so that the heart (sales), the brain (management), and the body (employees) all function in a more coordinated, productive, efficient, effective, and less stressful way.

Today's work practices must acknowledge that we work in an age where the majority of employees are employed to create and distribute intangible value. This is *very different* from the time when the majority of people were employed in factories and worked on production lines.

THE LAW OF TIME ACCUMULATION

The *law of time accumulation* (IIS8001.L5) states that we cannot look at activities in isolation—we must accumulate the effects of activities until we form an *enterprise-wide* understanding of their impact. This law states that:

> The amount of productive time and nonproductive time accumulates for each task and multiplies by the number of people performing that task throughout the organization over a full work year. By determining the number of times the task must be performed each year, across the organization, the aggregate effect of this task on organizational productivity can be determined.

Because the time and cost effects are determined over a full working year, we can compare and contrast the times required to perform various activities. By detailing every activity a *full activity map* of every activity an organization performs and how long it takes the organization to perform those tasks, especially within processes, can be determined.

APPLYING THE LAW OF TIME ACCUMULATION

All activities that occur within organizations have the potential to increase or decrease organization value. Consider phone calls. Let us assume that we are investigating a firm of 1000 staff. The average staff member[1] makes one 6-minute phone call each hour. If we only focus on a single employee, we may consider a phone call of 6 minutes to be an acceptable use of organizational time. Over an 8-hour workday, each staff member will accumulate 48 minutes of telephone usage, which may also be viewed as acceptable.

However, the feasibility of this practice changes dramatically when we understand the *accumulated effects*. If 1000 staff average one 6-minute phone call each hour over 8 working hours, the firm is actually allocating 800 hours ($1000 \times 6/60 \times 8$) of organizational time to phone call utilization *each day*. Over 5 days, the organization's 1000 staff have allocated 4000 hours to telephone usage. Over 50 weeks, this figure increases to 200,000 hours.

---

[1]This means that *some* employees will make zero phone calls, while others will make multiple phone calls per hour.

THE LAW OF ORGANIZATIONAL TIME DETERMINATION

The *law of organizational time determination* (IIS8001.L6) states that:

> For every hour of organizational time, the organization has access to a total amount of time equal to the number of employees working throughout the whole organization in that hour.

Hence, if an organization employs 50 staff it has access to 50 hours of potential productivity within any single organizational hour. Naturally, individual staff members can only have access to 1 hour each hour but as a group, they create 50 hours of potential productivity for the organization.

In the current example, 1000 staff give the organization access to 1000 hours of potential productivity each hour. Because 1000 staff are spending 6 minutes on phone calls, the organization is allocating 100 hours (1000 × 6/ 60) of this 1000 hours to phone calls. In the span of 8 hours, the organization would produce 8000 hours of potential productivity, although 800 hours of this total amount would have been allocated to phone calls.

If you are confused by the above, it is because you are looking at it from the *employee's* perspective and not the *organization's* perspective.

Employee's Perspective

One hour of employee time can only ever be worth 1 hour.

Organization's Perspective

One hour of organizational time is determined by the number of staff employed during that hour. If 1000 staff are employed, then each hour of organization time is worth 1000 hours.

The law of time accumulation has therefore determined that if each employee averages one 6-minute phone call each hour, at the end of a normal working year, the firm would have to allocate 200,000 hours to telephone utilization.

THE LAW OF TIME VALUATION

The *law of time valuation* is one of the most important laws in this book. It states:

> To correctly value a time savings requires (1) the value of a reduction in non-productive wage allocations to be added to (2) the potential increase in revenue generating capacity as determined by the Intangible Standard. (IIS8001.L7).

This law allows organizations to value time usage and potential cost savings brought about by time savings.

Employees can be paid for productive work or nonproductive work. If an employee is paid for productive work, then the organization generates revenue (say, $125/hour) at the expense of a productive wage allocation (say, $25/hour). However, if the employee is paid for nonproductive work (personal phone calls), the organization makes a wage payment (say, $25/ hour) that cannot be offset because the employee does not generate any organizational value (the phone calls costs the business productivity).

VALUING TIME SAVINGS

If management reduced telephone usage to an average of 4.50 minutes per call (through intangible management practices), this would generate a time savings of 50,000 hours each year (200,000 × (6 − 4.5)/6). To correctly value this time savings we require two components—a wage cost and the expected expansion in revenue.

DETERMINING WAGE COSTS

If employees charge an average of $15 per hour, then a saving of 50,000 hours will reduce nonproductive wage allocations by $750,000.

Most organizations have no understanding of how much phone usage, computer usage, meetings, information analysis, or interruptions cost their business each year. *Such costs have only been tolerated because they have remained unseen and not valued.*

DETERMINING REVENUE EXPANSION

International intangible standards provide assistance in determining an employee's average revenue contribution each hour. For simplicity, let us assume that the firm can generate revenue of $70 per hour for each of the released 50,000 hours. The revenue value of the time savings would be worth an estimated $3.5 million. Hence, the potential value of reducing phone calls from an average of 6 minutes per call to an average of 4.5 minutes per call would be $750,000 in wages and $3.5 million in potential revenue, or a total of $4.25 million.

Using the wage cost alone as a basis for measuring savings is *fundamentally* incorrect for two reasons: (1) Wage payments are satisfied from revenue—the creation of revenue allows wages to be paid (no revenue, no firm). (2) Wages, although employment related, are only one organizational expense. Marketing, production, advertising, legal, and other expenses must also be paid. Hence, using wages as the exclusive base ignores the fact that businesses exist to generate revenue, not pay expenses, and businesses experience a multitude of expenses, wages being just one type of expense.

Telephone conversations are simply a way in which organizations *acquire and distribute information and knowledge over time.* As such, it is essential to measure knowledge costs and information costs.

KNOWLEDGE COSTS AND INFORMATION COSTS

Knowledge costs and information costs are not generally captured by traditional management systems.

> By incorporating information in the category of intangibles and goodwill the problem [of valuing information] has been neatly avoided. However, the increasing importance of information as a factor of production in today's economic scene means that this position cannot be sustained for very much longer. —*Bill Mayon-White, London School of Economics*

The accounting industry is well aware of this growing problem:

> The components of cost in a product today are largely R&D, intellectual assets, and services. —*Arthur Andersen partner Edmund Jenkins*

Knowledge, time, and technology are playing an increasingly important role in both manufacturing and service industries:

> Even in the product heavy manufacturing environment, up to 75% of added value now comes from knowledge assets. —*Professor James Quinn, New Hampshire's Amos Tuck Business School*

Experts around the world have grappled, without success, with the problem of valuing information:

> No-one has found a viable formula to describe the value of information. —*Dr. Nigel Horne, member of the European Commission's DG III (Industry) Strategic Committee.*

This limited success, in valuing knowledge assets, has occurred because the valuation process has been approached from the "wrong perspective." *Information/knowledge is not an asset—it is an expense.*

Knowledge Assets—Valuation Principals

Lord Denning, a highly respected legal practitioner, many years ago, compared knowledge to a house. He stated that unlike a house knowledge decays and crumbles relatively quickly—it requires constant reinforcement if it is to maintain its structure and use in the immediate term. Knowledge is not solid; it is an intangible commodity that literally decays from the time it enters our mind. In fact, the *law of knowledge decay* states that:

> Knowledge decays at least 5% per day. (IIS8001.L15)

Within 30 days, newly acquired knowledge has eroded or decayed to a minimum state (100% decay does not occur). Even so, few organizations fully exploit the retained knowledge of their staff, customers, and processes.

> Organizations use only 20% of available intellectual capacity on a day to day basis. —*The Gottlieb Duttweiler Foundation*

Knowledge management is therefore required to ensure that the organization maximizes access to the firm's available intellectual capacity.

For many years management methods have focused attention on identifying, classifying, reporting, measuring, and managing the impact of tangible (observable) financial transactions on an organization's financial structure. From previous chapters, we have seen that financial transactions result from the creation or fulfillment of legal property rights. We also saw that intangible rights are competitive by nature. Such rights precede contracts and contract law. As a result, intangible costs escape detection by conventional management systems because they prevent financial transactions from occurring.

CHAPTER 9

Intangible Cost Management

Today there is a critical requirement to expand conventional management systems to measure intangible assets, intangible liabilities, intangible revenue, intangible expenses, and intangible capital. Because accounting systems already measure intangibles under goodwill it seemed only logical that all intangibles should be viewed as "assets."

In truth, accounting practice must be extended to capture the financial effects of intangible assets, intangible expenses, and intangible revenue. Intangible cost management offers significant assistance in facilitating this process.

MANAGING INTANGIBLE COSTS

It is not a well-known fact: *Intangible costs are every organization's biggest cost center.* Intangibles steal millions, or even billions, of dollars worth of productivity and profitability from organizations every year. Worse still—most executives don't even know it is happening.

WHAT ARE INTANGIBLE COSTS?

If you have ever walked into a store, received bad service, and walked out without buying, *then you understand intangible costs.* If you ever purchased something, but swore that you would never buy from that organization again, *then you understand intangible costs.* If you were going to do business with a firm, but cancelled because you realized they had no real knowledge of what they were selling, *then you understand intangible costs.* It is the total financial impact of intangible costs (unobservable financial transactions) that either makes or breaks managerial careers and organizations.

At a fundamental level, intangible costs can be internal or external. The examples above illustrate external intangible costs. *External intangible costs are therefore activities that prevent financial transactions from occurring.*

Internal intangible costs are far more sinister and harder to identify. If you have ever stopped reading a document because it was too long, you have experienced internal intangible costs. If you ever attended a meeting that lasted too long, you have experienced internal intangible costs. If you have ever felt stress as a result of dealing with others at work, you have experienced internal intangible costs. *Internal intangible costs are therefore activities that decrease the productive quality of operational costs.* Internal intangible costs have the effect of artificially increasing the financial costs of an organization due to intangible mismanagement.

At a broad level, intangible costs are *unobservable* financial transactions that reduce revenue, increase costs, decrease profitability, and decrease sustainability.

IDENTIFYING INTANGIBLE COSTS

To identify intangible costs, executives need to develop an "intangible instinct." The world's best executives possess a special form of "gut instinct" that informs them when internal or external intangible costs are being, or could be, created. This special form of gut instinct is referred to as *intangible instinct.*

Intangible instinct works in two key dimensions. The first dimension is that intangible instinct allows highly skilled executives to put processes and managerial systems into place that reduce intangible costs *before* those costs are incurred by the organization. In the second dimension, intangible instinct allows premium executives to attract new business to their organizations by (1) leveraging on the intangible costs within *competing* organizations and (2) creating future client bases. The result of both dimensions is superior financial performance and organizational sustainability. The first dimension focuses on reducing intangible costs. The second dimension focuses on increasing intangible revenue. The world's best executives are sought by companies all around the world due to their special skills and abilities in reducing intangible costs and increasing intangible revenues.

UNDERSTANDING INTANGIBLE COSTS

Before, we mentioned that if you have ever walked into a store, received bad service, and walked out without buying that you understood intangible costs. Intangible costs therefore occur *before* financial transactions occur. Hence, intangible costs exist at the commencement of every interaction with and within an organization.

Level 1 Intangible Cost Barriers

According to the International Intangible Standards, whenever a customer deals with an organization they will first encounter a level 1 intangible cost barrier. This cost barrier exists *each time* the organization interacts with a customer. Its purpose is to determine if the organization's knowledge quality and competitive quality is sufficient to warrant the customer's current time allocation to that organization.

> Level 1 intangible cost barriers (IIS4002.P1) explain why it is possible to walk into a store and then walk out without buying because you could not gain the attention of a salesperson, even though you wanted to buy from that store.

Level 1 intangible cost barriers refer to all activities that the customers perceive as wasting their time (Figure 9.1). These factors include presentation, professionalism, ambience, color, sound, heating/cooling levels, waiting times, and so on.

All level 1 intangible cost barriers occur before an interaction occurs with the organization's staff. For this reason, level 1 intangible costs are referred to as entry-level intangible costs (IIS4002.D30) because they occur *when* the customer enters the organization.

Interpreting L1 Cost Curves

International Intangible Standards define three fundamental types of intangible cost curves: type A, type B, and type C. As Figure 9.1 illustrates, the gradient (or slope) of an organization's L1 intangible cost curve can vary from steep (high L1 intangible costs per unit of time), such as curve A, to low such as curve C where L1 intangible costs are accumulated slowly over time. It is

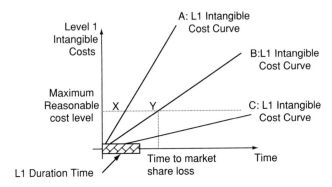

FIGURE 9.1   L1 intangible cost curves.

important to understand that L1 cost curves exist in all organizations. The critical factor is the gradient of the curve.

Time-to-Market Share Loss

Figure 9.1 also details *time-to-market share loss* (also known as *time to switch out*) on the horizontal (time) axis. This is the amount of time it takes for L1 intangible costs to accumulate to a level that causes the clients so much discomfort that they reallocate their time back to the market. Because L1 costs do not result in financial transactions, the cost of L1 intangible costs is a loss of market share, revenue, and profitability. If the organization has a type C L1 intangible cost curve it will take a significant amount of time until the customer is uncomfortable enough to switch to the competition.

From Figure 9.1, you can also see that type A organizations encounter significant intangible costs as denoted by point X. Point X represents the time at which customers become "locked out" of that organization's value creation process. A type B organization takes longer to lock customers out of its value creation process due to the impact of intangible costs. A type C organization takes a significantly longer period of time to lock customers out of its value creation process than do type A or B organizations.

L1 Duration Time

L1 duration time is the average amount of time required to *make contact* with a potential client (IIS4002.D43). For example, if a customer enters a shop and it takes an average of 5 minutes until organizational staff serve the customer, then 5 minutes is the L1 duration time of that organization. If an organization has a type A L1 cost curve, it will find that a significant loss in market value occurs during this initial 5-minute period as customers simply walk out of the door without purchasing. This loss of market value is due to L1 intangible costs.

Reversing L1 Intangible Costs

It seems almost counterproductive that organizations spend significant amounts of money to attract customers but then mismanage intangibles so that investment decreases in efficiency and effectiveness. To reverse L1 intangible costs, employees must realize that the costs are actually occurring. This requires managers to educate employees as to the costs of L1 intangibles and to implement systems to reduce those costs.

Level 2 Intangible Cost Barriers

If level 1 intangible costs are overcome, then the organization's value proposition has the potential to be explained to the customer. At this stage, it is the *quality, relevance,* and *quantity* of relationship assets and knowledge assets that create the customer expectations that determine if the sale has the potential to occur.

> Level 2 intangible cost barriers (IIS4002.P2) explain why you do not buy from a store: Because you have been spoken to, or interacted with, in a manner you didn't appreciate. Level 2 intangible cost barriers explain the concept of poor customer service.

Even if you manage to gain the attention of a salesperson, this does not mean that you will buy from that store—*even if you want to.* Level 2 intangible cost barriers exist to prevent organizations from establishing their value proposition.

> Level 2 intangible cost barriers explain why you do not buy from an organization: Because you feel they don't have the knowledge that you require. (IIS4002.D34)

Although an organization uses its knowledge assets and relationship assets to explain the value proposition of the organization, level 2 intangible costs *are always* generated. Some L2 intangible costs are reasonable and acceptable to customers. It is the unreasonable and unacceptable L2 intangible costs that cause customers not to buy.

It is useful to think of level 2 intangible costs as being like an invisible glue that is emptied into a customer's wallet as they talk to organizational staff. The higher the L2 intangible costs, the greater the amount of invisible glue that is poured into the customer's wallet. After a time, the customer will not be able to open the wallet to buy *even if they wanted to*, because the intangible glue (caused by intangible costs) has completely sealed it. The concept of intangible glue explains the "one strike and you are out" mentality that exists in the minds of consumers today. In truth, level 1 and level 2 intangible costs have sealed that customer's wallet to that organization. The customer knows it, but the organization may not.

> Level 2 intangible cost barriers explain why you will not return to an organization due to previous poor service.

Level 2 intangible costs are always created in every customer–organization interaction. The higher the level 2 intangible costs, the lower the resulting financial value of that sale (and potential repeat business) to the organization (Figure 9.2). Level 2 intangible costs directly influence the formation of customer expectations resulting from the organization's translated value proposition.

Just as L1 intangible costs have type A to C cost curves, so too do L2 intangible cost curves. L2 intangible costs result from inefficiencies in knowledge assets and relationship assets resulting from mismanagement of these assets, combined with a mismanagement of emotional assets and time assets.

After the level 2 barrier, base financial performance may occur but only if level 2 intangible costs that follow from the value proposition being established are low enough to permit a financial transaction to occur.

Level 3 Intangible Cost Barriers

After level 1 and level 2 intangible costs have been paid by the organization, the customer is now in a position to buy from the organization. The amount

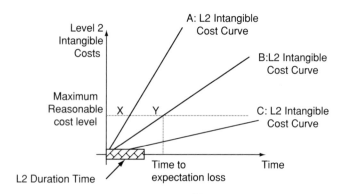

FIGURE 9.2   L2 intangible cost curves.

of expenditure the customer engages in is dependent on level 1 and level 2 costs, but also on level 3 intangible costs.

Level 2 intangible costs are communication costs that result when communicating customer value and level 3 costs are implementation costs that result from the implementation of the customer value proposition established at level 2 (IIS4002.P3). Most of the intangible costs that occur during level 3.

FINANCIAL PERFORMANCE IS ALWAYS DILUTED

An understanding of International Intangible Standards assists managers to understand that intangibles create financial transactions, hinder them, or prevent them from occurring at various stages of organizational performance. Conventional financial and accounting reports represent financial performance *after intangibles have diluted that performance*. Intangible financial reports are specifically designed to complement existing financial reports such as the income statement and the balance sheet by illustrating what financial performance the organization could expect by better managing intangible costs. Value dilution (IIS4002.D2) illustrates where value was gained or lost as a result of intangible management or intangible mismanagement.

$$\text{Value}_{\text{Dilution}} = \text{Financial}_{\text{Transactions}} - \left[\sum \left(\text{Internal}_{\text{Intangibles}} \right) + \sum \left(\text{External}_{\text{Intangibles}} \right) \right].$$

Because level 1, 2, and 3 intangible costs occur before financial transactions occur, financial performance cannot represent the total value creation of the business.

MEASURING INTANGIBLE COSTS

Because intangible costs occur before financial transactions occur (see IIS1001.C11, IIS2001.L1, IIS2001.L3, IIS2001.L4, IIS4001.L15, IIS4002.D2, and IIS17001.C11), we cannot measure intangible costs by simply assessing *recorded* financial transactions (IIS1001.C3). The only way to measure intangible costs is by linking emotional interactions (or human interactions) to how time has actually been allocated within the organization to create value. This process allows us to connect the currency of time and the currency of emotions to the currency of financial performance. Once these connections have been made, executives can use international intangible standards to determine the value of financial transactions the organization lost due to intangible costs—or gained due to intangible revenues.

Because intangible costs do not provide documentary evidence of their passing, we must use management and valuation systems that do not require such evidence to estimate value. Current management frameworks, such as return on investment (ROI), economic value added (EVA), discounted cash flow (DCF), free cash flow (FCF), and net present value (NPV), rely primarily on the currency of money to make estimations. Intangible costs are measured by combining the currency of time with the currency of emotions and the currency of money.

TIME MANAGEMENT CANNOT MEASURE THE CURRENCY OF TIME

When Frederick Taylor developed scientific management and time and motion studies, he threw the world into a worker-against-worker world. Because the quality and quantity of one worker's output was determined in accordance with the average output of the average worker, workers colluded to "go slow" so that they could work in a more sustainable manner with better payment conditions. The idea of time management was born from Frederick Taylor's work.

Time management allows an organization to allocate units of time to units of work. Such allocations under conventional time management systems are not sufficiently accurate to be used in accordance with International Intangible Standards to measure the currency of time.

EMOTION AND TIME STUDIES

The chairman of the International Intangible Management Standards Institute, Dr. Ken Standfield, has pioneered a special form of emotion and time studies that can be used to identify the value of intangible costs at various levels within an organization. These types of studies are discussed in detail in the next chapter.

Emotion and time studies allow an organization to reverse engineer the exact time conditions that created current financial performance. By determining where knowledge assets and relationship assets have lost efficiency and relevance, and in connecting this analysis with changes in emotional assets and time assets, it is possible to determine internal and external intangible costs. Once this connection is made, executives better understand the activities that an organization has undertaken in order to create the financial transactions as evidenced in the financial reports.

It is this new management ability that gives organizations the power to scientifically manage intangibles for the first time. It also allows the organization to determine the cost of intangibles and potential cost reductions that could occur if intangible costs were reduced in accordance with international intangible standards.

Emotion and time studies are insufficient, by themselves, to yield valuations on intangible costs. The International Intangible Management Standards Institute has developed numerous international standards that equip organizations with the skills and knowledge required to identify, classify, manage, report, and reduce internal and external intangible costs.

CHAPTER 10

Emotion and Time Studies

... there has been virtually no increase in the productivity of service work. — *Peter Drucker*

Emotion and time studies enhance organizational performance by identifying how the organization is experiencing intangible costs and benefits. The purpose of emotion and time studies is to identify, value, and reduce time-based costs.

Waste neither time, nor money, but make the best use of both. —*Benjamin Franklin*

As such, they are very different from time management as most people understand it (scheduling, to-do lists, priorities, etc.). For example, emotion and time studies would state "Attending this training seminar will cost you $450 in wages, *productivity* and other associated costs." Time management would inform you how to best organize your time before, during, and after the seminar. The two areas focus on time, but in very different ways.

BENCHMARKING STAFF PRODUCTIVITY

On average, each employee has a total of approximately 1800 working hours each year in which to apply their skills and talents. Consider a lawyer who can generate revenue of $250 per hour. If the lawyer has 1800 working hours, he can potentially generate $450,000 in revenue for the firm. These calculations are summarized in Figure 10.1.

In an ideal world, staff would be productive for the whole year. Common sense, and observation, informs us that this is not the case. Let us assume the employee charges out *half* of her available time to clients (900 hours). The other 900 hours are spent performing nonbillable activities such as paperwork, attending meetings, talking on the phone, keeping up to date with industry changes, attending seminars, training and other presentations, and so on. In this case, we can modify Figure 10.1 to incorporate the effects of these "nonproductive" activities, as shown in Figure 10.2.

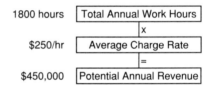

1800 hours	Total Annual Work Hours
	x
$250/hr	Average Charge Rate
	=
$450,000	Potential Annual Revenue

FIGURE 10.1   Relationship between time and revenue.

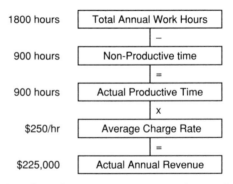

1800 hours	Total Annual Work Hours
	−
900 hours	Non-Productive time
	=
900 hours	Actual Productive Time
	x
$250/hr	Average Charge Rate
	=
$225,000	Actual Annual Revenue

FIGURE 10.2   Relationship among time, revenue, and nonproductive time.

This simple example illustrates that nonproductive time has already "cost" the organization $225,000.

We can also go one step further and assess what the value of this nonproductive time actually is. To do this we must determine the amount of time staff that *could* have been productive but were not, and then multiply this figure by how much money staff could have earned in that time. We can investigate the effects of productive and nonproductive activities simultaneously by incorporating the results of the previous two figures in Figure 10.3.

Enhancing Organizational Performance

Intangible management assists organizations in understanding how nonproductive overheads generate real competitive costs that the organization actually pays, but does not know it is paying. In the above case, the employee was performing at 50% productivity. Using intangible management standards, activities that generate little or no value to the firm would be sustainably managed to produce *at least* a 50% reduction in nonproductive time.

If nonproductive time is reduced from 900 to 450 hours, we effectively increase productive time from 900 to 1350 hours. Figure 10.4 illustrates

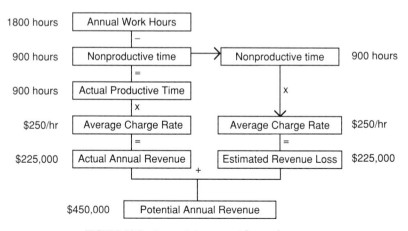

FIGURE 10.3   Determining potential annual revenue.

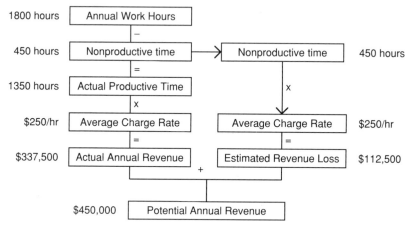

FIGURE 10.4   Effects of reducing nonproductive time.

these calculations: Although the *potential* earnings of the employee have not changed ($450,000), the increase in billable time (from 900 to 1350 hours) can generate an additional $112,500 in revenue for the firm—thereby increasing revenue from $225,000 to $337,500 for this employee. This increase in productive time also reduces the estimated revenue loss from $225,000 to $112,500.

THE EFFECTS ON REVENUE PER EMPLOYEE

If we assume that this firm has only one employee, then the revenue per employee has increased from $225,000 per employee to $337,500 per employee—a 50% increase—simply through applying intangible management standards.

By removing 450 hours of nonproductive activities from the employee's work year, that employee's job has been made considerably easier because she has less overheads to perform (paperwork, information analysis, etc.). By giving this staff member more time to do what he is actually paid to do (create organizational value), the employee will be more satisfied, happier, and probably under less stress (nonproductive interruptions can be very stressful).

The critical questions therefore become "How effective can intangible management be within my organization? How much room for improvement is there?"

HOW PRODUCTIVE IS YOUR STAFF?

According to Peter Drucker, up to 70% of an employee's day can be spent non-productively, performing work that adds no real value to the firm's operations. Alec Mackenzie, author of *The Time Trap* (AMACOM, 1997), comments that "the average manager spends ten hours a week in meetings, and 90% of managers say that half their meeting time is wasted" (p. 149). He also states that people can spend between "one to three hours each day" on paperwork (p. 157). Then there is the time spent on the phone, at an average of 6 minutes per call. There is also the time we spend socializing, taking breaks and being interrupted—it's a wonder that anyone actually gets anything done.

Because organizations have never scientifically managed intangible value, a significant amount of potential improvement is possible within every organization, through the application of intangible management standards.

As a minimum benchmark, employees are nonproductive for at least 40% of their day. Hence, a staff member employed for 1800 hours will be paid for 1800 hours of work, but is only productive for around 1080 hours.

DETERMINING WHAT YOUR ORGANIZATION IS REALLY WORTH

Assuming 1800 working hours a year and 40% nonproductivity, we can use the figures given in Table 10.1 to determine how much firms could earn if the

TABLE 10.1   Effects of Nonproductivity on Organizational Performance

Average charge rate	Annual potential earnings	Annual estimated earnings @ 40% nonproductivity	Estimated productivity loss
50	$ 90,000	$ 54,000	$ 36,000
70	$ 126,000	$ 75,600	$ 50,400
120	$ 216,000	$ 129,600	$ 86,400
180	$ 324,000	$ 194,400	$ 129,600
250	$ 450,000	$ 270,000	$ 180,000

employees charged different hourly rates to their clients. These figures only represent the effects for one staff member. In companies employing tens, hundreds, thousands, or hundreds of thousands of staff, the effects of nonproductivity are staggering. *The effects of intangible management can be equally profitable.*

In Table 10.2, the figures from the previous table have been expanded to attempt to define the intangible benefits and intangible costs of organizations with a varying number of employees and per-hour productivity rates. This table clearly illustrates that organizations do not generate 100% of their revenue potential. The larger the number of staff involved in the operation, the greater the magnitude of resulting intangible costs. Intangible management standards focus specifically on decreasing the intangible costs within organizations.

The critical issue is, therefore, what is the organization's contribution toward revenue per hour and what are the organization's intangible overheads?

ASSESSING ORGANIZATIONAL NONPRODUCTIVITY

In the first example, we assumed a legal professional worked 1800 hours and billed clients at $250 per hour. We also assumed the staff member was only productive half the time. Let us assume that the full details of the legal practice have been obtained. The legal practice generates $100 million and employs 850 staff. Relative performance is determined in accordance with the following formula:

$$\text{Relative performance} = \frac{\text{Total revenue}}{\text{Number of staff}}.$$

We can determine that the relative performance, or revenue per employee, is $117,647 ($100 million ÷ 850 staff). We can determine the average charge rate for the staff member given the total number of working hours in the year (1800 hours) and the average revenue per employee, as shown in Figure 10.5.

If we assume that staff average 1800 working hours, then we can determine that each staff member is contributing $65.36 per effective working hour to revenue. This figure clearly demonstrates that productive time is not being used effectively. Why? Because, legal professionals should be charging significantly more than $65 per hour for their services. If we assume that, on average, each staff member *should be* charging out at $245 per hour, then staff should be generating $245 per hour, not $65.36 per hour. In this case, we can

TABLE 10.2 Benchmarking Intangible Costs

Estimated intangible benefits (revenue)

Number of staff					
1	$54,000	$75,600	$129,600	$194,400	$270,000
10	$540,000	$756,000	$1,296,000	$1,944,000	$2,700,000
50	$2,700,000	$3,780,000	$6,480,000	$9,720,000	$13,500,000
100	$5,400,000	$7,560,000	$12,960,000	$19,440,000	$27,000,000
200	$10,800,000	$15,120,000	$25,920,000	$38,880,000	$54,000,000
500	$27,000,000	$37,800,000	$64,800,000	$97,200,000	$135,000,000
1,000	$54,000,000	$75,600,000	$129,600,000	$194,400,000	$270,000,000

Estimated intangible costs (productivity losses)

Number of staff					
1	$36,000	$50,400	$86,400	$129,600	$180,000
10	$360,000	$504,000	$864,000	$1,296,000	$1,800,000
50	$1,800,000	$2,520,000	$4,320,000	$6,480,000	$9,000,000
100	$3,600,000	$5,040,000	$8,640,000	$12,960,000	$18,000,000
200	$7,200,000	$10,080,000	$17,280,000	$25,920,000	$36,000,000
500	$18,000,000	$25,200,000	$43,200,000	$64,800,000	$90,000,000
1,000	$36,000,000	$50,400,000	$86,400,000	$129,600,000	$180,000,000

Potential annual earnings (leveraged earnings)

Number of staff					
1	$90,000	$126,000	$216,000	$324,000	$450,000
10	$900,000	$1,260,000	$2,160,000	$3,240,000	$4,500,000
50	$4,500,000	$6,300,000	$10,800,000	$16,200,000	$22,500,000
100	$9,000,000	$12,600,000	$21,600,000	$32,400,000	$45,000,000
200	$18,000,000	$25,200,000	$43,200,000	$64,800,000	$90,000,000
500	$45,000,000	$63,000,000	$108,000,000	$162,000,000	$225,000,000
1,000	$90,000,000	$126,000,000	$216,000,000	$324,000,000	$450,000,000

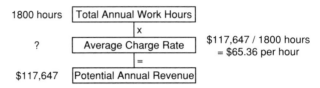

FIGURE 10.5   Relationship between time and revenue.

assume that the firm is exhibiting very low relative productivity. It also illustrates that the firm is not correctly applying international intangible standards to manage its productivity and revenue.

The firm is actually operating at 26.68% productivity ($65.36 / $245 × 100). But how do we arrive at this conclusion? Let's look at Figure 10.6.

ASSESSING ORGANIZATIONAL POTENTIAL

If the firm generates $100 million employing 850 staff at 26.68% productivity, it follows that, *other things being equal*, if the firm were to operate at 100% productivity, the firm would be capable of earning significantly more than it is now. If the firm were 100% productive then staff would actually be contributing $245 per hour to revenue (instead of $65.36). Over 1800 hours, the firm would be capable of generating $441,000 of revenue per employee. Given that the firm employs 850 staff, Figure 10.6 would need to be modified to allow the firm's potential value to be correctly determined as is done in Figure 10.7.

Figure 10.7 indicates that at 100% productivity, the firm would be capable of generating $374.85 million in revenue, which is considerably more than the firm's current revenue levels of $100 million.

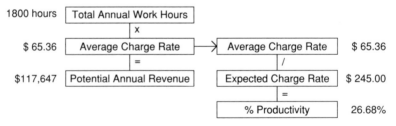

FIGURE 10.6   Benchmarking actual organizational productivity.

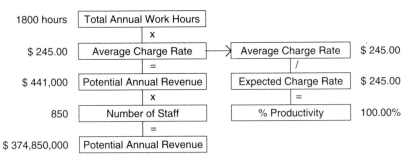

FIGURE 10.7   Assessing potential organizational value.

A Critical Issue

Even if the organization were to increase efficiency to 100%, the above revenue would only be guaranteed if the organization provided staff with increased business. Fortunately, decades of downsizing and restructuring have left many organizations with excess workloads where revenue is actually being lost because staff cannot satisfy current levels of demand. This factor guarantees that a fair percentage of any productivity improvements can be readily translated into increased profitability.

Benchmarking Revenue Productivity

Level 1 Revenue Productivity Benchmarking

The preceding analysis, introduced you to a specific form of productivity benchmarking, referred to in the International Intangible Standards as *level 1 revenue productivity benchmarking*, or L1RP benchmarking for short. L1RP benchmarking is designed to create a consistent and conservative starting point for the analysis of all organizations. As such, it does not seek to determine what productivity the organization *should* be making.

$$L1RP_{Benchmark} = \left(\frac{Relative_{Performance}}{1800}\right) = \left(\frac{\sum Revenue/Employees}{1800}\right).$$

For this example the L1RP benchmark is $65.36, which denotes that the average employee contributes $65.36 for each hour of *paid organizational time*. Even though employees may be paid for 1800 hours each year, they work far less than that. To determine the accuracy and practicality of the L1RP benchmark, we must initially determine how much annual work time has been lost to probable working overheads. This process is assisted through calculation of the IIS5001 Organizational Time Determination Statement (Figure 10.8). This analysis shows us that employees of the legal firm only work 65.75% of the year due to impacts of holidays, annual leave, sick leave, weekends, etc. An adjustment has been made to account for paid and unpaid overtime of 13 days.

Level 2 Revenue Productivity Benchmarking

We must now determine the impact of normal working conditions on the distribution of productive and nonproductive time. If staff work an average of 38 hours a week over 5 days over 240 effective workdays, then each staff member will accumulate around 1800 hours of actual work time. This work time does not take into account internal process inefficiencies, such as wasted time, tea/coffee breaks, toilet breaks, knowledge overheads, process overheads, etc. To gain a more realistic estimate of the actual productive time, we need to discount the 1800 hours by the benchmark of 40%. It is this discounting that gives us a more realistic and practical indication of the average employee contribution toward revenue. This new statistic is referred to as the *level 2 revenue productivity benchmark*, or L2RP benchmark for short:

$$L2RP_{Benchmark} = \left(\frac{Relative_{Performance}}{1800 \times (1 - 0.40)} \right) = \left(\frac{\sum Revenue/Employees}{1800 \times (1 - 0.40)} \right).$$

IIS5001 Organizational Time Determination Statement

Days in Year			365
Less Employment Overhead			
Weekends	104		
Annual Leave	20		
Absenteeism	1		
Sick Leave	5		
Holidays	7		
Other Leave	1		
Total Overhead Days		138	
Less Additional Overtime		13	
Total L1 Employment Overhead			125
Effective Annual Working Days			240
Percentage of days actually worked			65.75%
Percentage of days lost to L1 Employment OH			34.25%

FIGURE 10.8   Assessing the validity of the L1RP benchmark.

For this case study, the L2RP benchmark is $108.93. This number illustrates that staff, on average, contribute $108.93 to the productivity of the firm each effective work hour. This is only a benchmark indication, but it assists in the comparison of similar firms in determining which firm better manages its productivity.

L1 Operating Efficiency

Level 1 operating efficiency occurs when we attempt to estimate how industry best practices apply to the firm under analysis, without regard to potential productivity issues. In this case we take the figure of $245 per hour that is expected relative performance of the firm.

$$
\mathrm{L1Operating}_{\mathrm{Efficiency}} = \left(\frac{\mathrm{Relative}_{\mathrm{Performance}}}{1800} \right) \bigg/ \mathrm{RP}_{\mathrm{Expected}}
$$

$$
= \frac{1}{\mathrm{RP}_{\mathrm{Expected}}} \left(\frac{\sum \mathrm{Revenue/Employees}}{1800} \right)
$$

L1 Operating Deficit

L1 operating efficiency is 26.68%. This means that management is 73.32% below its expectations of organizational productivity. The figure of 73.32% is referred to as the *L1 operating deficit* and is calculated as follows:

$$
\mathrm{L1Operating}_{\mathrm{Deficit}} = 1 - \mathrm{L1Operating}_{\mathrm{Efficiency}}.
$$

L2 Operating Efficiency

Level 2 operating efficiency occurs when we attempt to estimate how industry best practices apply to the firm under analysis *with* regard to potential productivity issues. In this case we take the figure of $245 per hour that is expected relative performance of the firm.

$$
\mathrm{L2Operating}_{\mathrm{Efficiency}} = \left(\frac{\mathrm{Relative}_{\mathrm{Performance}}}{1800 \times (1 - 0.40)} \right) \bigg/ \mathrm{RP}_{\mathrm{Expected}}
$$

$$
= \frac{1}{\mathrm{RP}_{\mathrm{Expected}}} \left(\frac{\sum \mathrm{Revenue/Employees}}{1800 \times (1 - 0.40)} \right)
$$

In this case, revenue productivity of $245 is assessed against the $108.93 figure. This allows us to see that management is operating at 44.46% of level 2 benchmarked revenue productivity. The figure of 44.46% is referred to as *L2 operating efficiency.*

L2 Operating Deficit

L2 operating efficiency is 44.46%. This means that management is 55.54% below its expectations of organizational productivity. The figure of 55.54% is referred to as the L2 *operating deficit* and is calculated as follows:

$$\text{L2Operating}_{\text{Deficit}} = 1 - \text{L2Operating}_{\text{Efficiency}}.$$

L3 Operating Efficiency

Level 3 operating efficiency occurs when we attempt to estimate how *adjusted* industry best practices apply to the firm under analysis *with* regard to potential productivity issues. In this case we take the figure of $245 per hour that is expected relative performance of the firm. Executives know that even if staff can obtain the figure of $245 per hour of average contribution to revenue, staff may not necessarily be able to maintain that figure for the duration of 1 year. In this case, managers will dilute the ability expectations of the firm to hold consistent performance at $245 per hour per employee to a more sustainable level. International Intangible Standards recommend a 25% dilution rate as a benchmark. This dilution allows employees to maintain $245 per hour productivity 75% of the time. Hence, L3 operating efficiency is determined by:

$$\text{L3Operating}_{\text{Efficiency}} = \left(\frac{\text{Relative}_{\text{Performance}}}{1800 \times (1 - 0.40)} \right) \Big/ \text{RP}_{\text{Expected}} \times (1 - 0.25)$$

$$= \frac{1}{\text{RP}_{\text{Expected}} \times (1 - 0.25)} \left(\frac{\sum \text{Revenue/Employees}}{1800 \times (1 - 0.40)} \right)$$

In this case, revenue productivity of $245 is diluted by 25% to a figure of $183.75 and assessed against the $108.93 figure. This allows management to determine that they are operating at 59.28% of revenue productivity. The figure of 59.28% is referred to as *L3 operating efficiency*.

L3 Operating Deficit

L3 operating efficiency is 59.28%. This means that management is 40.72% below its expectations of organizational productivity. The figure of 40.72% is referred to as the *L3 operating deficit* and is calculated as follows:

$$\text{L3Operating}_{\text{Deficit}} = 1 - \text{L3Operating}_{\text{Efficiency}}$$

Understanding Revenue Productivity Analysis

International Intangible Standards use five levels of analysis when determining the impact of intangibles on an organization. The first three levels (covered above) all seek to benchmark revenue productivity with minimal information requirements (publicly available data are sufficient). Level 4 is a low-level auditing of the organization to determine intangible performance. Level 5 is a full audit of the organization that uses various International Intangible Standard–compliant measuring devices and software to assist in maximizing the accuracy of resulting figures.

To minimize the opportunity of creative accounting and misrepresentation, all levels of revenue productivity must be calculated (as Table 10.3 illustrates).

REDUCING INTANGIBLE COSTS

> You can only manage time in those moments when you are alert to what is going on within you and around you. —James McCay

Today, determining how employees use time is absolutely critical to the success of your firm. Intangible costs result from the nonproductive use of time. For this reason it is essential to understand how nonproductive time occurs and how it can be managed, as discussed in the next chapter.

TABLE 10.3 Revenue Productivity Analysis

RP Analysis	Level 1	Level 2	Level 3	Level 4	Level 5
		Benchmarked		Audited	
Legal Film	$ 100,000,000	$ 100,000,000	$ 100,000,000	$ 100,000,000	$ 100,000,000
Employees	850	850	850	850	850
Relative performance	$ 117,647	$ 117,647	$ 117,647	$ 117,647	$ 117,647
Gross working hours	1,800	1,800	1,800	1,756	1,645
Nonproductive OH	0%	40%	40%	44.97%	48.79%
Actual productive	1,800.00	1,080.00	1,080.00	966.33	842.40
Revenue performance	$ 65.36	$ 108.93	$ 108.93	$ 121.75	$ 139.66
Gross targeted RP	$ 245.00	$ 245.00	$ 245.00	$ 237.00	$ 225.00
Dilution	0.00%	0.00%	25.00%	28.75%	31.45%
Net targeted RP	$ 245.00	$ 245.00	$ 183.75	$ 168.86	$ 154.24
Operating efficiency	26.68%	44.46%	59.28%	72.10%	90.55%
Operating deficit	73.32%	55.54%	40.72%	27.90%	9.45%

CHAPTER 11

Identifying Nonproductive Time

Practically all activities employees perform have a component, either large or small, of nonproductive time.

INFORMATION COSTS

Let us assume that the legal firm from the previous chapter sends a daily update (between 5 or 10 pages) to 600 of the 850 employees. This update details changes, or articles of interest, relevant to each professional's area of specialization and takes approximately 25 minutes to read. The information is then stored in a file, where it can be referenced should the need arise.

Conventional management systems would not typically attach a financial cost to such an activity or a financial benefit. The purpose of International Intangible Standards is to assign a financial cost and a financial benefit to such activities.

On a daily basis, each staff member will be losing 25 minutes of productive time that could be charged to clients at the average rate of $245 per hour. This equates to daily "information cost" of $102.08 per employee, or $61,250 for the group. Over a 5-day working week, the cost of reading updates would be $306,250 per week. If staff are paid $25 per hour, then the wage allocation cost of reading the information will be $10.42 per staff member per day. For the group of 600 staff, this nonproductive wage allocation cost becomes $6,250, or $31,250 for a week. If we assume 4 weeks in a month, then the nonproductive wage allocation cost will be $125,000 and the associated productivity loss will be $1,225,000, creating a total real cost of $1,350,000 per month. This cost relates only to 600 out of 850 people at 25 minutes worth of information each day.

For your interest:
Why is reading the brief considered nonproductive time?

Let us assume that a legal executive has work to do, but devotes 25 minutes to reading the brief instead. In this instance, the legal professional *can* charge $245 per hour for services, but does not as the knowledge within the information has a higher perceived value than payment of the $245 by the client. *Because the time could have been used to perform productive activities, but was not, the time is classified as nonproductive time.*

REVIEW AND SEARCH COSTS

Over time, staff will wish to refer to information they read previously. To do this, staff will have to review (reread) the previously analyzed information, so *review costs* will be created. Before staff can reread relevant information, they will have to find that information, so there will also be a *search cost*. The search cost involves the time costs associated with finding the required information. If 25% of the employees need to engage in search and review activities on a daily basis and it takes an average of 3.5 minutes to find the article and then 5 minutes to read it, the costs are as Follows:

- *Daily search cost*: 150 staff (25% of 600) × 3.5 minutes = 525 minutes = 8.75 hours. If this activity is not charged to clients, the revenue cost is $2,143.75 per day in search costs.
- *Daily review cost*: 150 staff × 5 minutes = 750 minutes = 12.5 hours. Assuming this time is not billed to clients, the revenue cost at an average of $245 per hour, generates a daily review cost of $3,062.50.

Analyzing the Data

Our analysis of these information costs, at a very superficial level, can occur at many levels. For the sake of simplicity, we have included an individual daily analysis, a daily group analysis, and a weekly group analysis.

Individual Daily Analysis

Table 11.1 illustrates that the average employee will accumulate $13.96 in nonproductive wage allocations and around $136.79 in productivity losses from reading the 5 to 10 pages of information each day. This will result in a real cost associated with reading information of $151 per day for each individual staff member.

Typically wage costs are ignored in daily operational analysis because working with information is deemed to be part of an employee's job description. However, if the time required to analyze information can be reduced, then there is an intangible cost associated with removing employees from income-generating work.

Group Daily Analysis

Table 11.2 illustrates that for the 600 staff, they will accumulate $6,781.25 in nonproductive wage allocations and $66,456.25 in productivity losses

TABLE 11.1   Individual Daily Costs of Reading 5–10 Pages of Information

Individual daily	Productivity	Wage	Total
Reading/analysis cost	$ 102.08	$ 10.42	$ 112.50
Search cost	$ 14.29	$ 1.46	$ 15.75
Review cost	$ 20.42	$ 2.08	$ 22.50
Total real cost	$ 136.79	$ 13.96	$ 150.75

TABLE 11.2   Group Daily Costs of Reading 5–10 Pages of Information

Daily group	Productivity	Wage	Total
Reading/analysis cost	$ 61,250.00	$ 6,250.00	$ 67,500.00
Search cost	$ 2,143.75	$ 218.75	$ 2,362.50
Review cost	$ 3,062.50	$ 312.50	$ 3,375.00
Total real cost	$ 66,456.25	$ 6,781.25	$ 73,237.50

TABLE 11.3   Weekly Group Costs of Reading 5–10 Pages of Information

Weekly group	Productivity	Wage	Total
Reading/analysis cost	$ 306,250.00	$ 31,250.00	$ 337,500.00
Search cost	$ 10,718.75	$ 1,093.75	$ 11,812.50
Review cost	$ 15,312.50	$ 1,562.50	$ 16,875.00
Total real cost	$ 332,281.25	$ 33,906.25	$ 366,187.50

from reading the 5 to 10 pages of information each day. This will result in a real cost associated with reading information of $72,238 per day for the group.

Group Daily Analysis

Table 11.3 illustrates that for the 600 staff, they will accumulate $33,906.25 in nonproductive wage allocations and $332,281.25 in productivity losses from reading the 5 to 10 pages of information each day. This will result in a real cost associated with reading information of $366,188 per week for the group.

INFORMATION COST REDUCTION

In the previous example, the accumulated time effects of the reading time (25 minutes), search time (3.5 minutes), and rereading time (5 minutes) created a weekly group cost of $366,188. Because revenue losses ($322,281) are determined solely by the amount of nonproductive time, time reductions *will* generate cost reductions.

International Intangible Standards provide methods to convert nonproductive time allocations into productive time allocations. One such method is provided in the IIS21001 Knowledge Reengineering Standard. The IIS21001 Knowledge Reengineering Standard provides new ways in which to reformulate information so that concepts are communicated quickly and effectively to people who need to read information.

IIS21001 KNOWLEDGE
REENGINEERING STANDARD

The IIS21001 Knowledge Reengineering Standard is a powerful new way of communicating information that incorporates powerful learning systems to make understanding information quick and easy. The IIS21001 Knowledge Reengineering Standard is a guaranteed way to reduce information costs by at least 50%.

A QUICK INTRODUCTION TO IIS21001

All information is composed of thoughts or ideas expressed in words. The IIS21001 Knowledge Reengineering Standard counts how many unique thoughts or ideas or concepts are expressed and forms a "learning infrastructure" which communicates *all* these concepts as quickly and simply as possible. In the process of implementing IIS21001, concepts may be explained using different words (less jargon) and in a different sequence (one that is more understandable). Implementing the IIS21001 Knowledge Reengineering Standard reduces information costs at the source and forms the basis of an ongoing information cost management system.

The previous costs were created due to 25 minutes of analysis by 600 staff, where 25% of the group experienced search costs of 3.5 minutes and rereading costs of 5 minutes. The IIS21001 Knowledge Reengineering Standard can represent information in a more concise format so that comprehension, understanding, and retention are maximized in a minimum amount of time. Assuming that the application of the IIS21001 Knowledge Reengineering Standard could reduce reading time from 25 to 10 minutes, search time from 3.5 to 1.5 minutes, and rereading time from 5 to 2.5 minutes, the costs shown in Table 11.4 would be associated with the IIS21001 project.

The difference between the initial costs and the IIS21001 costs is shown in Table 11.5. Hence, implementation of the IIS21001 Knowledge Reengineering Standard should save the organization around $217,688 for each week it is applied to reducing the time taken to communicate the concepts in the daily 5- to 10-page brief. Later chapters will explore the application of the IIS21001 Knowledge Reengineering Standard.

OTHER NONPRODUCTIVE AREAS

The above example simply illustrated the potential costs associated with staff reading information on a daily basis. Many organizations encourage their staff to read the newspaper, magazines, and other articles during work time. Senior managers are often required to read reports that accumulate information relating to the company's markets, products, and competitors. Such reports also generate information costs that must be reduced. Circulars,

TABLE 11.4   Costs after Implementation of the IIS21001 Knowledge Reengineering Standard

Individual daily	Productivity	Wage	Total
Reading/analysis cost	$ 40.83	$ 4.17	$ 45.00
Search cost	$ 6.13	$ 0.63	$ 6.75
Review cost	$ 10.21	$ 1.04	$ 11.25
Total real cost	$ 57.17	$ 5.83	$ 63.00
Daily group	Productivity	Wage	Total
Reading/analysis cost	$ 24,500.00	$ 2,500.00	$ 27,000.00
Search cost	$ 918.75	$ 93.75	$ 1,012.50
Review cost	$ 1,531.25	$ 156.25	$ 1,687.50
Total real cost	$ 26,950.00	$ 2,750.00	$ 29,700.00
Weekly group	Productivity	Wage	Total
Reading/analysis cost	$ 122,500.00	$ 12,500.00	$ 135,000.00
Search cost	$ 4,593.75	$ 468.75	$ 5,062.50
Review cost	$ 7,656.25	$ 781.25	$ 8,437.50
Total real cost	$ 134,750.00	$ 13,750.00	$ 148,500.00

TABLE 11.5   Savings in Comparing Information Transfer Before and After IIS21001

Individual daily savings	Productivity	Wage	Total
Reading/analysis cost	$ 61.25	$ 6.25	$ 67.50
Search cost	$ 8.17	$ 0.83	$ 9.00
Review cost	$ 10.21	$ 1.04	$ 11.25
Total real cost	$ 79.63	$ 8.13	$ 87.75
Daily group savings	Productivity	Wage	Total
Reading/analysis cost	$ 36,750.00	$ 3,750.00	$ 40,500.00
Search cost	$ 1,225.00	$ 125.00	$ 1,350.00
Review cost	$ 1,531.25	$ 156.25	$ 1,687.50
Total real cost	$ 39,506.25	$ 4,031.25	$ 43,537.50
Weekly group savings	Productivity	Wage	Total
Reading/analysis cost	$183,750.00	$18,750.00	$202,500.00
Search cost	$ 6,125.00	$ 625.00	$ 6,750.00
Review cost	$ 7,656.25	$ 781.25	$ 8,437.50
Total real cost	$197,531.25	$20,156.25	$217,687.50

newsletters, reports, or manuals (standard operating procedures, etc.) also generate information costs.

When employees do paperwork, the time spent filling out that paperwork must be carefully audited. If employees spend 5 minutes filling out paperwork that could be filled out in 1 minute, then the firm experiences 4 minutes of unnecessary nonproductive time per staff member. Over the span of a day, small accumulations like this can easily steal hours of productive time and *result in thousands of dollars of unnecessary costs.* Meetings, interruptions, phone calls, seminars, and training are other areas in which nonproductive times are generated.

ONCE ACTIVITIES HAVE BEEN AUDITED

Because activities have both productive and nonproductive time components, it is essential to reduce the amount of nonproductive time to the minimum time possible. This minimum time is referred to as the '*core time*'.

For example, let us assume that an organization holds a regular 2–hour meeting to assess staff progress on important jobs. To reduce the time costs associated with this, the organization may look toward a formal intranet-based solution. For example, staff could simply fill out an intranet questionnaire indicating their job progress and make comments if required. This could then be submitted to the manager for analysis. This could easily reduce the time required from 120 to 5 minutes, thereby reducing the associated information costs by more than 90%.

A knowledge of International Intangible Standards assists executives, managers, and employees in creating value in accordance with the new economic principles that govern the current economic environment.

CHAPTER 12

Knowledge Application Costs

Previous chapters have illustrated that relative performance (revenue per employee) can be enhanced by leveraging intangible management standards. One key area where executives can enhance the relative performance of the organization is by controlling knowledge costs.

Knowledge costs are generated whenever staff apply, maintain, or enhance their skill and knowledge. Today, employees spend significant amounts of time using computers. Computers are complex by nature and require a reasonable degree of knowledge to operate satisfactorily. As such, the use of computers will be the first area for which knowledge costs will be discussed.

Today, practically all office employees are equipped with computers. These computers are typically linked to internal and external networks. Any event that requires understanding generates knowledge costs. Because the ability to use computers often requires an understanding of complex operations (hardware, software, networks, etc.), computer usage generates knowledge costs.

Applying Einstein's quote of only using "less than 10% of our brains," the majority of staff know less than 10% of the features of the software programs they use each day. This means that an average employee *does not* know 90% of the features of the computer programs they may use every day.

Organizations experience potentially large knowledge costs on a daily basis. These costs arise because employees take the "long way" when performing tasks, which increases nonproductive time. Increases in nonproductive time directly affect the firm's relative performance.

IIS8001 Intangible Project Management Standard uses methods and processes compliant with International Intangible Standards to determine what activities employees actually perform and the impact of those activities on the organization's intangible cost structure.

ESTIMATING COMPUTING KNOWLEDGE COSTS

When employees use computers they generate knowledge costs. Knowledge costs are identified, classified, measured, and managed by the IIS10001 Intangible Knowledge Management Standard.

Let's consider a staff member who spends 4 hours a day using a computer program. If this staff member could have performed the same work in 2.5 hours, *as a result of increased knowledge and skill*, what are the potential knowledge costs and benefits?

As we investigated earlier, productivity and wage costs for a single employee are not necessarily significant. But when those costs are aggregated across a whole organization they become significant.

BENCHMARKING SOFTWARE COSTS

Most organizations believe that the cost of software is the cost to license that software, plus customization plus training. In truth, the financial transactions relating to software costs are just the tip of the iceberg.

The major cost involved with software is the cost of staff using the software on a periodic basis. Let us assume that we are analyzing the financial performance of a management consulting organization. Table 12.1 shows this organization's financial data, which was taken from publicly available financial statements.

Today all employees require a computer to perform their work. In this example, we will assume that 90% of the employees use a computer for an average time according to IIS benchmarked statistics for this organization's industry, as represented in Table 12.2. This analysis illustrates that of the computer time that staff use (row B), some of it is nonproductive (row C).

Just as we investigated the concept of determining revenue productivity, we can also determine wage productivity using the revenue productivity con-

TABLE 12.1 Publicly Available Financial Data

Financial details Revenue in $US millions	As of 12/31/96	As of 12/31/97	As of 12/31/98	As of 12/31/99	As of 12/31/00
Revenue	75,947.00	78,508.00	81,667.00	87,548.00	88,396.00
Employees (actual figures)	240,615	269,465	291,067	307,401	316,303
Relative performance	315,637.01	291,347.67	280,578.01	284,800.64	279,466.21

TABLE 12.2 IIS10001 Intangible Knowledge Management Standard Data

IIS 10001 Intangible KM Standard Computer usage valuation	As of 12/31/96	As of 12/31/97	As of 12/31/98	As of 12/31/99	As of 12/31/00
A: Computer users	216,553.50	242,518.50	261,960.30	276,660.90	284,672.70
B: Daily computer usage (hours/day)	3.00	3.49	4.04	4.58	5.12
C: Nonproductive computer time (hours/day)	1.20	1.40	1.62	1.83	2.05
D: Annual payroll ($US millions)	14,075.98	16,078.98	17,708.52	18,972.02	19,706.47
E: Effective work hours per year (hours/year)	1,800.00	1,800.00	1,800.00	1,800.00	1,800.00
F: Nonproductive overhead (%)	40.00%	40.00%	40.00%	40.00%	40.00%
G: Effective work hours per year (hours/year)	1,080.00	1,080.00	1,080.00	1,080.00	1,080.00
H: L3 revenue productivity benchmark ($US/hour)	292.26	269.77	259.79	263.70	258.77
I: L3 wage productivity benchmark ($US/hour)	54.17	55.25	56.33	57.15	57.69

cept. In this example, Level 3 wage productivity is determined by the following formula:

$$L3WP = \left(\frac{Payroll_{Annual}}{1800 \times (1-0.4)}\right) = \left(\frac{\$14,075.98 \text{ million}}{1080}\right) = 54.17$$

With the results of L3RP (Level 3 revenue productivity) and L3WP (Level 3 revenue productivity), we can now benchmark the costs of staff using computers each day on (1) a per day per employee basis, (2) a per day per group basis, and (3) a weekly group basis (Table 12.3).

Using IIS10001 and other International Intangible Standards, it is possible to accurately pinpoint the costs that make up the aggregated costs given in Table 12.3. For example, IIS10001 may determine that 5% of the costs are due to slow computers that should be upgraded. That 5% therefore represents the "Deficient processing speed" cost, which is a category of "Processing overhead" (Table 12.4). Assuming a 40-week working year, the costs would be as shown in Table 12.4.

By graphing the data as Figure 12.1 we can see that processing costs are increasing for each year and are projected to increase in the future. Using

TABLE 12.3   Using IIS10001 Intangible KM Standard to Value Knowledge Costs

IIS 10001 Intangible KM Standard Computer usage valuation	As of 12/31/96	As of 12/31/97	As of 12/31/98	As of 12/31/99	As of 12/31/00
Per day employee analysis ($US)					
Productivity cost (L3)	350.71	376.59	419.83	483.11	529.95
Nonproductive wage allocation (L3)	65.00	77.13	91.03	104.69	118.14
Total daily (individual)					
Per day group analysis ($US millions)					
Productivity cost (L3)	75.95	91.33	109.98	133.66	150.86
Nonproductive wage allocation (L3)	14.08	18.71	23.85	28.96	33.63
Total daily (group)					
Per week group analysis ($US millions)					
Productivity cost (L3)	379.74	456.65	549.89	668.28	754.31
Nonproductive wage allocation (L3)	70.38	93.53	119.24	144.82	168.16
Total daily (group, week)	450.11	550.18	669.13	813.10	922.47

TABLE 12.4   Using the IIS10001 Intangible KM Standard to Categorize Knowledge Costs

IIS 10001 Intangible KM Standard Computer usage valuation	As of 12/31/96	As of 12/31/97	As of 12/31/98	As of 12/31/99	As of 12/31/00
Per week group analysis ($US millions)					
Processing overhead					
Deficient processing speed					
Productivity cost (L3)	18.99	22.83	27.49	33.41	37.72
Nonproductive wage allocation (L3)	3.52	4.68	5.96	7.24	8.41
Total daily (group, week) $US millions)	22.51	27.51	33.46	40.66	46.12
Annualized cost ($US millions)	900.23	1,100.36	1,338.26	1,626.21	1,844.95

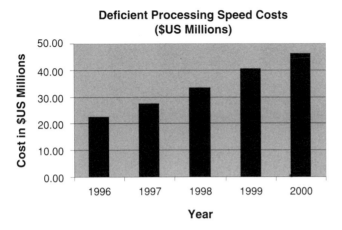

FIGURE 12.1   Determining trends in deficient processor costs ($US millions).

International Intangible Management Standards Institute financial modeling systems, we determine that deficient processing costs will continue to increase according to the following equation:

$$y = \frac{a}{(a + bx^c)} \qquad (12.1)$$

where:

a	=	0.74521252
b	=	−0.69933492
c	=	0.021186274
Standard error	=	1.0849233
Correlation coefficient	=	0.9986736

Using this analysis, IIS10001 would estimate that deficient processing costs would be $US 53.135 million in 2001 and $US 60.813 million in 2002.

DETERMINING INTANGIBLE BREAK-EVEN BUDGETS

Using International Intangible Management Standards Institute financial modeling systems, we estimate that the revenue of the firm fits this equation:

$$y = \frac{a + bx}{1 + cx + dx^2} \qquad (12.2)$$

where $a = -0.23114646$, $b = 1.0567827e + 009$, $c = 14343.722$, and $d = -50782.471$. Using this equation, we would predict revenue in the next year to be $US 93,410 million and 2002 revenue to be $US 97,821 million.

Over the same period, International Intangible Management Standards Institute financial modeling systems determined that employment was estimated by the following equation:

$$y = \frac{ab + cx^d}{b + x^d} \qquad (12.3)$$

where $a = 7.3772909$, $b = 1.5001117$, $c = 1246572.7$, and $d = 0.22345179$. Using this equation, it is estimated that employment in 2001 will be 326,945 and 335,320 in 2002.

An intangible break-even budget (IBB) is the amount of money that could be allocated to reducing an intangible cost to zero on a per employee basis. The IBB therefore represents the maximum amount of money the organization can spend without incurring additional costs, as illustrated in Table 12.5.

Break-Even Budgeting

Conservative executives can use the L1 intangible break-even budget (the wage budget) to determine how much money can be placed into an upgrading program simply to offset nonproductive wage allocation costs. More forward thinking executives can use the L2 intangible break-even budget (the productivity budget) to determine how much they can spend just to offset productivity losses. Because the real organizational cost is the combination of L1 and L2 costs, the sensible executive should use the L3 total break-even budget to determine the maximum amount that can be spent on a solution to offset intangible costs. In Table 12.5, we estimated the likely costs and benefits in 2001 and 2002.

TABLE 12.5 Using Intangible Standards to Determine the Intangible Break-even Budget

IIS 10001 Intangible KM Standard Computer usage valuation	As of 12/31/96	As of 12/31/97	As of 12/31/98	As of 12/31/99	As of 12/31/00	As of 12/31/01	As of 12/31/02
Per week group analysis ($US millions)							
Processing overhead							
Deficient processing speed							
Productivity cost (L3)	18.99	22.83	27.49	33.41	37.72	45.94	56.17
Nonproductive wage allocation (L3)	3.52	4.68	5.96	7.24	8.41	10.02	12.00
Total daily (group, week)($US millions)	22.51	27.51	33.46	40.66	46.12	55.96	68.16
Annualized cost ($US millions)	900.23	1,100.36	1,338.26	1,626.21	1,844.95	2,238.34	2,726.48
Intangible break-even budget ($US)							
L1 wage budget ($US)	650.00	771.29	910.35	1,046.91	1,181.44	1,361.84	1,589.90
L2 productivity budget ($US)	3,507.08	3,765.94	4,198.28	4,831.06	5,299.51	6,245.07	7,444.53
L3 total break-even budget ($US)	4,157.08	4,537.23	5,108.63	5,877.97	6,480.95	7,606.91	9,034.44

CHAPTER 13

Intangible Information Management

Intangible information management differs from conventional information management. Intangible information management is concerned with the management of intangible costs that accumulate when staff use, distribute, or apply information.

INFORMATION DEPENDENCY

All organizations are dependent on information. Information is required to coordinate staff, sell products, purchase inputs, communicate with the customers and the market, and for numerous other reasons. *Without information organizations would lose the ability to function.* To determine the information dependence of an organization, obtain feedback from employees regarding the consequences of not:

- Answering, or making, any phone calls
- Attending any meetings, reading any newspapers, journals, magazines, or other information

- Using computers
- Using the Internet or e-mail
- Using faxes, pagers, or mobile phones
- Not reading, writing, listening, typing, or talking

Today, the vast majority of organizations are almost completely dependent on information.

MANAGING CORPORATE INFORMATION FLOWS

Managers, executives and directors are moving from managing people and processes to managing information, knowledge, relationships, emotions, and time. Ensuring that the right people get the right information at the right time can be exceptionally difficult. Executives have to contend with an overwhelming abundance of information, which can often be contradictory and therefore requires further research.

A critical focus of IIS10010 (Intangible Information Management Standard) is to assist executives in streamlining information flows and ensuring that the costs of information flows do not outweigh the benefits those flows generate.

INFORMATION FLOW MANAGEMENT

Adopting an organizational policy of writing less, but of a higher quality, is critical to maintaining profitability in an era of fast-paced change. *Information flow management* is the area of intangible management that ensures internal and external communications are (1) cost justified, (2) create competitive advantage, and/or (3) maintain competitive advantage.

Information flow management generates profitable internal and external information flows. To generate profitable flows, the "corporate information culture" must be adjusted to reflect the realities of the current business climate.

> The global economy is here today. It is not waiting for us to adjust to it. —
> *Knowledge Exchange, Christopher Locke, Internet World*

ADJUSTING THE CORPORATE INFORMATION CULTURE

Today, people write to "prove their worth," as *The Economist* quote below illustrates:

They [white-collar workers] are given information to process and a computer to process it with and told to tell the boss when they have finished. Often they find the best way to prove their worth is to generate more information than anyone else. . . . The result is that managers are flooded with more data, some of it superfluous, than they can mentally process. —*Too Many Computers Spoil the Broth*, The Economist

Conventional organizations subscribe to the idea that "more is more." Let us suppose that an employee produces a 1200-page manual to be distributed to employees. Psychologically, employees know that a 1200-page manual will take a significant amount of time to read.

Understanding Information Lock

Information lock is the point at which people stop reading information due to a perceived unacceptable reduction in time assets. Figure 13.1 illustrates that if information lock sets in, reading will cease before information is completely analyzed. According to this figure, an average person analyzing the information will receive 6.25% of the real value of the document due to information lock.

Why Information Lock Generates Potential Costs

Because information is the lifeblood of business, it generates significant benefits. Let us assume that IIS5001 has determined that the value of the *complete* document (100%) could have been translated into $500,000 in additional

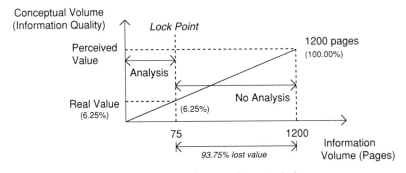

FIGURE 13.1   Explaining information lock.

revenue. Because information lock only released 6.25% of that document's full value ($31,250), the business would lose an estimated $468,750 in potential revenue due to the effects of information lock. Information lock is a significant business problem, which can now be solved by applying the IIS21001 Knowledge Reengineering Standard.

WHAT GENERATES INFORMATION LOCK?

Because information is only valuable *after* it is read, people must invest time first *before* they see a return. Because the return on information is not instant, people continually question whether they should be reading or performing more immediately profitable work. Because the time spent reading information is lost productive time, people are forced to reallocate their time from productive activities to information that may or may not enhance their productivity. Because staff only have a certain amount of productive time in each day, reading information leads initially to negative conversion.

EVER INCREASING NEGATIVE CONVERSION

Today, staff could spend every productive hour analyzing information and therefore never get any work done. Many people argue that "keeping up to date" has become a full-time occupation in its own right. When staff read information they must concentrate and focus on converting the raw information into understood knowledge. Understanding (information analysis), in itself, is an involved process.

HOW WE ANALYZE INFORMATION

Reading and understanding a book while someone is speaking to you is practically impossible. Analyzing information requires concentration (undivided attention) and *focus*. For example, if you are trying to read something important, and someone continually interrupts you, you will "lose your train of thought" or "lose track" of where you are. Figure 13.2 illustrates how people convert information into knowledge.

In fact, understanding is the process of (1) "making sense" of information (analysis), (2) putting all the new pieces of information together (integration), and then (3) "restructuring and reformatting" that information into a form that makes sense to us on an *individual* and *personal* level.

How We Analyze Information

Time is required to -

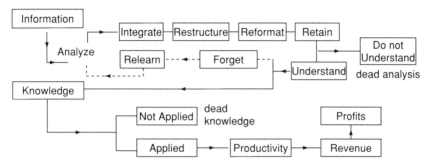

FIGURE 13.2   IIS21001.P5 (Knowledge Reengineering Standard): how information is analyzed.

What we understand, we retain; what we do not understand becomes "dead information." *As much as 50% of technical information eventually ends up as dead information.* Our understanding erodes over time as we forget. As we forget we must continually relearn information. What we remember *and* understand is called *knowledge.* Knowledge derived within an organization should be used to increase the value-generating abilities of the organization. Because knowledge is gained at the expense of productive time, gained knowledge should be used for productive purposes. Due to the complexity of learning, it is little wonder that staff must temporarily cease productive work when gaining knowledge. The problems caused by the temporary suspension of productive activities are addressed by information flow management.

THE INFORMATION QUALITY TEST (IIS21001.P10)

Within an organization, all information should be passed through the information quality test to determine if the information should be communicated to staff. This test requires people to ask several important questions:

- If this information is read, *will staff become immediately more productive?* If the answer is no, do not communicate the information.
- Assuming the preceding step, what is the estimated value of the potential increase in productivity caused by the new knowledge?
- Assuming all the preceding steps, what steps have been taken to ensure that the *value of increased productivity has been maximized?*
- Assuming all the preceding steps, *has the information been written as clearly, concisely, and simply as possible?*

- Assuming all the preceding steps, is the information being communicated *in as few words as possible?*
- Assuming all the preceding steps, has technology been used to leverage the time of the organization so that *information costs and nonproductive time are being minimized?*

IIS21001.P10 (Figure 13.3) ensures that information that genuinely enhances the organization's competitive position is communicated.

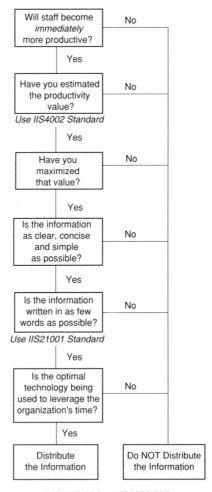

FIGURE 13.3   IIS21001.P10.

INFORMATION DESKILLING

In 1991, *The New Scientist* magazine estimated that the amount of information around the world was doubling every 20 months. Malthus's law of information states that new information content is doubling every year and that the time spent on information is practically constant.

> The sum total of human knowledge changed very slowly prior to the relatively recent beginnings of scientific thought. It has been estimated that by 1800 it was doubling every 50 years; by 1950, doubling every 10 years; and that presently [1972] it is doubling every 5 years. Computer technology may make a frighteningly high rate of increase possible for centuries. —The Computer Society, *J. Martin and A. Norman, Penguin, 1973*

Information overload occurs because our ability to convert information into knowledge (our "analysis capacity") is considerably less than the rate of growth in available information ("information growth") (Figure 13.4).

Information deskilling is the process of losing *relative* expertise due to information growth. If you knew 100% about your discipline this minute, in 12 months time (using Malthus's law of information), provided you had not read anything related to your field, you would only know 50% of your subject, because the knowledge in your field would have doubled. The major problem is that the 50% you know could well be out of date and irrelevant, as the following statement illustrates:

> Everyone of us lives closer to the brink of obsolescence. Each one of us that is adult and qualified feels menaced in some degree by the push of new developments which establish themselves only by discarding the methods and techniques and theories that he has learnt to master. . . . The rapidity of change in social conventions

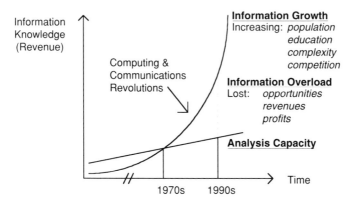

FIGURE 13.4   Information, knowledge, and information overload.

and moral attitudes, associated with technological transformations in the mode of living, renders a person's experience of the world a generation ago largely irrelevant to the problems of today. —Sleepers, Wake! Technology & The Future of Work, *Oxford University Press, 1982, p. 181*

IIS21001 uses a completely new method of analyzing information that represents a quantum leap in how we can analyze and understand information.

> The significant problems we face cannot be solved at the same level of thinking we were at when we created them. —*Albert Einstein*

KNOWLEDGE REENGINEERING

The task of every manager, director, and employee is to maximize the conversion of organizational productive time into value (revenue, share price, etc.). IIS21001 explains why we have not been able to increase the speed at which we analyze information.

AUTONOMOUS PROCESSING RATE

The *autonomous processing rate* (APR) is the time required for an average person to read and understand 1 page of information (IIS21001.D4). The APR for the average person is approximately 5 minutes per page. Hence, a 10-page document will take approximately 50 minutes to *convert* into knowledge. If the information is highly complex, containing complex terminology, the APR will increase. Conversely, well-written easy-to-understand information, with pictures and diagrams, typically lowers the APR.

Information Value Dilution Rate

When people "scan" or "skim" information they attempt to understand a substantial amount of information *without reading* its contents fully. When people used skimming technique, they may only require 1 minute per page, or less, but this activity leaves the reader with an inaccurate picture of the information. For example, if skimming takes 1 minute per page, where a full analysis takes 5 minutes per page, skimming will give 20% or less of the value of a full analysis. The information value dilution rate (IVDR) in this case is equal to 80%. That is:

$$\text{IVDR} = \left[1 - \left(\frac{\text{SkimRate}}{\text{APR}} \right) \right] \times \frac{100}{1} = \left[1 - \left(\frac{1}{5} \right) \right] \times \frac{100}{1}$$
$$= [1 - (0.2)] \times \frac{100}{1} = 80\%$$

The IVDR therefore measures the value reduction in the individual's ability to translate information into knowledge. By artificially lowering the APR people may assume that they are obtaining greater access to information and knowledge by lowering the value of the information's quality and reading more. While there is truth that people appear to have greater *information efficiency* (reading more in less time), those same people have lower *information effectiveness* (transfer of information into knowledge).

Time-Revenue Suspension

The *law of time-revenue suspension* (IIS21001.L2) states that:

> Every time an employee reads information during organizational hours, the organization's revenue generating capabilities will be temporarily suspended. (IIS21001.L2)

Organizations permit staff to read information; the understanding gained *after* the analysis should lead to an increase in skills and therefore productivity. This skill increase is believed to *pay back* the lost productive time that results from reading the information. If we return to the 1200-page manual example, the *time-revenue suspension diagram*, IIS21001.P7, would appear as shown in Figure 13.5.

Figure 13.5 shows that the time spent attempting to understand the information results in decreased productivity. However, when the analysis is finished, increased productivity is used to "pay back" the cost of obtaining that information. When conducting information flow management, it is critical to minimize the effects of time-revenue suspension and to maximize the after-analysis productivity rate.

IIS21001 KNOWLEDGE REENGINEERING STANDARD

We understand by reading, analyzing, and integrating information. IIS21001 presents analyzed and integrated information in as few words as possible. If you think of knowledge as a dartboard, the *closer* you are to the middle, the *more* important the knowledge is (Figure 13.6). Hence, the bull's-eye has the highest value. The IIS21001 Knowledge Reengineering Standard provides techniques that illustrate how to present the most important concepts first in an easily understood structure.

The IIS21001 Knowledge Reengineering Standard

- Represents a quantum leap in the ability to summarize information. Conventional summary seeks to extract the most important *words*.

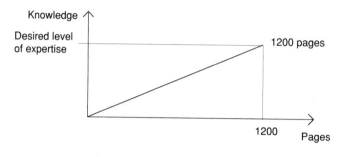

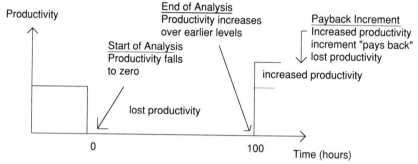

FIGURE 13.5   IIS21001.P7: time-revenue suspension.

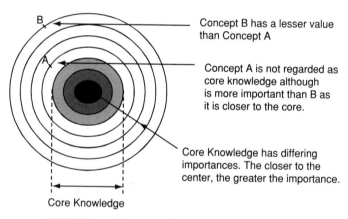

FIGURE 13.6   Illustrating the concept of core knowledge.

- Provides new analytical techniques to give people skill in extracting the most important *concepts*.
- Restructures and recommunicates (using advanced learning systems) and presents what the document is *trying* to say in the fewest number of words.

- Ignores the words and focuses, instead, on the underlying meaning of the information: the *concepts*.

By using fewer words to express the same content, IIS21001 ensures that time-revenue suspension is minimized. IIS21001 uses advanced learning systems, like *exponential learning*, to ensure that even fewer words are required to express information content.

IIS21001 also uses a number of techniques to maximize understanding and retention. The goal of IIS21001 is to:

- Minimize information costs as measured through intangible cost analysis
- Maximize after-analysis productivity rates.

Figure 13.7 shows how writing less, but communicating the same content, saves time, which saves money.

Critical Mass

IIS21001 Knowledge Reengineering Standard presents information at its *critical mass*. The critical mass is the least number of words required to express the information's *total* content.

To explain critical mass, assume that four employees write documents (A, B, C, and D) on the same issue. *All documents cover the same information*, except document A does this in 10 pages, document B in 22 pages, document C in 45 pages, and document D in 60 pages (Figure 13.8). From Figure 13.8, we see that document A will communicate 100% of its value through 10 pages. At the APR of 5 minutes per page, full knowledge will be reached with 50 minutes of analysis. Document B takes 22 pages to convey its meaning and will take 110 minutes to be fully converted into knowledge at the APR of 5 minutes per page. Because documents A and B are conceptually equal, reading document A in preference to document B will save each employee 60 minutes of analysis time.

Document C communicates its conceptual value in 45 pages and will take the average person 225 minutes (3.75 hours) to convert into knowledge. Because document A has the same conceptual value as document C, the average employee would save 175 minutes (nearly 3 hours) by analyzing document A in preference to document C.

Document D has 60 pages (300 minutes or 5 hours of analysis) and would appear to be the most valuable document according to the old conventions of assessing document quality (conceptual value) by document volume (the number of pages). Because document D has the same conceptual content as document A, however, reading document A will save the average employee 250 minutes (over 4 hours) of analysis.

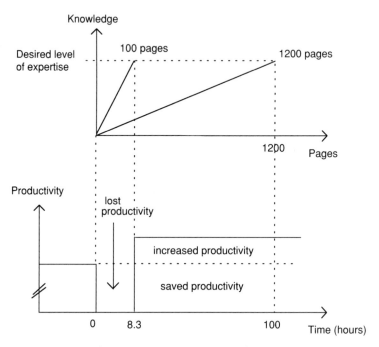

FIGURE 13.7 Explaining time-revenue suspension after IIS21001 reengineering.

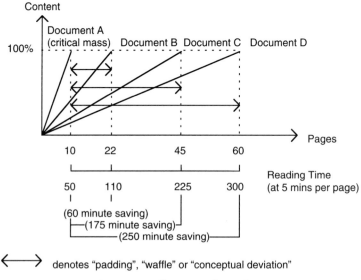

←——→ denotes "padding", "waffle" or "conceptual deviation"

FIGURE 13.8 Illustration of critical mass.

Documents A, B, C, and D were formed by employees with different information presentation abilities. Document A is the length the document can be written at using the IIS21001 standard. Because each page can potentially take 5 minutes to understand fully, by reducing the number of pages to the critical mass, the recipient of the information can save significant amounts of reading time without experiencing *information value dilution* or *information lock.*

Because information also contains intangible benefits, the firm gains access to those benefits more quickly and can capitalize on those benefits before the competition can (to create a competitive advantage).

CHAPTER 14

IIS21001 Knowledge Reengineering Standard

CORE CHARACTERISTIC

If information is correctly reengineered using the IIS21001 Knowledge Reengineering Standard, that information results in the total analysis time being reduced *without increasing the information value dilution rate* because the conceptual content remains the same.

For example, an 8-hour training seminar would be compliant with the IIS21001 Standard *if* the seminar were reengineered into a 4-hour seminar, *if and only if* the 4-hour seminar had the same conceptual content as the 8-hour seminar. In other words, a person attending the 4-hour IIS21001 seminar would have to have an understanding of the content equal to that of a person attending the original 8-hour seminar. *The IIS21001 standard is typically applied to information, but can be applied to any activity, any technology, or any process.*

IIS21001 APPLIED TO INFORMATION

The IIS21001 Knowledge Reengineering Standard, when applied to information, ensures that the conceptual content of the original information on the left side of the scale shown in Figure 14.1 is equal in terms of content (conceptual value) to the reengineered information on the right-hand side of the scale.

IIS21001 AND SUMMARY

IIS21001 knowledge reengineering is a "significant upgrade" on normal summary methods. The upgrade differences between the two methods are seen in how the information is formed:

- Summary: formed by subjective *exclusion* of words
- IIS21001 reengineered information: formed by *inclusion* of concepts

A summary, as most people understand it, is formed by *excluding* information that is of little or no value. The danger with this approach is that "one person's food is another person's poison." Hence, summaries often exclude information that is potentially important to someone, *but not to the person forming the summary*. IIS21001 knowledge reengineering does *not* exclude words; it reengineers, compresses, rearranges, and represents *concepts* using *new* words and *new* presentation techniques. The differences between summary and IIS21001 knowledge reengineering are represented diagrammatically in Figure 14.2.

EXPLAINING THE FIGURE

Figure 14.2 illustrates how 100% of the value of the document is reached on the 100th page. A linear (straight-line) association between document value

FIGURE 14.1   Illustrating how the IIS21001 Knowledge Reengineering Standard maintains conceptual value.

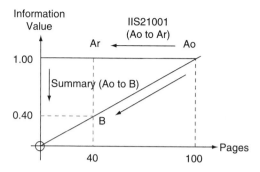

FIGURE 14.2   Illustration of how summary and IIS21001 knowledge reengineering differ.

and information quantity has been used in this example. On the 40th page, it is assumed that 40% (0.40) of the document's information value has been analyzed (converted into knowledge). This 40% position can be referred to as point B. At the 100th page, 100% (1.00) of the document's information value is assumed to be analyzed. The full document analysis point is denoted by Ao.

Conventional Summary

Excluding information value through the exclusion of words forms a summary. As such a 40-page summary represents a movement from point Ao to point B in Figure 14.2 and a reduction in information value from 100% (1.00) to 40% (0.40).

IIS21001

If the 40-page summary were formed according to the rules of International Intangible Standard IIS21001, the value of the information would be maintained at 100% but the number of pages required to communicate that value would be reduced from 100 to 40 pages. In this case, the movement in Figure 14.2 is from Ao to Ar.

Because information creates value, any *excluded* information can lead to a loss of revenue-generating potential. This decrease therefore leads to intangible costs being generated.

How IIS21001 Knowledge Reengineering Works

All information contains "units of thought" called *concepts*. *Words communicate concepts*. Different people can explain a concept in just a few words while others may require several pages. The IIS21001 Knowledge Reengineering Standard extracts all the concepts from the original information and using simpler words and explanations explains all of these concepts in the minimum number of words possible (the document's critical mass).

Critical Mass

The IIS21001 Knowledge Reengineering Standard is much like a weight loss program except for information, not people. For example, if someone loses weight, the "real person" underneath suddenly emerges into clear sight. By applying the IIS21001 Knowledge Reengineering Standard to information the "real information"—the information the writer was actually trying to convey—emerges into clear sight. *IIS21001 knowledge reengineering simply uncovers the real value of the information.*

Information Anorexia

If IIS21001 knowledge reengineering is "weight loss for information," then writing fewer pages than the *critical mass* amant results in a reduction in information value, or *information anorexia*. Hence, anyone trying to write less than the critical mass of a document creates a reduction in information value. In short, IIS21001 knowledge reengineering also provides guidance in understanding what the document's critical mass actually is.

IIS21001 KNOWLEDGE REENGINEERING METHODS

IIS21001 knowledge reengineering achieves reengineering by applying a wide range of methods as discussed next.

INFORMATION RESTRUCTURING

Information restructuring works in a way similar to how our mind *actually* attempts to understand information. The mind, as shown earlier, travels through a number of processes in order to present information in a state that can be understood by the reader. Similar concepts are grouped, and concepts are built on top of each other to form a knowledge structure.

FOUNDATION ANALYSIS

The law of sequential analysis (IIS21001.L4) states that "The brain processes new information sequentially." For example, if you were learning 18 areas (for example, each new area could be a chapter of a book), you would read them in order (Figure 14.3).

KNOWLEDGE REFORMULATION

Each incremental concept added to our existing knowledge of an area changes the understanding of that area. That is, as new information is added to existing knowledge, our understanding changes. It is therefore vital to know how a new concept relates to all other concepts as *conceptual linkages* influence our understanding. For example, let us assume that a document conveys five concepts. Under conventional learning and analysis techniques, most people would hold a conceptual structure like the one shown in Figure 14.4.

Using the IIS21001 standard, the concepts would be restructured in accordance with their relative value to each other. Knowledge reformulation (IIS21001.P10) *defines the conceptual associations and value dependencies of one concept group to other group(s) of concepts* (Figure 14.5). From Figure 14.5, you can see instantly that C1 is the foundation of understanding for C2 and supports an understanding of C4. C4 requires C3 and C1 to be understood because C1 and C3 contain concepts that are required to understand C4. C5 is

FIGURE 14.3   The law of sequential analysis.

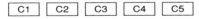

FIGURE 14.4   Conventional formulation.

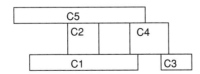

FIGURE 14.5   Knowledge reformulation (IIS21001.P10).

based on C2 and on C4 (to a lesser extent). You will also notice that C1 has conceptual width meaning that it has a number of foundation concepts. C4 has conceptual height as it builds a number of concepts on top of each other rather. C2 is in the middle of C1 explaining that C2 is dependent on *core concepts* relating to C1 (remember the bull's-eye). C4 is on the edge of C1 explaining that C4 builds on peripheral concepts of C1 and C3. Significant understanding is embedded in information by using knowledge reformulation techniques.

FOUNDATION MAPPING

To create a complete understanding, our mind must create a "total structure" based on all of the information being analyzed. The role of IIS21001 foundation analysis is to visually create that structure.

Foundation mapping uses the concept of *knowledge depth* to create a three-dimensional picture of the interrelationship between groups of concepts. You can see in Figure 14.6 that A1 is the foundation of A2, A3, A12, A13, etc. You can also see that A1 has more than twice the number of concepts of A2, and A3 has about one-third of the concepts of A2. This analysis makes it easy to understand the *relative importance* of different areas.

ERASURE ANALYSIS

The law of knowledge erasure (IIS21001.L7) states that:

> The furthest nonreinforced area will have the highest amount of erasure (the highest erasure factor).

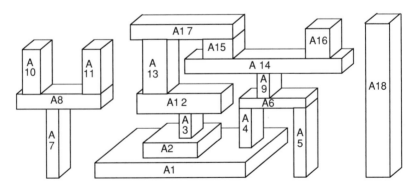

FIGURE 14.6   Foundation learning diagram for 18 areas.

This means that as you pass from area 1 (A1) to A2, your understanding of A1 will start to erode. As you pass from A2 to A3, your understanding of A2 and A1 will erode, but A1 will have eroded more than A2. As you start analyzing A4, your understanding of A3, A2, and A1 will erode. However, the furthest nonreinforced area (A1) will have the maximum amount of erasure.

Erasure Rounds

An *erasure round* (IIS21001.D11) occurs whenever time is devoted to another area of knowledge. Each time you move to another knowledge area, the previous knowledge areas are erased by an amount equal to your *erasure factor*. Some people have high erasure factors; others have lower erasure factors. *Someone with a high erasure factor will forget new information very quickly.*

> In the example of Figure 14.6, a movement from A1 to A2 to A3 to A4 to A5 creates four erasures of A1, three erasures of A2, two erasures of A3, and one erasure of A4 (in accordance with the law of erasure).

Erasure is increased when areas are not reinforced with learning. Our minds are designed to forget nonreinforced information, so the law of erasure follows the biochemical laws of the brain. As such, people who do not possess the ability to draw connections between different concepts have great difficulty remembering or applying new knowledge. It is only when concepts are connected that they can be understood.

Erasure Diagrams

An *erasure diagram* (IIS21001.D14) determines how quickly an individual will reach their maximum erasure level. It also shows how total understanding is never lost; it is just reduced to a minimal level. For example, the erasure diagram of Figure 14.7 illustrates that over seven erasure rounds, this person has been subject to an 80% erasure factor. Hence, the person will recall an average of 20% of the subject matter.

RELEARNING ANALYSIS

The law of knowledge reinforcement (IIS21001.L10) states that the only way to offset erasure is through the constant reconnection and reinforcement of conceptual linkages between concepts. The relearning factor is always greater than the erasure factor because when information is analyzed a residual trace

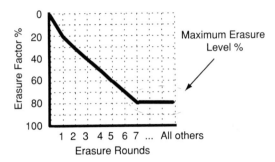

FIGURE 14.7   An erasure diagram.

of that knowledge remains within the brain. It is the reinforcement of conceptual content (relearning) that creates knowledgeable staff.

INFORMATION ENHANCEMENT

There are times when an author may incorrectly assume that the reader has the required knowledge to understand what is being read. A major focus of the IIS21001 Knowledge Reengineering Standard is to communicate information in a way such that people are equipped with (or can easily access) the required fundamentals.

EXPONENTIAL LEARNING TECHNIQUES

Accelerated learning is a faster way to learn than normal learning. *Exponential learning* is an even faster way to learn than accelerated learning. Exponential learning allows people to spend less time working with information and more time applying it. Exponential learning was developed specifically for the IIS21001 Knowledge Reengineering Standard.

BOTTOM LINE ORIENTED

With excess competition, increasing workloads, and excessive stress, individuals can no longer afford to "learn for learning's sake." Any sacrifice of productive time *must be paid for* by increased productivity. The purpose of the IIS21001 Knowledge Reengineering Standard is to communicate information as practically and quickly as possible so that the skills people are *trying* to attain are *actually* attained. Those skills can then be used to generate superior returns for the organization as individuals improve their quality, depth, and number of knowledge assets, relationship assets, emotional assets, and time assets.

CHAPTER 15

Examples of IIS21001 Knowledge Reengineering

About 250,000 Americans suffer from *narcolepsy*, an embarrassing, mysterious, and, on occasions, dangerous sleep disorder. Narcoleptics cannot remain awake during the day no matter how much sleep they have the night before. Despite his or her best efforts, the narcoleptic remains permanently susceptible to "sleep attacks:" the sudden, overwhelming requirement for 5 to 20 minutes of sleep. To an observer, such people behave like sleep addicts; they cannot be reasoned with, cajoled, or threatened into wakefulness. They fall asleep in the midst of conversation, while talking with their boss, even while making love.

EXAMPLE 1: 73% COMPRESSION AND REENGINEERING

IIS21001 knowledge reengineering has numerous tools at its disposal to concentrate information value. One of the most useful is the IIS21001 concept flow diagram. An IIS21001 concept flow diagram visually represents words in a format similar to a standard flow diagram. This visual representation is designed to uncover the underlying structure or critical mass of the information under analysis. The IIS21001 concept flow diagrams for the narcolepsy information is illustrated in Figure 15.1.

The original quote was 93 words. Below is an IIS21001-compliant version of the information (25 words, a 73.11% decrease in the words required to transfer value):

> Narcolepsy, a sleep disorder, causes about 250,000 Americans to fall asleep, anywhere or anytime, for up to 20 minutes during which they cannot be woken.

The words that we retain as understanding are represented in bold and underlined in Figure 15.1 to show the difference between the original information and the words that have meaning to the average person.

The IIS21001 concept flow diagram shows that very little understanding has actually been omitted. For example, the section stating "They fall asleep in the midst of conversation, while talking with their boss, even while making love" really means that sufferers fall asleep "anywhere or anytime." By using different words, we have captured the value of the information.

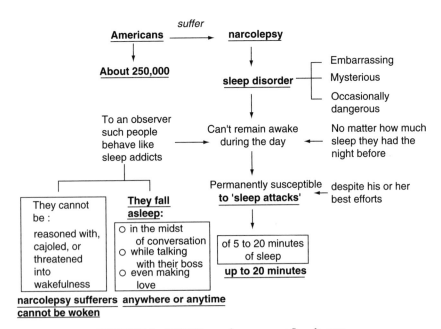

FIGURE 15.1   IIS21001 narcolepsy concept flow diagram.

ASSESSING THE BENEFITS

This example has illustrated that you can read 73% less and still have a near perfect understanding of the subject matter. IIS21001 knowledge reengineering was not designed to reengineer small chunks of information. It was designed to reengineer significant volumes of information.

EXAMPLE 2: 58% COMPRESSION AND REENGINEERING

IIS21001 knowledge reengineering can be applied to *any* subject at *any* level of learning. Consider the quote below:

> Advertising includes those activities by which visual or oral messages are addressed to the public for the purposes of informing them and influencing them either to buy merchandise or services or to act or be inclined favorably toward ideas, institutions, or persons featured.

The IIS21001 knowledge reengineering version reduces the original 43 words to 18 words—a 58% reduction with little, if any, *real* loss of value. Here is the reengineered version:

> Advertising informs and influences the public to buy goods or services, or support featured ideas, institutions, or persons.

The IIS21001 concept flow diagram for this example is covered in Figure 15.2.

Knowledge reengineering allows organizations to quickly convert masses of information into meaningful knowledge. Many people actually find that reengineered information is easier to remember. It also helps to avoid the problems of *information overload* and *information fatigue syndrome*.

REDUCING INFORMATION OVERLOAD

Information overload (too much information) converts productive time into nonproductive time because information *only* creates value *after* analysis has ceased. For example, if you spend 60 minutes reading something, the information is *only* useful *after* the 60 minutes has been invested.

> One of the most formidable opponents your organization may face is information overload. . . . Information overload is the dark side of the information age. Dealing with this growing problem will be one of the most strategic challenges that managers will face. —Making the Right Moves, Canadian Datasystems, Grant Buckler

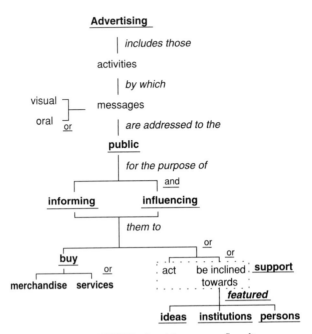

FIGURE 15.2   IIS21001 advertising concept flow diagram.

Every business and individual faces the problem of information overload on an almost daily basis. Too much information is a severe problem. People require *time* to convert information into knowledge—time that organizations and individuals cannot afford to spend.

> We are drowning in information but starved for knowledge. —*John Naisbitt, Megatrends.*

Today, organizations must reward staff for producing *less information that is of a higher conceptual quality.* Because less information can be understood more quickly, time costs are reduced, information can be converted into knowledge more quickly, and organizations increase potential profitability (because employees spend more time applying knowledge and less time reading information).

EXAMPLE 3: 91% COMPRESSION AND REENGINEERING

> Anyone who has spent a moonless night in the country, in a forest, or at sea knows how very dark it can be when the sun is on the other side of the earth. At

early dawn, objects that we could not see a few minutes earlier begin to take shape. The details sharpen, colors appear and brighten, and daylight begins. It is the light from the sun, rising above the horizon in the east, that gives shape, detail and color to our world.

The sun, the stars, lamps, even lightning bugs give off light. They are called luminous bodies (from the Latin word *lumen*, meaning light). Other objects—trees, grass, the pages of this book, for example—are nonluminous. They are visible only when they receive light from some luminous source and reflect it to our eyes.

> Whether a body is luminous or nonluminous depends as much on its condition as on the material from which it is made. By changing the conditions we can make many familiar substances luminous or nonluminous at will. The filament, or fine wire, inside an electric light bulb is nonluminous unless it is heated by an electric current passing through it. We can take a cold piece of iron and make it glow red, yellow, or white by heating it in a bed of burning coals or over a gas flame. When solids and such liquids as melted metals are heated to temperatures above 800xC (about 1500 degrees Fahrenheit), they become sources of light. Such heated materials are known as incandescent bodies.

Of the three paragraphs above (261 words) the IIS21001 reengineered version can be represented in just 26 words (a 90% reduction). The various examples given simply serve to illustrate the Following 26 words:

> Objects can either create light (luminous bodies) or reflect light (nonluminous bodies). An incandescent body is a nonluminous body that becomes luminous when heated above 800°C.

EXAMPLE 4: 86% COMPRESSION AND REENGINEERING

> Only a small portion of the understanding one gains in face-to-face interaction comes from words. One prominent authority claims that a mere 35% of the meaning of communication derives from words; the remainder comes from body language. Albert Mehrabian stated in a widely quoted article that in situations he examined, only 7% of the impact was verbal—the remaining 93% was nonverbal.

The IIS21001 reengineered version follows:

> Understanding is derived mainly from body language, not words.

This simple example yielded an 86% reduction in the amount of words required to explain the concept. Remember, a concept is what the idea is *really* about—it ignores the finer detail of what the words state and focuses on the bigger picture of what knowledge needs to be obtained. Considering we forget a large portion of what we read almost instantaneously due to being continually bombarded by information overload and information lock, making fine detail an "important issue" does not make sense.

Today, it is common practice for employees, regardless of industry, to spend several hours working with information such as:

- Paperwork
- Reports (research, product reports, etc.)
- Daily circulars, organizational news informing employees of internal changes (job openings, organizational acquisitions, strategic directions, etc.)
- E-mail
- Organizational plans
- Intranet or Internet information
- Legal documentation
- environmental scanning reports (press clippings regarding industry, competitor and organizational news)
- Other types of information

If we assume that the average employee spends 2.5 hours each day working with information, then over 240 effective working days *the average employee will spend approximately 600 hours each year working with information.*

By reducing the time required by employees to understand information by at least 50%, we would estimate that after IIS21001 knowledge reengineering, the average employee could have an estimated 300 hours of *additional* productivity each year in which to generate *additional* organizational wealth. As previous examples have shown, this increased productivity does not reduce understanding. In fact, IIS21001 knowledge reengineering (for large volumes of information) is designed the exponentially enhance understanding through the application of exponential learning.

If we assume that the average employee can contribute $95 per hour to organizational wealth if time is used productively and they are paid an average of $14 per hour in wages, then increasing productive time by 300 hours per employee will create an IIS21001 reengineered productivity benefit of approximately $34,200 per employee. For an organization of 10 such employees the savings would be $342,000.

As we investigated in previous chapters, the costs associated with information are significant. For this reason, it is essential to understand an organization's intangible cost structure, as discussed in the next chapter.

CHAPTER 16

Intangible Cost Structures

Our language has much to blame for our lack of progress in the management and valuation of intangible costs. Current understandings of the word *intangible* define intangibles as being (1) nonmaterial and (2) hard to describe. It is because intangibles are *perceived* that they escape physical definition. Intangibles do not possess material qualities and are difficult to define or describe in physical terms. Conventional theory also states that intangibles are unquantifiable assets or qualities (such as trust, duty, honor, respect, etc.).

PUTTING INTANGIBLES IN CONTEXT

Because intangibles create perceptions and perceptions cannot be readily transferred between parties, it stands that intangibles cannot be possessed in the same way as we would possess a tangible object. For example, you can possess a chair, but the perception of that chair is unique to each person. If you tried to own that perception, you would have great difficulty in (1) transferring *your exact perception* to others, (2) *owning* other people's perceptions, (3) enforcing your right of "ownership" in other people's perceptions, and (4) proving and claiming legal damages for any infringement of ownership rights in (3). Despite these problems, intellectual property law was created to assist people in enforcing intangible rights on others. Trademarks, patents, designs, copyrights, or other forms of intellectual property have been given legislated protection (the government passed acts). To recover damages from infringed intellectual property rights, it became essential to be able to value intellectual property. As the value of intangible assets became known, the discipline of *intellectual asset management* was developed to acquire, license, and sell intellectual property (IP). Over time, it became more and more important to manage specific types of intangibles, such as knowledge and relationships. Knowledge was better managed through *knowledge management* than asset management. *Customer relationship management* was developed to better manage customer relationships. More holistic management thinkers started to develop *intellectual capital management* as a method of managing intangible value across the whole organization from a market perspective.

BENEFITS AND COSTS

There is no benefit without a cost and no cost without a benefit. Today the source of greatest benefit (intangibles) is also the source of the greatest costs (intangibles).

FINANCIAL TRANSACTIONS

Conventional management uses techniques that identify, classify, measure, and manage *financial transactions*. It then equates changes in financial transactions to changes in organizational value. The current system of *accounting* was developed more than 500 years ago to specifically record changes in financial transactions through a process that has become widely known as *double-entry bookkeeping*. This system of value management records the sources and uses of money and ensures that they are kept in balance, requiring debits to equal credits. These concepts led to the development of the balance sheet, the income statement, and the cash flow statement. It is these financial reports that the management of private and public organizations use to manage their organizations. In summary, the value equation managers have used to manage value is:

$$FT = FP, \tag{16.1}$$

where FT equals financial transactions and FP equals financial performance.

It is widely understood at the top levels of the accounting, finance, and economics industries that measuring financial transactions to report financial performance through financial reports is becoming an increasingly inaccurate way to measure value. The development of intellectual capital reporting, triple bottom-line accounting, the Balanced Scorecard, and intangible accounting attest to this fact.

EXTENDING MANAGEMENT SYSTEMS

Intangible management complements existing management methods because it allows executives and managers to put more management issues on their radar screen to manage. It is useful to think of the organizational value creation process like a football game. The game has four quarters and the game is won or lost in the final quarter. Like a football team, there are players, managers, investors, and a coach. We can think of the coach as the accounting profession. We'll show you that financial transactions are the *third quarter result* of the value creation process. The four quarters of the current value creation process are discussed next.

Quarter 1: Precontractual Rights

This is the period required to convince the customer that organizational knowledge assets, relationship assets, emotional assets, and time assets are of significant quality to allow the customer to purchase value from the organization. For every 100 customers an organization services, a certain percentage will find that the precontractual rights are below their intangible return on investment. Such customers will leave the firm without purchasing.

Quarter 2: Contractual Performance

This is the period of time required to perform contractual rights according to the customer's value expectations. Because significant competition exists in all industries, the only sources of competitive advantage are competencies relating to knowledge assets, information assets, emotional assets, and time assets. Let us assume that for every 100 customers the organization receives in quarter 1, 20% of these do not acquire value due to inefficient and ineffective intangible assets. This leaves 80 customers for quarter 2. Of these customers, let us assume that 20% (16 customers) realize that their expectations will not be met due to inefficient and ineffective intangible assets. These 16 customers will break their contract due to nonperformance. This leaves 64 customers who actually purchase.

Quarter 3: Financial Performance

Financial performance is the money we collect from customers less the money we spent to get those customers to buy. In this case, financial performance will be derived from 64 customers (not 100). Assuming the average customer value is $100, the organization will have generated $6400 from the day's trading.

What executives need to understand and manage are the *dilution rates* that accompany doing business in severely competitive markets. For example, is this $6400 representative of what customers *should* be purchasing? From a very basic perspective we understood that we started with 100 customers. If each of these customers were willing to pay $100, then organizational revenue could have been $10,000—not $6400. If the organization could somehow capture this $3600 of additional value, it would be able to increase its revenues from $6400 to $10,000. This would mean that the organization has the potential to increase *value capture* by 56.25% ($3600/$6400). Such an action would result in the organization moving to 100% value creation ability from 64% ($6400/$10,000). Such a movement to 100% value creation would be impossible for practically any organization, but a move to 80 to 90% would not be impossible provided knowledge assets, relationship assets, emotional assets, and time assets were scientifically managed.

A second understanding is that the figure of $100 in average customer value represents a *diluted value amount* as defined by IIS12001, Intangible Return on Investment Standard:

> A diluted value amount is the level of a financial transaction that occurs with knowledge asset inefficiencies, relationship asset inefficiencies, emotional asset inefficiencies, and time asset inefficiencies factored into that amount. (IIS12001.D5)

In short, the $6400 of value recorded by the financial transactions is less than the financial transaction amount the firm could have generated if it better controlled its intangibles. If we assume that the price customers were willing to pay was $120 per transaction, then the value of $6400 represents the diluted value amount. The undiluted value amount would therefore be $7680 (64 × $120). From a very simplistic viewpoint we could state that the organization is operating at 83.33% of its *immediate revenue operating ability*. IIS12001.D10 defines this as follows:

> Immediate revenue operating ability is the ability of a firm to initially remove inefficiencies and effectiveness from knowledge assets, relationship assets, emotional assets, and time assets to immediately increase the value of received financial transactions. (IIS12001.D10)

After assessing the business for immediate revenue operating ability, we determine that the $6400 of business we assessed against a potential value of

$10,000 now needs to be reassessed against the figure of $12,000 (100 × $120). The organization is therefore operating at 53.33% of its revenue operating efficiency, not 64% as was initially thought. To create consistency and conservatism, IIS12001 uses various levels of metric to distinguish between different intangible metrics.

Quarter 4: Organizational Performance

Organizational performance is not the same as financial performance. We have seen a business that could service 100 customers at $120 each shrink to an organization that serviced 64 customers at $100 each due inefficient and ineffective intangible management. Organizational performance deals with what happens the next time customers visit the organization. It would be safe to assume that in the next competitive round, there may not be 100 customers visiting the store, there may not even be 64 customers visiting the store. Organization performance is defined by IIS12001.D15 as follows:

> Organizational performance refers to the factors that influence the future viability of the organization as a going concern, such as expectation satisfaction, repeat business, and referred business. (IIS12001.D15)

As such, it attempts to estimate what flow-through effects the business will encounter in the next time period. Expectation satisfaction defines how many of the 64 customers in quarter 3 will no longer visit the organization due to nonperformance of intangible assets. Repeat business defines how many customers will return to the store due to superior intangible asset performance. It also refers to the customers who will no longer return to the organization due to competitive forces. Referred business defines the number of customers that flow from customers who have found the organization's value proposition superior. To keep the example simple, let us assume that the estimates shown in Table 16.1 have been made. This table illustrates that over four competitive periods the organization will steadily lose its customer value. Table 16.1 was generated under the assumption that the market is closed and has a market growth factor of zero (no growth in the customer base).

In competitive period 1, 100 customers will visit the organization and 20 will leave as they receive an unacceptable return on intangible investment. Of the 80 that progress to the next level 20% of these (16) will leave due to contractual nonperformance brought about by inefficient or ineffective intangible management. Of the 64 that purchase, 20% of these (12.80) will not revisit the organization in the future due to the organization's mismanagement of intangibles. This leaves 51.20 people for the organization to create repeat and referred business. Of these 51.20, 20% (or 10.24) will take their business to other competitors. At the start of competitive period 2, 40.96

TABLE 16.1   Analyzing Organizational Performance

	Period 1	Period 2	Period 3	Period 4
Customers	100.00	40.96	16.78	6.87
Quarter 1 dilution	20%	20%	20%	20%
Quarter 1 value loss	20.00	8.19	3.36	1.37
Quarter 2 entry level	80.00	32.77	13.42	5.50
Quarter 2 dilution	20%	20%	20%	20%
Quarter 2 value loss	16.00	6.55	2.68	1.10
Quarter 3 entry level	64.00	26.21	10.74	4.40
Quarter 3 dilution	20%	20%	20%	20%
Quarter 3 value loss	12.80	5.24	2.15	0.88
Quarter 4 entry level	51.20	20.97	8.59	3.52
Quarter 4 dilution	20%	20%	20%	20%
Quarter 4 value loss	10.24	4.19	1.72	0.70

people will be available to the organization to access. You can see that the dilution rates continue even though we have captured business with these customers before. This is because the value created from intangible assets needs to be experienced every time a customer buys.

Competitive Periods

Competitive periods are measured in terms of *competitive waves*. Just like the wave of an ocean, a competitive wave crashes against industries and washes their value away with new technologies, new concepts, and new processes. Competitive waves in highly competitive industries are larger, more frequent, and more destructive than competitive waves in slow-growing industries.

Understanding Growth Factors

The above example deliberately constrained market growth to zero to illustrate the effects of saturated markets. Saturated markets occur when the value proposition of one firm is conceptually identical to that of the competition. For example, many people are insensitive to buying the latest computer from one supplier as opposed to another, because they feel there is no real difference between the computers on offer. Highly competitive markets are subject to strong customer interest (high growth rates)—highly destructive and frequent competitive waves combined with short product life cycles.

Understanding Referral Factors

If intangibles are leveraged correctly, more value is obtained at each stage of the value creation process. The most successful organizations in the world create their business based on *referrals*. A referral occurs when one person introduces another to the organization's value network due to a personal recommendation. Referrals reduce advertising and marketing costs and expose the organization to customers with a higher tolerance to intangible inefficiency and intangible ineffectiveness (due to their association with an existing customer). Referral factors are the only true source of sustainable competitive advantage in any economic system.

MANAGING INTANGIBLE COSTS

Now that you understand more about how intangible inefficiency and intangible ineffectiveness reduce organization performance, we can discuss intangible costs.

Intangible costs are not "costs" in the true accounting sense of the word. An accounting cost is "the price which must be paid to obtain or hold a good or service."[1] Intangible costs measure the financial impact of knowledge assets, relationship assets, emotional assets, and time assets on the organization's financial performance. Even so, intangible costs are costs (or expenses) in that they reduce profit and profitability. Intangible cost-generating activities decrease an organization's ability for customers to capture the value the organization produces and hence affects the organization's revenue-earning capacity.

MEASURING INTANGIBLE COSTS

The easiest way to measure intangible costs is to determine how activities increase nonproductive wage allocations and productivity losses. Whereas financial transactions are recorded because of their incidence, intangible transactions are recorded in accordance with their absence.

THE WAGE–REVENUE NEXUS

If an employee's time can be sold to a client at $120 per hour, the business will not pay that person $120 in wages. Why? Because the purpose of *revenue* is to satisfy:

---

[1] *The Penguin Macquarie Dictionary of Economics & Finance*, Penguin Books, 1988, p. 64.

- Staff costs (wages, bonuses, salaries, commissions, etc.)
- Expense costs (rent, electricity, marketing, accounting, etc.)
- Debt servicing
- Return to shareholders
- Business expansion

Whereas it is true that debt can be also used to satisfy these ends, debt requires a cash flow (generated, or eventually generated, from revenue) capable of repaying the debt.

Revenue generation, therefore, is a critical determinant of a firm's success.

THE ROLE OF EMPLOYEES

"If employees are nonproductive for every hour of their employment, how much revenue will the firm make?" In most cases, the organization will not make any revenue. Hence, there is an almost perfect correlation, and causal effect, between an organization's employment levels and the revenue it is capable of generating. When one organization generates *more* revenue than another organization of the same size in the same industry, it is because the high-performing firm is leveraging its knowledge assets, relationship assets, emotional assets, and time assets more effectively. In other words, the factor that distinguishes high-performing firms from low-performing firms is the management of intangibles, or executive skill in the field of *intangible management*.

ASSESSING INTANGIBLE MANAGEMENT EFFICIENCY

The Financial Accounting Standards Board (FASB) has long argued that intangibles need to be measured. The FASB has encountered difficulties in the measurement of intangibles and their disclosure in publicly available reports primarily on the grounds of *reliability*. If an intangible measure is not reliable then it may lead investors and executives into making incorrect decisions. Reliable measures need to create high *investor security* and *economic stability*. International Intangible Standards assist in providing reliable measures for intangibles. The *EFTE intangible efficiency ratio* is one such example.

EFTE Intangible Efficiency Ratio

Consider a group of organizations in the same industry with the same number of employees, but with differing financial performance. Let us assume that the performance of these firms is graphically represented in Figure 16.1. International Intangible Standard IIS6001 (Intangible Finance Standard) deals with the financial analysis of organizations from a stock market perspective. Under IIS6001.P5, the EFTE intangible efficiency ratio is determined by this process:

> The EFTE intangible efficiency ratio is the ratio of gross revenue to equivalent full-time employees (EFTEs) as measured from publicly available data. This measure gives an investor a single financial measure that explains how well the organization is managing intangibles from an external perspective. (IIS6001.P5)

Applying this process in Figure 16.1, intangible efficiency is 40,000 for Firm A, 20,000 for Firm B, and 10,000 for firm C. This shows, from a bird's-eye perspective, how well the firm is managing its value creation process. The EFTE intangible efficiency ratio provides a useful starting point for an intangible finance assessment, but this statistic needs to be used in conjunction with a wide variety of other intangible analysis statistics to form a balanced opinion of an organization's intangible performance. Generally, the higher the EFTE intangible efficiency ratio the greater the ability of the firm to manage its intangibles.

Determining Organizational Intangible Cost Structures

According to IIS4002.L1, every business has (1) a tangible cost structure *and* (2) an intangible cost structure. Whereas a significant body of knowledge exists on identifying, controlling, and managing the tangible costs that result from financial transactions, this textbook represents the fundamental foundation for identifying, controlling, and managing intangible costs at an enterprise-wide level.

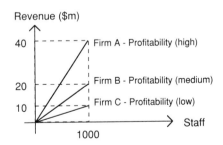

FIGURE 16.1   Assessing intangible efficiency.

By determining activities that generate intangible costs and valuing those costs accordingly, managers increase their ability to identify, control, and manage the intangible cost structure of the organization's for which they work. Correctly analyzing intangible cost structures requires an understanding of how knowledge assets, relationship assets, emotional assets, and time assets influence organizational performance.

Negative Conversion

The previous statistic, the EFTE intangible efficiency ratio, gave a measure that could be used to compare financial performance between various organizations. All that was required was a gross revenue figure and the number of equivalent full-time employees.

> ... the people who do most of the knowledge and service work in organizations ... carry a steadily growing load of busy work, additional activities that contribute little or no value and that have little or nothing to do with what these people are qualified and paid for. —Managing for the Future, *Peter F. Drucker, Butterworth Heinmann, p. 86*

To understand negative conversion, it is important to understand that organizations pay money to individuals in exchange for productive time. Productive time is the amount of time that individual's are actually productive (it does not include overheads and nonproductive time). International Intangible Standard IIS4002 (Intangible Cost Management) deals with the identification, classification, measurement, and management of intangible costs. According to this standard, an intangible cost is defined as follows:

> Any activity within an organizational context that decreases the efficiency, effectiveness, or useful life of knowledge assets, relationship assets, emotional assets, or time assets. (IIS4002.D5)

Negative conversion occurs when employees knowingly or unknowingly *convert* productive time into nonproductive time due to the incidence of intangible cost-generating activities.

NONPRODUCTIVE TIME

Every staff member encounters nonproductive and productive time (Figure 16.2). Nonproductive time is essentially "dead time." It is time where the opportunity to create value has been lost. Nonproductive time is either *voluntary* (a personal phone call, socializing with other staff, extended breaks, etc.) or *involuntary* (network downtime, organizational lags, knowledge lags,

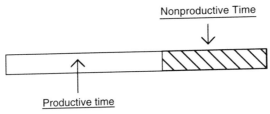

FIGURE 16.2   Productive and nonproductive time.

process lags, etc.). Today, most nonproductive time is *involuntarily* generated. This involuntary generation has occurred due to the transition between the economic eras.

> Time is the scarcest resource, and unless it is managed, nothing else can be managed. —*Peter Drucker*

Let us assume that an employee makes a personal phone call for 15 minutes. During this time, the employee may appear productive, but is actually "on strike" and not generating any value for the organization.

If an employee is reliant on the organization's computer network, and the network ceases to operate due to some technical problem, the employee is forced into nonproductive time as he waits until the problem is fixed. This waiting time is conceptually equivalent to the employee making a personal phone call (and therefore being on strike).

PRODUCTIVE TIME

Productive time is the time in which employees *apply* their skills and talents to generate, or assist in the generation of, organizational wealth. Staff can only create value during productive time.

If an employee reads a document for 45 minutes, the employee's application of skill *only occurs at the end of the 45 minutes. Hence, the 45 minutes of reading time is essentially nonproductive time.* As staff only become productive when they apply information, knowledge reengineering should be used wherever possible.

Negative Conversion

When productive time is translated into nonproductive time, *negative conversion* occurs (IIS4001.D20)—see Figure 16.3. Negative conversion decreases

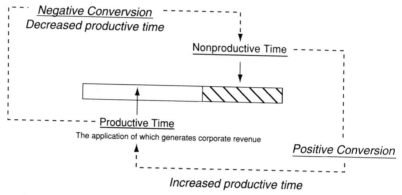

FIGURE 16.3   Relationship between productive and nonproductive time.

organizational profitability. Average employees lose 40% or more of their productive time due to the impact of nonproductive activities.

> The average worker is productive only 55 percent of the time. —*James Field, Los Angeles Times*

Negative Conversion Generates Intangible Costs

Whenever negative conversion occurs, intangible costs always follow (IIS4001. L51). By tracking the incidence of negative conversion, you can identify activities that generate intangible costs.

Positive Conversion Reduces Intangible Costs

Positive conversion is the opposite of negative conversion. Positive conversion occurs when nonproductive time is converted into productive time (IIS4001. D21). By converting nonproductive time into productive time, you decrease the costs generated by time, people, and knowledge. *Positive conversion reduces intangible costs* (IIS4001.L52).

Positive Conversion and Artificial Employment

Increasing productive time increases revenue generation capacity *without* the associated wage and other costs typically associated with increased employment (IIS4001.L53). Time captured by positive conversion allows a firm to engage in *artificial employment* (IIS17001.C3).

To understand artificial employment, consider four employees (employed for 1800 hours each year) working at 50% productivity. As a group, the employees create 3600 hours (4 × 900 hours) for the organization, out of a potential 7200 hours (4 × 1800 hours). If the group could decrease negative conversion by 1800 hours, this would be equivalent to hiring two additional employees (because each employee was only originally productive for 900 hours) at $0 wage cost (because no additional employment has occurred).

Because most organizations are seriously understaffed, this artificial increase in employment has the potential to generate significant amounts of revenue for the firm while lowering overall costs.

> Creating, facilitating, and managing artificial employment needs to be a major priority within firms.

Getting What You Pay For

If an organization pays $25,000,000 in employee expenses, then it is reasonable for the business to want 100% of the value associated with that payment. If employees are 50% productive, the organization only receives 50% of the value, but pays 100% of the cost. Intangible management assists organizations to get what they paid for—paying 100% of the cost and receiving the maximum amount of sustainable value.

NONDISRUPTIVE CHANGE

Working smarter not harder is the focus of intangible management. By strategically identifying activities that can enhance productive time, while reducing intangible costs, the organization gains access to increased productivity and artificial employment and decreases its relative cost base.

For example, leveraging knowledge through knowledge management practices can create significant gains. If employees use computers for the majority of their day, teaching them touch-typing could increase productivity dramatically because the intangible costs associated with time assets are decreased. Usually staff will use two or more programs on a regular basis—train them in the use of these programs to dramatically increase the productivity of knowledge assets.

Making life easier for staff by strategically managing knowledge, relationships, emotions, and time creates higher productivity, higher quality, reduced costs, and greater revenue. Most importantly, this type of change is significantly less disruptive than the change created by restructuring, process reengineering, downsizing, etc.

INTANGIBLE COST ANALYSIS

Intangible cost analysis allows executives to identify, measure, and reduce costs that the organization has always been aware of, but has not been able to previously measure and control.

Practically every preceding chapter has illustrated that intangible management provides new ways of increasing productivity and profitability while simultaneously cutting costs. These new ways are designed to reflect the realities of today's economic environment. Today, we cannot simply assess an activity on the strength of its "tangible cost." *This is because, when producing "intangible goods" (services), the majority of the benefits of the product are intangible and the majority of the costs of producing that product are also intangible.*

IIS4002 INTANGIBLE COST MANAGEMENT STANDARD

If a coin has two sides, then the IIS4002 standard is the other side of the accounting industry's standards. Whereas the accounting industry expertly measures financial transactions, IIS4002 expertly measures activities that generate intangible costs. Today, organizations require an accounting analysis and an IIS4002 analysis to determine the true costs and true benefits associated with managing operations.

An organization with knowledge of only one or the other type of costs has only a part of the picture. Today, executives need to have access to both sides of the coin. For corporate governance issues, managers and executives need to understand tangible and intangible costs. Without both sides of the costing picture, executives can potentially make decisions that could adversely affect the profitability and performance of their organization.

LOWEST TANGIBLE COST RULE

Traditionally people have applied the *lowest tangible cost rule* to determine the value of activities. This rule states:

> The choice between two competing alternatives is typically made by selecting the alternative (1) with the lowest tangible cost, and/or (2) that generates the lowest ongoing financial costs. (IIS4002.L5)

This old rule can lead people to make incorrect decisions. Decisions based on the lowest tangible cost rule ignore the fact that activities have numerous cost components (not just one). These components include knowledge costs, relationship costs, emotional costs and time costs. The solution to the lowest tangible cost rule is to use the *lowest total real cost rule*. The lowest total real cost rule assists people to make the most profitable decision based on all facts:

> The choice between two competing alternatives must be made by selecting the alternative with the lowest total real cost (tangible costs + intangible costs). (IIS4002.L10)

A COMPLEMENTARY SKILL: COST QUALITY

The IIS4001 standard extensively supports existing accounting frameworks by assisting executives to understand how changes in financial transactions can either increase or decrease intangible costs. IIS4002 is therefore a bridge between conventional management and intangible management.

Cost Quality

As previous chapters have shown financial transactions influence intangible transactions and vice versa:

Financial transactions ⇔ Intangible transactions

When we are referring to costs, costs can do a wide variety of things to intangible transactions. IIS4002 deals with the potential consequences on intangible transactions of changing financial transactions.

IIS4002 Inferior Cost Quality

If a financial cost is decreased, but the reduction in that cost causes a chain of events that increases intangible costs, then that cost reduction activity is said to have *inferior cost quality*. Twelve types of inferior cost quality interactions are identified under International Intangible Standards and are discussed in the Following sections.

Level 1 Inferior Cost Quality

This occurs when only one intangible asset is decreased due to a change in expenses. Four level 1 inferior cost quality types can result from a decrease in expenses and four level 1 inferior costs can result from an increase in expenses (Table 16.2).

Level 2 Inferior Cost Quality

This occurs when any two intangible assets are decreased due to a change in expenses. Six level 2 inferior cost quality types can result from a reduction in expenses and six can result from an increase in expenses (Table 16.3).

TABLE 16.2   Level 1 Inferior Cost Quality Categories

↓↑	IIS4002 code	Knowledge assets	Relationship assets	Emotional assets	Time assets
↓ Expense	IIS4002.C100	↓			
↓ Expense	IIS4002.C101		↓		
↓ Expense	IIS4002.C102			↓	
↓ Expense	IIS4002.C103				↓
↑ Expense	IIS4002.C100i	↓			
↑ Expense	IIS4002.C101i		↓		
↑ Expense	IIS4002.C102i			↓	
↑ Expense	IIS4002.C103i				↓

TABLE 16.3   Level 2 Inferior Cost Quality Categories

↓↑	IIS4002 code	Knowledge assets	Relationship assets	Emotional assets	Time assets
↓ Expense	IIS4002.C201	↓	↓		
↓ Expense	IIS4002.C202	↓		↓	
↓ Expense	IIS4002.C203	↓			↓
↓ Expense	IIS4002.C204		↓	↓	
↓ Expense	IIS4002.C205		↓		↓
↓ Expense	IIS4002.C206			↓	↓
↑ Expense	IIS4002.C201i	↓	↓		
↑ Expense	IIS4002.C202i	↓		↓	
↑ Expense	IIS4002.C203i	↓			↓
↑ Expense	IIS4002.C204i		↓	↓	
↑ Expense	IIS4002.C205i		↓		↓
↑ Expense	IIS4002.C206i			↓	↓

Level 3 Inferior Cost Quality

This occurs when any three intangible assets are decreased due to a change in expenses. Four level 3 inferior cost quality types can result from a decrease in expenses and another four can result from an increase in costs (Table 16.4).

Level 4 Inferior Cost Quality

This occurs when all four intangible assets are decreased due to a change in expenses. The two level 4 inferior cost quality types are shown in Table 16.5.

IIS4002 Superior Cost Quality

The opposite of inferior cost quality is superior cost quality. Superior cost quality occurs when a change in tangible costs leads to an increase in one or more intangible assets.

Level 1 Superior Cost Quality

This occurs when only one intangible asset is increased due to a change in expenses. Four of the eight level 1 superior cost quality types relate to a reduction in expenses and four to an increase in expenses (Table 16.6).

Level 2 Superior Cost Quality

This occurs when any two intangible assets are increased due to a change in expenses. The twelve level 2 superior cost quality types are shown in Table 16.7.

TABLE 16.4   Level 3 Inferior Cost Quality Categories

↓↑	IIS4002 code	Knowledge assets	Relationship assets	Emotional assets	Time assets
↓ Expense	IIS4002.C301	↓	↓	↓	
↓ Expense	IIS4002.C302	↓		↓	↓
↓ Expense	IIS4002.C303		↓	↓	↓
↓ Expense	IIS4002.C304	↓	↓		↓
↑ Expense	IIS4002.C301i	↓	↓	↓	
↑ Expense	IIS4002.C302i	↓		↓	↓
↑ Expense	IIS4002.C303i		↓	↓	↓
↑ Expense	IIS4002.C304i	↓	↓		↓

TABLE 16.5   Level 4 Inferior Cost Quality Categories

↓↑	IIS4002 code	Knowledge assets	Relationship assets	Emotional assets	Time assets
↓ Expense	IIS4002.C401	↓	↓	↓	↓
↑ Expense	IIS4002.C401i	↓	↓	↓	↓

TABLE 16.6   Level 1 Superior Cost Quality Categories

↓↑	IIS4002 code	Knowledge assets	Relationship assets	Emotional assets	Time assets
↓ Expense	IIS4002.C131	↑	–	–	–
↓ Expense	IIS4002.C132	–	↑	–	–
↓ Expense	IIS4002.C133	–	–	↑	–
↓ Expense	IIS4002.C134	–	–	–	↑
↑ Expense	IIS4002.C131i	↑	–	–	–
↑ Expense	IIS4002.C132i	–	↑	–	–
↑ Expense	IIS4002.C133i	–	–	↑	–
↑ Expense	IIS4002.C134i	–	–	–	↑

TABLE16.7   Level 2 Superior Cost Quality Categories

↓↑	IIS4002 code	Knowledge assets	Relationship assets	Emotional assets	Time assets
↓ Expense	IIS4002.C231	↑	↑	–	–
↓ Expense	IIS4002.C232	↑	–	↑	–
↓ Expense	IIS4002.C233	↑	–	–	↑
↓ Expense	IIS4002.C234	–	↑	↑	–
↓ Expense	IIS4002.C235	–	↑	–	↑
↓ Expense	IIS4002.C236	–	–	↑	↑
↑ Expense	IIS4002.C231i	↑	↑	–	–
↑ Expense	IIS4002.C232i	↑	–	↑	–
↑ Expense	IIS4002.C233i	↑	–	–	↑
↑ Expense	IIS4002.C234i	–	↑	↑	–
↑ Expense	IIS4002.C235i	–	↑	–	↑
↑ Expense	IIS4002.C236i	–	–	↑	↑

Level 3 Superior Cost Quality

This occurs when any three intangible assets are increased due to a change in expenses. The eight level 3 superior cost quality types are shown in Table 16.8.

Level 4 Superior Cost Quality

This occurs when all four intangible assets are increased due to a change in expenses. The two level 4 superior cost quality types are shown in Table 16.9.

Statistical Combination Theory

Those familiar with mathematics and statistics will note that superior and inferior cost quality elements have been determined by combination theory, a subset of probability theory in statistics. To determine how many types of level 2 inferior cost quality elements there are, simply apply the standard combination formula:

$$C(n, \ k) = 2\left(\frac{n!}{k!(n-k)!}\right), \tag{16.2}$$

TABLE 16.8   Level 3 Superior Cost Quality Categories

↓↑	IIS4002 code	Knowledge assets	Relationship assets	Emotional assets	Time assets
↓ Expense	IIS4002.C331	↑	↑	↑	–
↓ Expense	IIS4002.C332	↑	–	↑	↑
↓ Expense	IIS4002.C333	–	↑	↑	↑
↓ Expense	IIS4002.C334	↑	↑	–	↑
↑ Expense	IIS4002.C331i	↑	↑	↑	–
↑ Expense	IIS4002.C332i	↑	–	↑	↑
↑ Expense	IIS4002.C333i	–	↑	↑	↑
↑ Expense	IIS4002.C334i	↑	↑	–	↑

TABLE 16.9   Level 4 Superior Cost Quality Categories

↓↑	IIS4002 code	Knowledge assets	Relationship assets	Emotional assets	Time assets
↓ Expense	IIS4002.C431	↑	↑	↑	↑
↑ Expense	IIS4002.C431i	↑	↑	↑	↑

where n is the total number of elements under analysis (Four in this case: knowledge assets, relationship assets, emotional assets, and time assets) and K is the number of elements we are analyzing at each stage. For example, for a level 2 analysis, $k = 2$. For a level 1 analysis, $k = 1$, and for a level 4 analysis, $k = 4$. The term $n!$ means n factorial. For example, $4! = 4 \times 3 \times 2 \times 1$; $3! = 3 \times 2 \times 1$; $2! = 2 \times 1$; $1! = 1$; and $0! = 1$. The result is multiplied by 2 because superior and inferior cost quality is brought about by two options: decreasing cost or increasing cost. Hence, if you need to determine how many inferior level 2 cost quality elements an organization may experience, the equation (and workings) would be:

$$C(n,\ k) = 2\left(\frac{n!}{k!(n-k)!}\right) = C(4,\ 2) = 2\left(\frac{4!}{2!(4-2)!}\right)$$

$$= 2\left(\frac{4!}{2!(2)!}\right) = 2\left(\frac{4 \times 3 \times 2 \times 1}{2 \times 1(2 \times 1)}\right) \tag{16.3}$$

$$C(4,2) = 2\left(\frac{4 \times 3 \times 2 \times 1}{2 \times 1(2 \times 1)}\right) = 2\left(\frac{4 \times 3}{2 \times 1}\right) = 2\left(\frac{12}{2}\right) = 2(6) = 12.$$

This figure agrees with International Intangible Standard IIS4002.

IIS4002 Hybrid Cost Quality

The inferiority or superiority of changing an expense will typically result in a combination of value changes in knowledge assets, relationship assets, emotional assets and time assets. It is reasonable for some intangible assets to increase in value whereas others may decrease in value or remain constant. Hybrid cost quality is used to measure potential combinations of changes in *intangible value* when compared to changes in financial value.

Level 1 Hybrid Cost Quality

By definition, hybrid value changes require more than one intangible asset to change in value. As such, there cannot be any level 1 hybrid cost quality measures.

Level 2 Hybrid Cost Quality

This occurs when there is a change in any two intangible assets due to a change in expenses. There are 24 potential cost quality changes at the level 2 hybrid cost quality level, as shown in Table 16.10.

TABLE 16.10 Level 2 Hybrid Cost Quality Categories

↓↑	IIS4002 code	Knowledge assets	Relationship assets	Emotional assets	Time assets
↓ Expense	IIS4002.C251	↑	–	↓	–
↓ Expense	IIS4002.C252	↑	–	–	↓
↓ Expense	IIS4002.C253	↑	↓	–	–
↓ Expense	IIS4002.C254	↓	↑	–	–
↓ Expense	IIS4002.C255	↓	–	↑	–
↓ Expense	IIS4002.C256	↓	–	–	↑
↓ Expense	IIS4002.C257	–	↑	↓	–
↓ Expense	IIS4002.C258	–	↑	–	↓
↓ Expense	IIS4002.C259	–	↓	↑	–
↓ Expense	IIS4002.C260	–	↓	–	↑
↓ Expense	IIS4002.C261	–	–	↑	↓
↓ Expense	IIS4002.C262	–	–	↓	↑
↑ Expense	IIS4002.C251i	↑	↓	–	–
↑ Expense	IIS4002.C252i	↑	–	↓	–
↑ Expense	IIS4002.C253i	↑	–	–	↓
↑ Expense	IIS4002.C254i	↓	↑	–	–
↑ Expense	IIS4002.C255i	↓	–	↑	–
↑ Expense	IIS4002.C256i	↓	–	–	↑
↑ Expense	IIS4002.C257i	–	↑	↓	–
↑ Expense	IIS4002.C258i	–	↑	–	↓
↑ Expense	IIS4002.C259i	–	↓	↑	–
↑ Expense	IIS4002.C260i	–	↓	–	↑
↑ Expense	IIS4002.C261i	–	–	↑	↓
↑ Expense	IIS4002.C262i	–	–	↓	↑

Level 3 Hybrid Cost Quality

This occurs when any three intangible assets are decreased due to a change in expenses. There are 24 level 3 inferior cost quality types that can result from a decrease in expenses and 24 that can result from an increase in costs. The 24 hybrid events for a decrease in expenses are shown in Table 16.11 and the 24 hybrid events for an increase in expenses are shown in Table 16.12.

TABLE 16.11   Level 3 Hybrid Cost Quality Categories for a Decrease in Expenses

↓↑	IIS4002 code	Knowledge assets	Relationship assets	Emotional assets	Time assets
↓ Expense	IIS4002.C350	↑	↑	↓	–
↓ Expense	IIS4002.C351	↑	↑	–	↓
↓ Expense	IIS4002.C352	↑	↓	↓	–
↓ Expense	IIS4002.C353	↑	↓	↑	–
↓ Expense	IIS4002.C354	↑	↓	–	↓
↓ Expense	IIS4002.C355	↑	↓	–	↑
↓ Expense	IIS4002.C356	↑	–	↑	↓
↓ Expense	IIS4002.C357	↑	–	↓	↓
↓ Expense	IIS4002.C358	↓	↑	↑	–
↓ Expense	IIS4002.C359	↓	↑	↓	–
↓ Expense	IIS4002.C360	↓	↑	–	↓
↓ Expense	IIS4002.C361	↓	↑	–	↑
↓ Expense	IIS4002.C362	↓	↓	↑	–
↓ Expense	IIS4002.C363	↓	↓	–	↑
↓ Expense	IIS4002.C364	↓	–	↑	↓
↓ Expense	IIS4002.C365	↓	–	↑	↑
↓ Expense	IIS4002.C366	↓	–	↓	↑
↓ Expense	IIS4002.C367	↓	–	↓	↑
↓ Expense	IIS4002.C368	–	↑	↓	↓
↓ Expense	IIS4002.C369	–	↑	↑	↓
↓ Expense	IIS4002.C370	–	↓	↑	↓
↓ Expense	IIS4002.C371	–	↓	↑	↑
↓ Expense	IIS4002.C372	–	↓	↓	↑
↓ Expense	IIS4002.C373	–	↓	↓	↑

Level 4 Hybrid Cost Quality

International Intangible Standards identify 24 level 4 hybrid cost quality types for a decrease in expenses (Table 16.13) and 24 level 4 hybrid cost quality types for an increase in expenses (Table 16.14).

SUMMARIZING COST QUALITY

It is essential to understand that for every increase or decrease in a financial transaction, there is a potential change to knowledge assets, relationship

TABLE 16.12   Level 3 Hybrid Cost Quality Categories for an Increase in Expenses

↓↑	IIS4002 code	Knowledge assets	Relationship assets	Emotional assets	Time assets
↑ Expense	IIS4002.C350i	↑	↑	↓	–
↑ Expense	IIS4002.C351i	↑	↑	–	↓
↑ Expense	IIS4002.C352i	↑	↓	↓	–
↑ Expense	IIS4002.C353i	↑	↓	↑	–
↑ Expense	IIS4002.C354i	↑	↓	–	↓
↑ Expense	IIS4002.C355i	↑	↓	–	↑
↑ Expense	IIS4002.C356i	↑	–	↑	↓
↑ Expense	IIS4002.C357i	↑	–	↓	↓
↑ Expense	IIS4002.C358i	↓	↑	↑	–
↑ Expense	IIS4002.C359i	↓	↑	↓	–
↑ Expense	IIS4002.C360i	↓	↑	–	↓
↑ Expense	IIS4002.C361i	↓	↑	–	↑
↑ Expense	IIS4002.C362i	↓	↓	↑	–
↑ Expense	IIS4002.C363i	↓	↓	–	↑
↑ Expense	IIS4002.C364i	↓	–	↑	↓
↑ Expense	IIS4002.C365i	↓	–	↑	↑
↑ Expense	IIS4002.C366i	↓	–	↓	↑
↑ Expense	IIS4002.C367i	↓	–	↓	↑
↑ Expense	IIS4002.C368i	–	↑	↓	↓
↑ Expense	IIS4002.C369i	–	↑	↑	↓
↑ Expense	IIS4002.C370i	–	↓	↑	↓
↑ Expense	IIS4002.C371i	–	↓	↑	↑
↑ Expense	IIS4002.C372i	–	↓	↓	↑
↑ Expense	IIS4002.C373i	–	↓	↓	↑

assets, emotional assets, and/or time assets. In the analysis above we identified 172 cost quality types, which are categorized in Table 16.15.

THE MANAGEMENT RAMIFICATIONS OF COST QUALITY

Currently management uses management systems that are not compliant
with International Intangible Standards. As a result, a *reduction in expenses* is

TABLE 16.13   Level 4 Hybrid Cost Quality Categories for a Decrease in Expenses

↓↑	IIS4002 code	Knowledge assets	Relationship assets	Emotional assets	Time assets
↓ Expense	IIS4002.C451	↑	↓	↓	↓
↓ Expense	IIS4002.C452	↑	↑	↓	↓
↓ Expense	IIS4002.C453	↑	↓	↑	↓
↓ Expense	IIS4002.C454	↑	↓	↓	↑
↓ Expense	IIS4002.C455	↑	↑	↑	↓
↓ Expense	IIS4002.C456	↑	↑	↓	↑
↓ Expense	IIS4002.C457	↑	↑	↑	↓
↓ Expense	IIS4002.C458	↑	↓	↑	↑
↓ Expense	IIS4002.C459	↓	↑	↑	↑
↓ Expense	IIS4002.C460	↓	↓	↓	↑
↓ Expense	IIS4002.C461	↓	↓	↑	↓
↓ Expense	IIS4002.C462	↓	↑	↓	↓
↓ Expense	IIS4002.C463	↓	↑	↑	↑
↓ Expense	IIS4002.C464	↓	↓	↑	↑
↓ Expense	IIS4002.C465	↓	↑	↓	↑
↓ Expense	IIS4002.C466	↓	↑	↑	↓
↓ Expense	IIS4002.C467	↓	↓	↓	↑
↓ Expense	IIS4002.C468	↓	↓	↑	↓
↓ Expense	IIS4002.C469	↓	↓	↓	↑
↓ Expense	IIS4002.C470	↓	↑	↓	↓
↓ Expense	IIS4002.C471	↑	↓	↓	↓
↓ Expense	IIS4002.C472	↑	↑	↑	↑
↓ Expense	IIS4002.C473	↑	↑	↓	↑
↓ Expense	IIS4002.C474	↑	↓	↑	↑

typically always regarded as an activity that increases profit. From the above analysis, we know that a great number of factors intervene between a change in a financial transaction and the ultimate profitability of the organization. Managers and executives need to be aware and know how a change in a financial transaction could influence knowledge assets, relationship assets, emotional assets, and time assets and how these changes could influence financial performance.

$$\Delta \text{ Financial transaction} \to \Delta \text{ Intangible asset} \to$$
$$\Delta \text{ Organizational performance} \to \Delta \text{ Financial performance}$$

TABLE 16.14 Level 4 Hybrid Cost Quality Categories for an Increase in Expenses

↓↑	IIS4002 code	Knowledge assets	Relationship assets	Emotional assets	Time assets
↑ Expense	IIS4002.C451i	↑	↓	↓	↓
↑ Expense	IIS4002.C452i	↑	↑	↓	↓
↑ Expense	IIS4002.C453i	↑	↓	↑	↓
↑ Expense	IIS4002.C454i	↑	↓	↓	↑
↑ Expense	IIS4002.C455i	↑	↑	↑	↓
↑ Expense	IIS4002.C456i	↑	↑	↓	↑
↑ Expense	IIS4002.C457i	↑	↑	↑	↓
↑ Expense	IIS4002.C458i	↑	↓	↑	↑
↑ Expense	IIS4002.C459i	↓	↑	↑	↑
↑ Expense	IIS4002.C460i	↓	↓	↓	↑
↑ Expense	IIS4002.C461i	↓	↓	↑	↓
↑ Expense	IIS4002.C462i	↓	↑	↓	↓
↑ Expense	IIS4002.C463i	↓	↑	↑	↑
↑ Expense	IIS4002.C464i	↓	↓	↑	↑
↑ Expense	IIS4002.C465i	↓	↑	↓	↑
↑ Expense	IIS4002.C466i	↓	↑	↑	↓
↑ Expense	IIS4002.C467i	↓	↓	↓	↑
↑ Expense	IIS4002.C468i	↓	↓	↑	↓
↑ Expense	IIS4002.C469i	↓	↓	↓	↑
↑ Expense	IIS4002.C470i	↓	↑	↓	↓
↑ Expense	IIS4002.C471i	↑	↓	↓	↓
↑ Expense	IIS4002.C472i	↑	↑	↑	↓
↑ Expense	IIS4002.C473i	↑	↑	↓	↑
↑ Expense	IIS4002.C474i	↑	↓	↑	↑

TABLE 16.15 The 172 Cost Quality Types Identified by IIS4002

Level	Inferior cost quality	Superior cost quality	Hybrid cost quality	Totals
1	8	8	N/A	16
2	12	12	24	48
3	4	4	48	56
4	2	2	48	52
Total	26	26	120	172

INTANGIBLES AND ORGANIZATIONAL PERFORMANCE

International Intangible Standards were used to determine 172 potential intangible effects that could occur when expenses were increased or decreased
in an organization. Once we know how the organization's intangible assets
have been affected, we need to determine the financial impact of a changed
intangible asset value on the organization's performance. To do this, IIS4002
makes the link between intangible asset performance and organizational performance.

How Intangible Performance Affects
Organizational Performance

The value proposition of the majority of for-profit organizations can be
reduced to a simple diagram (Figure 16.4). This diagram illustrates that it is
the intersection between organizational capabilities and market opportunities
that generates value for an organization. The quality and quantity of knowledge assets, relationship assets, emotional assets, and time assets *directly
influence* the size of the value intersection.

The value proposition of the majority of government and non profit organizations can also be reduced to a simple diagram (Figure 16.5). This diagram
illustrates that it is the intersection between the government's capabilities and
the public's requirements (and opportunities) that generates value for the
government and for the economy as a whole. Again, the quality and quantity
of knowledge assets, relationship assets, emotional assets, and time assets
directly influence the size of the value intersection.

The government also plays a key role in the private sector. International
Intangible Standards acknowledge that government policies can either

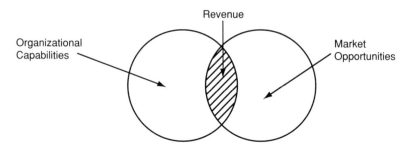

FIGURE 16.4   Linking intangible performance to organizational performance.

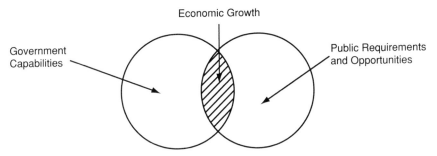

FIGURE 16.5   Linking intangible performance to government performance.

increase or decrease corporate value creation in the private sector. Government policies aimed at employment, interest rates, exchange rates, inflation rates, and taxation rates all influence corporate performance. Often government employees will state that "the government does not make money" and is therefore different from private enterprise. International Intangible Standards view the role of government differently. Governments can make, or break, an economic system and determine the level of investment security, GDP, social capital, personal security, and many other factors that are directly related to an economic system's inherent prosperity. In this sense, government is looked as the enabler of business and the value of an initiative can be distributed across an industry or the whole economic system. International Intangible Standards also acknowledge that democratic governments create policies that balance economic development against public interest. As such, unfavorable policies can be passed that decrease the election attractiveness of the reigning political power. Typically, government policies will tend to give an advantage one economic interest group over another.

In today's economy, the quality and relevance of corporate and government knowledge assets, relationship assets, emotional assets, and time assets are the factors that attract business or repel business from an organization, an industry, a sector, or a whole economy.

DETERMINING INTANGIBLE VALUE

International Intangible Standards assess value creation, maintenance, expansion, and management by assessing value changes in knowledge assets, relationship assets, emotional assets, and time assets.

Old Methods: Why They Cannot Solve the Problem

Many people have attempted to reformulate *old* management methods and principles to solve the new problem of intangibles. While the application of old techniques to an incremental change in the complexity of an *existing* problem can yield positive results, the application of old techniques to a totally new problem yields poor results at best, or misleading results, or diversionary results at worst.

Traditional management systems were designed to measure the flows of financial transactions that resulted from tangibles. The balance sheet captured the value of the business as the total financial value of the assets of the business. The income statement measured the wealth generated from leveraging tangible assets. Ownership of tangibles (factories, raw materials, etc.) was critical if the business was to compete effectively against its rivals. Economies of scale and scope resulted from mass production, which led to lower prices and greater market penetration. Assets, capital, equity, and debt were the critical issues. All of these factors were "glued together" by assessing the financial transactions in which business engaged. Traditional systems therefore managed value by identifying, classifying, recording, analyzing, valuing, and reporting changes in financial transactions. Intangible issues were ignored, because they did not obey the old rules. In other words, intangibles were "off the radar screen" (and still are) of conventional management systems.

New Methods: Solving the Problem

International Intangible Standards put intangibles on the management radar screen of corporate, private and government organizations by using a completely new system of identifying, classifying, recording, analyzing, measuring, reporting, and managing *intangible* value.

To understand International Intangible Standards, you need to regard all products and services simply as a bundle of knowledge assets, relationship assets, emotional assets, and time assets. You need to see through the tangible façade and look at what customers are actually purchasing: *expectations of future value.*

If customers today are buying expectations of future value across the four categories of intangible assets (knowledge assets, relationship assets, emotional assets, and time assets), then the value proposition of the intangibles needs to be first established. Quarter 1 (precontractual rights) of the value creation process explains that customers must spend time determining if organizational intangible assets meet the customer's specific requirements and needs. If the return on intangible investment is too low for the customer, that customer will switch out of the organization and have their needs fulfilled by another, more capable, competitor(s).

Hence, time needs to be expended by the customer to understand the value of the bundle of intangible rights inherent within the product or service. Time also has to be spent by employees in explaining the unique value proposition to the customer.

The second quarter describes the effectiveness of the organization in leveraging its knowledge assets, relationship assets, emotional assets, and time assets to deliver customer value (performing the contract). If the return on intangible investment is too low, the customer will rescind (nullify) the contract and switch out of the organization and have their needs fulfilled by another, more capable, competitor(s).

Again, time needs to be expended by the customer to understand how well the organization delivers the value of the bundle of expected intangible rights inherent within the product or service. Employees also have to spend time supplying that value to the customer.

In quarter 3, the money for successfully satisfied contracts is collected. In the game of business, the third quarter always comes after the first and the second. Many business executives feel that the third quarter is the only one they need to manage. This book has shown that organizations that only manage the third quarter will fail in the intangible economy. It is now critical to manage *all* quarters of the game.

In the fourth quarter, the customer assesses if he will ever "play ball" with the organization again. Customers will assess their overall return on intangible investment and determine if the firm has the capability to deliver the expected quality that customer demands *again*. If the customer decides to go back to the firm again (repeat business), that customer will assess the business at every stage. If the return on intangible investment is too low, even once, the customer will switch out and not give the organization repeat business again. Today, the "one strike and you are out" mentality dominates the thinking of most customers.

Throughout this discussion, *time* has been identified as a component of value creation in organizations. That time is divided between various categories:

1. *Employee time*: The time that staff are employed to work.
2. *Organizational time*: The sum of all individual employee times.
3. *Customer time*: The attention that customers give the organization's products and services on an individual basis.
4. *Firm time*: The sum of all customer times for the business.
5. *Industry time*: The sum of all firm times for the whole industry.
6. *Sector time*: The sum of all the industry times for specific sectors.
7. *Economic time*: The sum of the sector times for that economy.

8. *Economic impact time:* The sum of all economic times for the trading partners of an economy. Such times can be represented at any of the levels 1 to 7 above.

Where old value methods track the stock and flow of money, International Intangible Standards track the stock and flow of time and then use that to understand the stock and flow of money. Before we can launch into how these factors are used to measure intangible value, it is essential to understand intangible strategic management.

INTANGIBLE STRATEGIC MANAGEMENT

Many management methods argue that the only way for a business to be successful is to correctly implement and manage its strategy. From this perspective strategy is viewed as being top-down and rigid. Key performance indicators are put in place to assess the performance of staff and managers based on that strategy. In theory, such a system makes great sense. In practical terms, great difficulties surround the implementation of such systems.

The greatest difficulty is that markets now undergo *discontinuous* change. In the past markets were not subject to significant change because global markets were *unsaturated*. Geographical boundaries and tariff protection sheltered local producers from *competitive waves*. Today, the world is awash with competitive waves that become shorter and more destructive over time. With local tariffs all but removed and local economies subject to significant foreign investment, it is harder for companies to devise a strategy that will remain relevant for any period longer than 12 to 24 months. The competitive landscape of the past was a very different place: 30 to 40 years ago managers made 15- to 25-year plans, now strategic plans seldom cover more than 2 years at a time.

Intangible strategic management acknowledges the new rules of the Intangible Economy and formulates strategies with these facts in mind. Because markets now discontinuously change, it is important to move past setting strategies on the basis of continuity. A market now and that same market in 12 months time will be very different. The strategy applied to the market now may work, but in 12 months' time the same strategy may bankrupt an organization.

Intangible Strategic Measurement

Strategy in the past was measured with reference to key performance indicators, or KPIs. Staff were assessed against KPIs as were managers and executives. Those familiar with the concept of intellectual capital will understand that conventional intellectual statements are really nothing more than a collection of KPIs grouped under specific headings.

We can measure the impact of strategy in two ways: (1) through strategy-dependent measures (referred to as subjective methods) and (2) through strategy-independent measures (referred to as objective methods).

Objective measures do not reduce the strategic importance or applicability of subjective measures, because the two areas perform different tasks. Subjective measures are used for internal decision making with a focus on implementing a cohesive *continuous* strategy. Objective measures assume that strategy will become discontinuous at some stage and therefore create a strategic measurement system that can be applied to the organization regardless of its strategy.

Subjective Strategic Measures

The two types of subjective strategic measures are (1) point measures and (2) indices. *Point measures* seek to identify various key success factors and key performance indicators within a business that are believed to drive business performance. For example, point measures may include time to establish a new office (time), percentage of employees under a certain age (%), the average training expenditure per employee ($), and so on. *Indices* seek to aggregate point measures into indexes that can be tracked over time. Much like the consumer price index (CPI), a bundle of representative goods is chosen and a weighting given to that bundle. It is the changes in the index that managers are most interested in measuring. Subjective measures although very powerful management tools, are "subjective" because they are chosen with respect to the company's strategy. To illustrate how subjectivity arises, let us consider four *identical* firms in the same industry. Each firm has a different strategy, as shown in Table 16.16. In accordance with each strategy, 20 key success factors (KSFs) are chosen. Each success factor will focus on the firm's core strategy. For example, the focus of Firm D (intelligence) will be different from that of Firm A (growth), and Firm C's focus (cost) will be different from that of Firm B (social responsibility). The key issue here is that while subjective methods assist management to work cohesively toward the

TABLE 16.16   Corporate Strategies of Four Identical Firms in the Same Industry

Firm	Firm's core strategy
A	To gain 100% market share
B	To be the leader in socially responsible production
C	To be the lowest cost producer
D	To be the "smartest firm" in the industry

firm's core strategy (which is critical), they do not give investors stable tools to make consistent investment decisions and uniform investment comparisons. This instability is due to three very sound reasons: (1) incorrect formation, (2) comparability, and (3) underlying component changes.

Downfall 1: Incorrect Formation

Subjective strategic measures disobey a fundamental mathematical law—the *law of mathematical consistency*. This law says that to maintain mathematical validity, you should only compare "apples to apples" and not "apples to oranges." In this sense, if you have three point measures—time (200 hours), money ($250,000), and a percentage (45%)—and you seek to aggregate them into an index, you are really making mathematical "fruit salad" because 200 hours, $250,000, and 45% cannot be mathematically compared because they are not the same units of measurement. Hence, the law of mathematical consistency ensures that only like units of measurements can be compared. Subjective strategic measurements are subjective because they create an apparently objective number (an index) that is formed from subjective quantities of dissimilar units that cannot reasonably be compared. As such, investors do not have enough information to make an objective and comparable investment decision.

Downfall 2: Comparability

Investors make investment decisions by comparing data. To illustrate, let us consider Firms A, B, C, and D from Table 16.16. Because each firm has different strategies, different point measures have been derived and different indices have been formed. For example, if the human capital index in Firm A rises by 12% and the human capital index rises by 10% for Firm D, how do investors know what firm creates a better investment decision? If the strategies of the firms were not accurately communicated, then an investor could select Firm A (aggressive growth) over Firm D (intelligence). Immediately different issues spring to mind: an increase of 10% from what? The basic trouble with indices is that they are relative measures (10% and 12%) instead of absolute measures ($10 million and $120,000).

Downfall 3: Underlying Component Changes

Most people have heard of "creative accounting," the practice of manipulating accounting data to make financial performance appear to be better than it actually is. It should come as no surprise then that a form of creative accounting can also be easily applied to subjective measures. For example, let's assume that investors only make decisions based on movements in subjective indices. If Firm C has the highest increase in a specific subjective index, it will gain investment funds at the expense of the other firms. If Firm A is an unscrupulous firm that wants to aggressively attract funds to pursue its aggressive market dominance strategy, all it needs to do is change the underlying components of its subjective index so that the resulting figure is greater than that of other firms. There are many easy ways to this. Assuming the index was composed of 20 key success factors (selected from 100), where 11 factors were high performing and the remaining 9 were well below average, the firm only needs to discard the 9 low-performing factors and replace them with 9 high-performing factors from the 80 nonincluded factors. Another method: Simply increase the weightings of the 11 high-performing factors and significantly decrease the weightings of the low-performing 9 factors. Another method: Simply discard the low-performing measures all together. Another method: Readjust the values of the low-performing measures to make them high-performing measures. All of these methods artificially increase the perception of value of a firm.

To solve the significant problems associated with subjective strategic measures, objective strategic measures were developed by the International Intangible Management Standards Institute.

Objective Strategic Measures

When you lodge your tax return with the IRS, the IRS is neutral to your strategy. It doesn't let you pay *less* tax because you wish to pursue aggressive sales growth (Firm A) as opposed to a knowledge maximization strategy (Firm D). It just wants the money! In much the same way, investors just want to be ensured that they are investing their hard-earned dollars in a firm that will generate sustainable value. If an executive decision potentially destroys sustainable value for short-term gain, International Intangible Standards provide tools to help decipher the potential financial impacts.

According to the Intangible Finance Standard, an objective measurement metric must possess eighteen (18) fundamental characteristics:

1. *Universal comparability.* One firm's strategy needs to be objectively comparable to another firm's, irrespective of either firm's strategy or industry. Objective strategic measures ignore strategy and concentrate on how the firm actually created value. (IIS6001.L1)
2. *Strategic security.* The methods, techniques, and processes that an organization uses to creates organizational value represent a premium knowledge asset to the organization. If an organization were to communicate this premium strategy to its competitors, it would find its margins

and profits decreasing as the competition used the organization's strategy against itself (IIS6001.L11). Objective strategic measures are measured in time and/or dollars and therefore do not convey *how* the results were obtained. Strategic security is essential in reducing the potential of competitive harm brought about through disclosure. (IIS6001.L5)

3. *Consistency, verifiability, and auditability.* Investors need assurances that the underlying conceptual basis on which a strategic measure is formed will not change over time (i.e., a reweighting of indices or a shuffling of underlying point measures (IIS6001.L3)). Hence, the same factors must be used from one year to the next and to the next, in all industries. Objective strategic measures use the common metric of time to measure the effectiveness and efficiency of an organization's strategy.

4. *Metric solidity.* Objective strategic measures are formed in accordance with the laws of mathematical consistency (IIS6001.L3) (remember "apples to apples").

5. *Strategy independence.* Objective strategic measures are formed without any regard to a firm's strategy. This alleviates any problems with subjectively choosing one key success factor over another, or subjectively weighting one factor higher than another. Only time is measured, from multiple perspectives. (IIS6001.L4)

6. *Nonvolatile financial results.* Objective strategic measures are universally comparable, between firms, industries, departments, divisions, and the like because they are measured from a consistent time basis. This time basis is then compared to the firm's actual financial performance, and through a series of calculations we can determine how applied time was used to create financial value. The reverse engineering of actual financial performance into intangible performance creates a more detailed picture of how an organization created value. Such results are nonvolatile because they are derived from the organization's actual performance and therefore reflective of current competitive, economic, and other factors. (IIS6001.L5)

7. *Reliable recognition.* International Intangible Standards create an extremely reliable picture of the *operational value* of intangibles because these values are derived specifically from how the organization uses time to create financial performance. Fundamentally, time performance is matched against intangible performance and actual financial performance. Investors therefore know how the company has made its money without understanding how the result was actually achieved through the implementation of organizational strategy. (IIS6001.L12)

8. *Supplemental to conventional reports.* Using IIS5001 it is now possible to report the operational value of intangibles using a familiar (yet different) financial reporting model. IIS5001 allows businesses to create intangible

balance sheets, intangible income statements, and intangible cash flow statements. These statements are constructed in accordance with IIS5001 and supplement conventional accounting reports. (IIS6001.L14)

9. *Complementary results.* Accounting performance (third quarter performance) is actually financial performance that has been diluted (or decreased) due to the mismanagement of knowledge assets, relationship assets, emotional assets, and time assets. As such, the importance of financial results and financial reporting is unchanged by the introduction of International Intangible Standards. Intangible results are used to show performance in Q1 (precontractual), Q2 (contract performance), and Q4 (organizational performance) and how improvements in intangible assets can be used to increase the performance in Q3 (financial performance). (IIS6001.L15)

10. *Investor assessment or voluntary disclosure.* International Intangible Standards that relate to intangible finance allow investors to assess the intangible performance of practically any organization from a superficial level. Often unique initiatives exist within organizations that increase the value of knowledge assets, relationship assets, emotional assets, and time assets. Voluntary disclosure by organizations is a way to ensure that investors are aware of special initiatives that build intangible value within the organization. Voluntary reporting gives organizations a better chance of attracting capital and building the value of their organization. (IIS6001.L16)

11. *Easily generated internal reports.* Using the IIS5001 standard, it is relatively easy for organizations to generate periodic intangible reports that can be used to better manage the value creation process of the organization. Due to the advanced nature of International Intangible Standards, it is now possible to determine intangible value movements in all divisions of a business, including support departments (which were previously only regarded as cost centers). (IIS6001.L17)

12. *Cost center value assessment.* Although implied in the preceding point, International Intangible Standards can calculate value for cost centers such as information technology, human resources, engineering, research and development, administration, technical support, and so on. Departments were regarded as cost centers under conventional management methods because managers did not possess the tools or knowledge to attach value to departments that did not directly produce revenue. As such, support departments were frequently starved of funding. IIS5001 assists in understanding total value creation. (IIS6001.L17)

13. *Ignores old factors of production.* Land, labor, and capital were the old wealth creators—the old "factors of production." Because knowledge assets, relationship assets, emotional assets, and time assets are now

responsible for the creation and delivery of wealth, it is these factors of production that must be measured and managed. More than 70% of the workforce is employed in the services sector of the economy (producing services, defined by economics as "intangible goods"), so it is essential to ignore old factors of production such as land and capital, because they are not critical to this economic system's value creation process. (IIS6001.L18)

14. *Holistic value management.* Objective strategic measures connecting decision quality to movements in cycle time, productivity, revenue, market value, and share price across revenue-generating divisions and support divisions. (IIS6001.L8)

15. *Universal application.* International Intangible Standards are applicable to government departments, private unlisted firms, insurance companies, nonprofit organizations and publicly traded corporations (IIS6001.L9). Objective measures are applicable to any type of business in any type of industry. (IIS6001.L10)

16. *Value focused.* Substantial differences exist among cost, value, and price. Cost is the financial transaction required to create value. Prices are set in accordance with average perceived competitive value to customers. As such, value is the key issue, not cost. If a product or service is of no value to a customer, then the price is immaterial, because the customer will not buy. Organizations must stop focusing on cost and start focusing on value because it is value that creates organizational performance. Objective strategic measures financially measure the value of time within an organization, and this value can be used as the basis of decisions to increase or decrease costs by understanding how costs impact intangible performance. (IIS6001.L7)

17. *Relevance.* The most important issue regarding intangible value determined by IIS5001 is that the value is exceptionally relevant to decision making. (IIS6001.L6)

18. *Beyond financial transactions.* In the past, the measurement of intangibles was strictly limited to recording or estimating financial transactions. For example, *goodwill* (the sale of a business for more than the book value of its assets) could only occur when the sale was made (because the sale involved an exchange of money). If the financial transaction did not occur, then the business (assuming a private unlisted corporation) would have $0 goodwill. As we have seen above, financial performance is the third quarter of the value creation process and is derived from the intangible performance of the first and second quarters. International Intangible Standards acknowledge that it is intangibles that create financial transactions, not the other way around (as was previously thought). (IIS6001.L18)

The Traditional Economic Approach to Measuring Economic Profit

ANDREW TORRE

School of Economics, Deakin University

Most firms supplying the domestic market possess some degree of market power at different points in time over the course of their effective life. As a firm's market power increases, so does its insulation from competitive pressures, such that it is able to raise its prices or withhold the introduction of new technology. This can be done without concerns about the actions of its competitors, and without suffering a substantial reduction in its total revenue, because its customers lack reasonable alternatives to which to turn. Conversely, as a firm's market power decreases, the ability of the firm to raise prices or to market inferior products and utilize inferior technologies while excluding competition declines. Trade practices legislation and its equivalent in other jurisdictions requires that a firm have a substantial degree of market power as a prerequisite to committing some offenses. Consequently, it is important to be able to make some assessment of this issue. One potential although not unambiguous indicator of whether a firm possesses market power is to ascertain whether it is consistently earning economic profits over a sustained period of time.[1] Assuming that sustained economic profits are symptomatic of market power, theoretically they should attract new entrants into the industry until they are competed away, and in the absence of collusion the firm's market power would decline.

The benchmark that economists use in making a judgment about the existence of economic profit is the relationship between a firm's total revenue and its total cost. Economic profit is defined as an excess of total revenue over total cost. If a firm's total revenue is equal to its total cost then the firm is not earning any economic profit, only a normal rate of return. There is a slight difference between how accountants and economists compute these relationships.

THE THEORETICAL SPECIFICATION OF ECONOMIC PROFITS

To more clearly illustrate core concepts, much of the subsequent argument is illustrated with reference to an important and growing industry in the high-technology sector, computer hardware and software. One of the dominant players in the software subsector, Microsoft Corporation, has been the subject of a government antitrust action. The extent of this corporation's market power is a contentious issue. The U.S. Department of Justice says that Microsoft has monopoly power in the operating system market, while the defense argues that any monopoly power it may possess is only temporary and beneficial to society rather than permanent and harmful. The principal basis of competition in the operating systems market is product quality competition driven by innovation, research and development, and advertising rather than decreases in price.

Figure A.1 shows diagrammatically how economic profit is traditionally measured. The production of software requires labor (programmers) and capital (primarily software development tools and computers). Programmers write source code in a programming language; however, before programs can be executed, they must be translated into machine-readable object code. This

[1]Persistent economic profits over time is not a sufficient indicator of market power since a firm operating in a perfectly competitive market could be earning these over time not because it possesses any market power, but because it is more efficient than all or some of its rivals in the sense of having a lower cost structure. A firm in a perfectly competitive industry possesses no market power because it has absolutely no discretion over the price it can charge. Similarly a firm that does have some discretion over the price that it charges may confront a cost structure that does not allow it to earn economic profits. A less ambiguous indicator of market power is the firm's perception of the value of its own price elasticity of demand, which it confronts when it prices its products. A discussion of this is beyond the subject matter of this chapter.

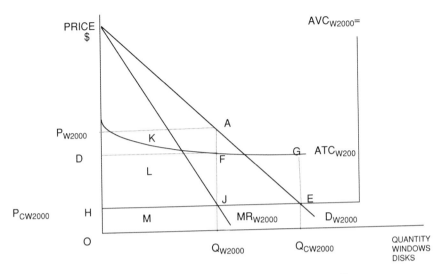

FIGURE A.1   Traditional way of measuring economic profit.

translation is accomplished by compilers, software that translates entire programs at once, or by interpreters, software that translates source code a line
at a time. Consequently, the output of a given quality of Windows disks
containing operating system programs per time period depends on programmers' services (person-hours per time period) and capital services (machine
hours per time period). Different rates of output per time period are accomplished by altering the use of capital and labor services per time period,
subject to the constraint of a maximum number of labor and machine hours.
This maximum is determined by the number of programmers, support
staff, and software development tools and computers employed by Microsoft.

Figure A.1 shows the profit maximizing price and output of Windows
2000 software disks. To obtain this information we need Microsoft's demand
function, marginal revenue function, and marginal cost function. The down-
ward sloping demand function labeled as D_{W2000} simply shows how many
Windows disks Microsoft can sell at different prices. As the price increases,
fewer disks will be sold, holding constant all of the other factors that motivate
a purchaser's decision to buy Microsoft Windows operating system software.
If any of these change and result in more Windows 2000 disks being bought
at each price, then the demand curve would shift to the right. Corresponding
to the demand curve is a downward-sloping marginal revenue curve labeled
MR_{W2000}. The marginal revenue curve shows the extra revenue to Microsoft

from selling one extra Windows disk and since price must be lowered to sell more disks, extra revenue will fall as more are sold.

What happens to Microsoft's costs as more Windows disks are produced is shown by the average total cost curve, ATC_{W2000}, and the average variable cost curve, which also equals the marginal cost curve, $AVC_{W2000} = MC_{W2000}$. Average total cost is the unit cost of producing a given number of Windows disks and is equal to average variable cost plus average fixed cost. Variable costs vary as the output of Windows disks changes. These are the cost of embedding PC software on the disk and the marketing, packaging, documentation, and distribution costs for the disk. Average variable cost is the unit variable cost of producing a given number of Windows disks. The marginal cost is the extra cost to Microsoft of replicating an additional disk. Initially average variable and marginal cost are constant; however, a maximum number of disks can be produced in a given time period for a given number of labor and machine hours. When this maximum is reached when the AVC = MC cost curve becomes vertical.[2]

The great majority of Microsoft's costs in producing software are fixed. These consist of the operating system software's share of the salaries and research and development effort of the knowledge workers, and the cost of the computers, other specialized equipment, and the premises. Total fixed costs are independent of the number of Windows disks Microsoft manufactures. However, as more Windows disks are replicated and sold, average or unit fixed costs fall, since a given total fixed cost is allocated over more and more Windows disks. This is why the average total cost curve in Figure A.1, ATC_{W2000}, is declining. The cost of producing an extra Windows 2000 disk is very low compared with the unit or average total cost. This is typical of network industries whose cost structure typically consists of high fixed and joint costs and low marginal costs. A network is a collection of points or nodes that are connected to each other. Industries characterized by networks include telecommunications, electricity, water, gas, payment services, and computer software and hardware.

On the assumption that Microsoft maximizes its profits it will produce Q_{W2000} windows disks at a price of P_{W2000}. The output level is found by going to the point where the marginal revenue curve MR_{W2000} intersects the marginal cost = average variable cost curve, $AVC_{W2000} = MC_{W2000}$, and the price is found by going up to point A on the demand curve and then across to P_{W2000} on the vertical axis. At this profit maximizing output and price in Figure A.1, total revenue is equal to $OP_{W2000}AQ_{W2000}$ and total cost is equal

---

[2]Another factor that may eventually cause average variable and marginal costs to rise is diminishing returns on each dollar spent on marketing and distribution. This is because there may be a decreasing effectiveness of marketing and distribution in maintaining customers' loyalty.

to $ODFQ_{W2000}$. The excess of total revenue over total cost, which is $DP_{W2000}AF$, is the economic profit. Over time, if this successfully attracts new entrants into the industry so that this excess disappears then this is consistent with a lack of market power over time in the product market. Conversely, if the excess persists because potential entrants cannot successfully enter the industry, then this is consistent with market power in the product market over time.

The key to grasping the economic definition of economic profit, the excess of total revenue over total cost, is to understand the notion of opportunity cost. The variable and fixed costs in Figure A.1 are all opportunity costs. In economic theory, opportunity cost is the cost of the foregone next best alternative.[3] In Figure A.1 total variable costs $OHJQ_{W2000}$ represent the minimum amount that Microsoft must pay in order to attract and keep the variable inputs to produce the corresponding output of Windows 2000 disks Q_{W2000}. It cannot pay less and expect to keep them. The nonspecialized labor must be paid a salary equal to what it could get in its next best alternative employment. This would be equal to the going market wage rate in the packaging industry and yields what economists call a normal return to this type of labor. A normal return is the minimum return required by the labor that packages and distributes the disks to induce those workers to stay employed with Microsoft. If it is not earned the labor will leave Microsoft. Any return in excess of this minimum (the opportunity cost of this sort of labor) is called an *economic rent* and may be paid by Microsoft to reward special worker talents or attributes that it wants to retain. These rents are part of the cost of this type of labor to Microsoft, and would be included along with the opportunity cost in the area $OHJQ_{W2000}$.

The area $HP_{W2000}AJ$ accrues to the fixed inputs of which there are three categories: specialized labor, specialized equipment, and the shareholders or owners of Microsoft. All of the fixed inputs, like the nonspecialized labor, must earn at least a normal rate of return if they are to continue to be associated with Microsoft. The specialized labor comprises computer programmers, software engineers, other knowledge workers, and managers, who are all likely to be paid in excess of their opportunity cost. These rents along with the opportunity cost of the specialized labor are found in the area HDFJ. Also to be found in HDFJ is the economic income over the relevant time period from Microsoft's specialized assets. These include the computers and the equipment used to embed the software onto disks. As an example suppose

---

[3]Some examples of opportunity cost are as follows. Workers will not remain employed as drivers for $200 a week if they can receive $600 a week employed as shop assistants. The opportunity cost of staying employed as a driver is $600 a week. Lenders will not lend $200,000 at 5% if they can get 10% and a property owner will not rent a property for $200 a week if the market rate is $500. The opportunity costs are $20,000 per annum and $500 a week, respectively.

that at the start of the accounting period the embedding equipment has a market value of $1000 and it produces $300 of net receipts at the end of the accounting period. However, its market value is only $850. Nominal economic income from the asset is $150 ($300 net receipts less the $150 loss in market value of the asset). If the asset had no alternative use or zero market value, then the nominal economic income would be the entire $300.

The remaining part of the area HDFJ comprises that part of the payments to shareholders (the owners of Microsoft) by Microsoft, which represents a normal rate of return. In making a decision about whether or not to continue investing in Microsoft, shareholders will compare their rate of return from owning Microsoft shares with the rate of return they can obtain by investing their funds in the next best alternative. This is the opportunity cost of their funds. Payments made by Microsoft to its shareholders are therefore a cost to them. Consequently, the condition that in the absence of any economic profit the firm's total revenue will equal its total cost means that the firm's owners are earning only a normal rate of return on their investment. This is just sufficient to induce them to keep their money in the firm. If total revenue exceeds total cost, then the owners of the firm will be earning rents or a rate of return in excess of the opportunity cost of their invested funds. These rents are equivalent to the area $DP_{W2000}AF$ in Figure A.1 and their source is the ability of the firm to earn economic profits.

THE EMPIRICAL MEASUREMENT OF ECONOMIC PROFITS

According to Figure A.1, the setting of price and output requires knowledge of the demand curve, the marginal cost curve, the marginal revenue curve, the average variable cost, and the average total cost curve. Estimates of all of these are hard to make accurately and many businesspeople are probably unfamiliar with all of these concepts. Furthermore, in practice, many businesses use a cost-plus markup in searching for the right price. Onto the wholesale cost of an item is added a percentage markup adequate to cover overhead costs and to yield a reasonable profit. However, this is consistent with the diagrammatic marginal analysis of Figure A.1. Markup pricing is a rule of thumb for price setters offering a starting point for a continual search. On the assumption that one's competitors sustain the same cost increases or decreases, the markup would be adjusted as these costs change. If a mistake is discovered, adjustments will be made. The diagram portrayed in Figure A.1 is the economic theorist's way of explaining how mistakes are discovered and rectified in the search for the most profitable price. For example, in Figure A.1 if Microsoft sets the price of a Windows 2000 disk below OD then it will quickly move into a loss situation since total revenue will be less than total cost.

Different methodologies can be used to estimate a firm's economic profit in a particular time period. The method adopted here is that suggested by Copeland, Koller and Murrin (1996).[4] They utilize the expression

$$\text{Economic profit} = \text{Net operating profit} - \text{Adjusted taxes} - \text{Invested capital} \times \text{Weighted average cost of capital.} \quad \text{(A.1)}$$

Expression (A.1) is estimated for a sample of five firms in the software and programming industry in the technology sector from published U.S. accounts.[5]

The sample of five firms only uses equity capital without any debt to finance its operations. Consequently the weighted average cost of capital is the imputed opportunity cost of shareholders' equity, and the capital asset pricing model (CAPM) is used for this purpose. The CAPM postulates that the opportunity cost of equity is equal to the return on risk-free securities, plus the companies' systematic risk (beta), multiplied by the market price of risk (market risk premium) (Copeland *et al.*, 1996). The equation for the cost of equity is as follows:

$$C_E = r_f + \left[E(r_m) - r_f \right](\beta), \quad \text{(A.2)}$$

where

r_f	= the risk-free rate of return
$E(r_m)$	= the expected rate of return on the overall market portfolio
$E(r_m) - r_f$	= the market risk premium
β	= the systematic risk of the equity.

To implement the CAPM approach, estimates of three things are needed: the risk-free rate, the market risk premium, and the systematic risk beta. The risk-free rate is the return on a security or portfolio of securities that has no default risk and is completely uncorrelated with returns on anything else in the economy. Copeland *et al.* (1996) recommend a 10-year treasury bond rate. Monthly rates were obtained online from the Federal Reserve Board of Governors and the median value taken for each year. The results are shown in Table A.1.

The market risk premium or the price of risk is the difference between the expected rate of return on the market portfolio and the risk-free rate, $E(r_m) - r_f$. It has been recommended that a market risk premium of 5 to 6% be used for U.S. companies (Copeland *et al.*, 1996) and 6% is utilized in this

---

[4]Tom Copeland, Tim Koller, and Jack Murrin, (1995). *Valuation: Measuring and Managing the Value of Companies*, Second Edition. John Wiley & Sons, New York, ISBN: 0–471–08627–4 (paperback).
[5]These were obtained on line at www.marketguide.com.

TABLE A.1   Median Values of 10-Year U.S. Treasury Bond Rates

1997	1998	1999	2000
6.36%	5.48%	5.84%	6.02%

exercise. Finally the beta values of each of the selected companies are published online. Table A.2 lists the company name, the industry to which it belongs, and the published beta value. Table A.3 provides information about the value of each company's shareholders' funds, and Table A.4 shows net operating profit (loss) less adjusted taxes for the 3-year period from 1998 to 2000.

The estimated cost of equity capital or shareholders' funds for each company in each of the three years is found by substituting values for the risk-free rate (Table A.1), beta (Table A.2), and a market risk premium of 6% into Eq. (A.2). The results are shown in Table A.5.

The value of shareholders' equity in Table A.3 is now multiplied by the estimated cost of equity capital in Table A.5 to give the imputed opportunity cost of shareholders' funds (Table A.6). The difference between adjusted net operating profit in Table A.4 and the imputed cost of shareholders' funds in Table A.6 yields economic profit. The estimates are shown in Table A.7.

The extent of Microsoft's market power is a contentious issue with the U.S. Department of Justice, which argues that Microsoft has monopoly power in the operating system market. The basis for this argument is that irrespective of the definition of the market used, Microsoft's market share is very high andstable and entry barriers for aspiring competitors to its Windows operating system are high. The defense argued inter alia that there are no high barriers to entry into PC software since the supply of critical inputs—venture capital and programmers—is ample and mobile. In addition, there is a worldwide network of scientific journals and conferences over which technical

TABLE A.2   Beta Values for Selected Companies in the Software and Programming Industry

Industry	Company	Published beta value
Software	Actuate Corporation	0
	Adobe Systems, Inc.	1.16
	Advent Software	1.16
	BMC Software	1.44
	Microsoft	1.78

TABLE A.3   Value of Shareholders' Equity for Selected Companies in the Software and Programming industry for the period 1998–2000 (millions of U.S. dollars)

Company	2000	1999	1998
Actuate Corporation	$ 57.0	$ 31.6	$ 26.0
Adobe Systems, Inc.	$ 752.5	$ 512.2	$ 516.4
Advent Software	$ 209.6	$ 160.7	$ 60.2
BMC Software	$ 1,780.9	$ 1,334.4	$ 877.7
Microsoft	$ 41,368.0	$ 28,438.0	$ 16,627.0

TABLE A.4   Net Operating Profit (Loss) Less Adjusted Taxes for Selected Companies in the Software and Programming Industry for the period 1998–2000 (millions of U.S. dollars)

Company	2000	1999	1998
Actuate Corporation	$ 6.6	$ 3.0	($ 3.9)
Adobe Systems, Inc.	$ 394.9	$ 191.1	$ 102.8
Advent Software	$ 28.8	$ 16.4	$ 3.0
BMC Software	$ 232.9	$ 396.3	$ 183.8
Microsoft	$ 10,206.0	$ 9,054.0	$ 5,314.0

TABLE A.5   Estimated Cost of Equity Capital for Selected Companies in the Software and Programming Industry for the period 1998–2000 (%)

Company	2000	1999	1998
Actuate Corporation	6.02	5.84	5.48
Adobe Systems, Inc.	6.00	6.02	6.08
Advent Software	6.00	6.02	6.08
BMC Software	6.00	6.07	6.22
Microsoft	5.98	6.12	6.40

TABLE A.6   Imputed Opportunity Cost of Shareholders' Funds for Selected Companies in the Software and Programming Industry for the period 1998–2000 (millions of U.S. dollars)

Company	2000	1999	1998
Actuate Corporation	$ 3.43	$ 1.46	$ 1.42
Adobe Systems, Inc.	$ 45.15	$ 30.83	$ 31.39
Advent Software	$ 12.57	$ 9.67	$ 3.66
BMC Software	$ 106.854	$ 80.731	$ 54.59
Microsoft	$ 2473.8	$ 1740.4	$ 1064.12

TABLE A.7 Estimates of Economic Profit (Loss) for Selected Companies in the Software and Programming Industry for the Period 1998–2000 (millions of U.S. dollars)

Company	2000	1999	1998
Actuate	$ 3.17	$ 1.54	($ 4.91)
Adobe Systems	$ 349.75	$ 160.27	$ 71.41
Advent Software	$ 16.23	$ 6.73	($ 0.66)
BMC Software	$ 126.046	$ 315.56	$ 129.21
Microsoft	$ 7732.2	$ 7313.6	$ 4249.88[a]

[a] The estimated economic profit for Microsoft in 1997 was $ 3154.56.

information is transmitted and because the "look and feel" of software enjoys only limited intellectual property protection, entrants face low imitation costs.

The estimates in Table A.7 suggest that the alleged absence of high entry barriers has not been successful in eroding Microsoft's economic profits during the past 4 years. These have continued to increase steadily and they are considerably higher than some other firms in the industry and this may suggest considerable market power. An alternative explanation is that Microsoft confronts a highly competitive market for some or all of its products; however, because it is more efficient in the sense of having a lower cost structure, it has earned and sustained economic profits over this 4-year period. Intangible management techniques and concepts, the subject matter of this book, provide a richer categorization and conceptualization of the firm's total revenue and total cost than is employed in traditional accounting statements. The emphasis is on intangible revenue and costs. For example a distinction is made between productive and nonproductive wage costs, and total revenue is broken down into intangible effectiveness and more traditional sources. These techniques may permit a more thorough analysis of the extent of economic profits in corporations than has been provided here.

INDEX